*Aldabra Alone*

# ALDABRA ALONE

TONY BEAMISH

FOREWORD BY SIR JULIAN HUXLEY

*San Francisco – SIERRA CLUB*

PRINTED IN GREAT BRITAIN
*in 11 point Plantin type*
BY JOLLY AND BARBER LIMITED, RUGBY

Until very recently, Aldabra meant nothing except to a few scientists, the local fishermen and, as we have now learnt, to the Anglo-American military planners who wanted to build an airfield there.

And it was almost lost to the world of science before the general public was reminded of its existence. A scientific tragedy of the greatest magnitude was averted only at the last minute.

For Aldabra is unique. The huge Indian Ocean atoll is one of the few unspoiled islands that remain in the tropics and it is in even greater need of protection today than it was when Charles Darwin and his friends first appealed for its preservation nearly a hundred years ago.

Aldabra's importance to science can hardly be exaggerated. On its elevated coral platforms, almost undisturbed by man, there are opportunities for the study of evolution and biological processes that can be undertaken nowhere else. The atoll has a big and varied community of plants and animals, including many species and sub-species found nowhere else. It is the last home of the giant Indian tortoise in the wild state. It is an important breeding base for multitudes of sea birds and marine turtles and has the most remarkable population of land birds to survive in any island of the region. Other aspects of its wild life are now being studied closely for the first time and there is every indication that they will prove as interesting as the tortoises and the birds.

Tony Beamish's vivid description of the atoll and of the fight to save it is timely, for the threat to develop Aldabra has only been suspended, and it is a pity that there was no book like this at the time the airfield proposals were made. The most charitable verdict on such a disastrous scheme is that it was formulated in ignorance of both the intrinsic difficulties and the irreparable damage it would inevitably have caused, for it is hard to believe that there were really no other suitable military alternatives.

This book with its beautiful photographs demonstrates the unique quality of a wild life evolved in isolation. It also shows convincingly how persistent pressures from lovers of unspoilt nature can cause the authorities to change their minds and how international is the concern felt today for the preservation of the few such places that are left.

In the campaign to spare Aldabra, American conservationists and scientists joined their British colleagues in giving unstinting support to the Royal Society and great help was also rendered by the British and American press, the BBC and many MPs. Useful lessons were learnt in this fight in defence of an atoll that was British only in the sense that it happened to be marked red on the map.

As a natural treasure house, Aldabra must belong to the whole world.

To sacrifice such a legacy for temporary strategic gain would be an act of vandalism. I hope that Tony Beamish's book will bring the issues at stake to the widest attention and help to prevent such threats from arising again, and if they do come, to provide some indication of how they may be met.

*Aldabra Alone* is an exciting story of exploration and of a dramatically successful conservation campaign. It is both a reassurance and a challenge.

JULIAN HUXLEY

# Acknowledgments

After the showing of the film 'Island in Danger' on BBC Television, someone wrote to ask: 'Where do I stay on Aldabra?'. There is no Hilton, of course, and I hope there never will be, but I mention this only because it is the sort of question I might myself have asked a year earlier. At that time I hardly knew the place existed. So my grateful thanks go not only to the many friends who helped me with this book but also to those who enabled me to get to the 'Lost Corner' . . . and back.

In the first place His Excellency the Governor of the Seychelles, the Earl of Oxford and Asquith and the lessee of Aldabra, Harry Savy. I also owe a big debt of gratitude to Captain Sauvage and his crew of the *Lady Esmé*, particularly to Esmé Jumeau my cabin mate, and to my fellow explorers Guy Lionnet and Harold Hirth, who were both let down by the camp-beds I bought for the expedition in Mombasa. Mercifully we never had real need for the mosquito nets. Philippe Lousteau-Lalanne's early advice about the birds was invaluable and the film would never have reached home safely without the help of Tony Bentley-Buckle and Chloe Compton in Kenya. Frank Sager and Ivan Polunin achieved the impossible in getting my equipment to the atoll in time.

Thanks to the impressive warnings of Malcolm and Mary Penny and others of the Bristol University Expedition to the Seychelles, of Alan Bosworth, leader of the BBC Expedition of 1966, Christopher Wright of the British Museum of Natural History and other friends, most pitfalls on the 'champignon' were avoided. The message 'climbing boots and polythene bags' got home.

Jeffery Boswall gave unstinting support from the shaky beginning and any success the expedition had on the television and radio front is largely due to him and his colleagues John Sparks, John Burton, Keith Hopkins, David Leonard and Pamela Everett and, of course, to Peter Scott in whose series the film featured and who made a moving introduction to it.

In writing the book I relied heavily on the guidance of the Royal Society, where David Griffin of the secretariat of the Aldabra Committee fed me with up-to-date information, on the *Smithsonian Institution Atoll Research Bulletin* No. 118 and on the Librarian of the Royal Geographical Society.

My very warm thanks go to Sir Julian Huxley for his encouragement and for honouring the book with his Foreword. For aid in innumerable ways and for guidance on the scientific facts I am deeply indebted to Roger Gaymer, Malcolm Penny, David Stoddart and William Bourne all of whom read the manuscript and offered their advice. I was much helped too by Sir Tufton Beamish, René E. Honegger, Richard Fitter,

Graham Howarth, Tom and Beryl Wood, Peggy Oxenford and Mrs Harvey Todman.

No lover of wild nature studying the Aldabra affair could feel anything but gratitude to the British and American press for the part they played and I hope I have done justice to their championship by my quotations. It was William Bourne, of the Seabird Group, author of the Appendix on the birds of Aldabra, who collected them for me.

The photographs of the atoll, which supplement my own, were taken by Tony Diamond, John Frazier, Roger Gaymer, Tony Graham, Peter Grubb, Tony Hutson, Siegfried Köster, John Peake, Malcolm Penny, Harry Stickley and David Stoddart. I am extremely grateful for the loan of these adornments to the book and to the Royal Society for allowing the use of those taken on their expeditions of 1967/8.

I have had so much co-operation and expert guidance in writing *Aldabra Alone* that all that I can claim to be entirely mine are the prejudices.

*Langore St Stephens*                                    TONY BEAMISH
*Launceston*
*Cornwall*

# Contents

# Illustrations

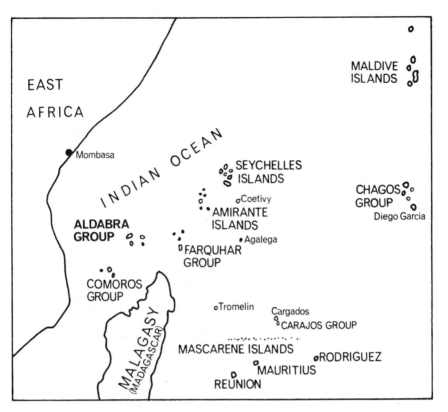

THE LOST CORNER

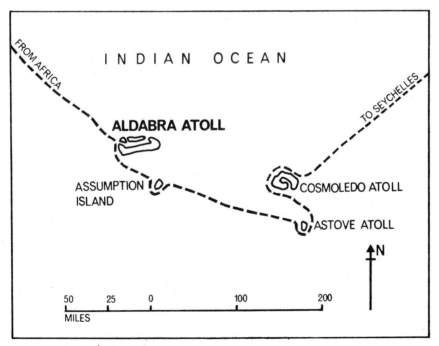

- - - - Course of 'Lady Esme'

THE ALDABRA GROUP

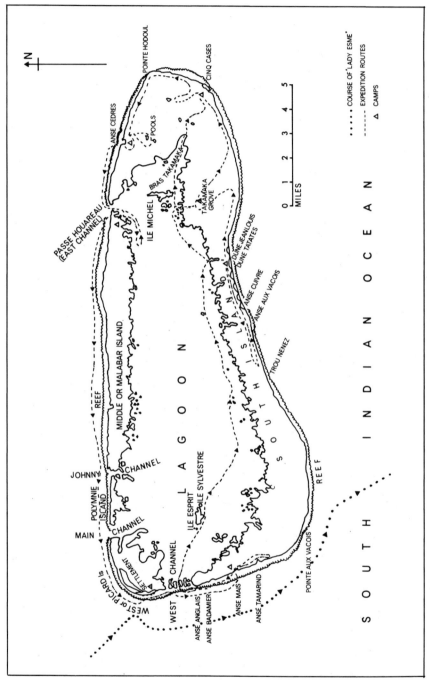

ALDABRA ATOLL

# I *Somewhere in an Empty Ocean*

'IF we miss Aldabra, we'll see an awful lot of blue water. No land for weeks!'

I glanced quickly at the captain poring over his ancient chart. Was he joking? I could never tell. It was a curious feeling to be in the 'lost corner' of the Indian Ocean without a ship's wireless. The old machine had broken down; it had no range anyway.

'Should see the atoll just after dawn. If the waves aren't too big . . . it's got no height and it's flat as a pancake. No wonder there've been so many wrecks.'

The captain threw his instruments aside, I strolled on deck – a member of the crew off-duty – wondering.

It was the late afternoon of our third day at sea. The wind had risen slightly and the *Lady Esmé* had started to roll badly. Above the louder noise of the engines I heard a sudden shout from the other deck. I rushed over to see what had happened. There, a hundred yards away, surfacing lazily, was a whale. To have a closer look, the ship turned round her – she moved so gracefully in the water I ascribed the female sex – and for ten minutes we watched her swimming unhurriedly and apparently undeflected from her course by the antics of our strange ship. A last blow and twist of her enormous tail and she was gone, the only living creature larger than a flying fish we had seen since leaving the East African coast.

The captain told me later it was unwise to be too curious at sea, particularly if it happened to be a whale and motionless. A ship he was in once approached such an object. It proved to be a gigantic bloated carcass. The moment they came alongside to investigate, it burst with a shattering report. It took days of scrubbing to clean up the debris!

By contrast our journey had been uneventful. I'd had time to get to know my fellow explorers. Guy Lionnet from the Seychelles, a fellow bug-hunter, who was to lead the expedition, and the American professor, Harold Hirth, a green turtle expert with such singleness of purpose that he spoke of little else. I had even begun to share his affection for the reptile. It was more like a pleasure cruise than the start of a journey into the unknown. We ate well too, cuisine à la Seychelloise. Dinner that last night was especially good. I wasn't quite sure what we were eating, but having suffered no ill-effects in the wilds of Asia from exotic foods like roast Vietnamese water-beetle, python steak, the nameless complicated biota in Chinese fish soup and those unforgotten tiger-meat sandwiches I once offered to my grateful guests in Laos, I had long ceased to be concerned with the provenance or taxonomy of a tasty dish. It was Harold Hirth who asked what it was.

'This is one way, probably the best, of cooking green turtle,' he was told. But there was nothing left on the dish when it was taken away.

Soon after dawn I was on deck. The engines had stopped and the rolling too. The American was already up and to be seen studying the eastern horizon through binoculars. A faint mist was rising from the deep blue water which shaded through purple to green as I followed his gaze. At first all I could see ahead was a long strip of cloud stretched above the horizon, like a thin band of grey tape.

'There it is,' said Hirth quietly. 'I should really bow three times to Aldabra, Mecca of the green turtle. I never thought I'd have the chance to see it.'

1. Giant tortoises of the Indian Ocean sheltering from the midday sun near Cinq Cases. Aldabra is their last home in the wild state. (*The Author*)

2.    Display of the comoro blue pigeon. *(Roger Gaymer)*

As he spoke the mist was clearing and now I could see the atoll. What I had thought was a cloud was its dead coral wall, fringed by white sand in the section we were facing. To the north, a deeply undercut cliff cut the sky, making the promontory look like the bows of a warship. Small white breakers marked the line of a reef ahead and a fantastic change in sea colour to emerald green, mottled here and there with the mauve of underwater rocks. Above the pale beach small squares of white were beginning to shine in the morning sun. The settlement.

The voice of the captain was behind me.

'We shan't be able to land for an hour or two. Have to wait for the right tide to get through the reef. I am going to anchor here as long as the weather holds. The manager will be coming out in a pirogue to fetch you.'

Looking at the silent land on this cloudless morning, it was hard to believe we had indeed arrived at Aldabra. Then I glanced up at the sky, brightening above the line of vegetation on the horizon; speckling it to a height of several thousand feet were innumerable black dots, soaring and wheeling like small aircraft, the frigate birds from their huge colonies on Malabar Island, north of the lagoon.

There was no doubt now. This placid coast was indeed mysterious Aldabra, the biggest in a vast chain of islands straddling the western Indian Ocean yet the only one so far unspoiled by man. Some called it the island man forgot; from all accounts it was a pity it had ever been remembered.

As we waited for the pirogue to take us ashore, with the sea around now criss-crossed by flights of fishing boobies and terns, far away in London and Washington the first shots were being fired in what was to prove the biggest conservation battle of all time. It was February 27, 1967.

I glanced again at my map and notes and at Fryer's report of 1911 which Guy Lionnet had brought along as a bible. Like Harold Hirth, I never thought I'd make it to Aldabra, one of the most inaccessible islands in the world. I looked across the water. No, it wasn't a mirage.

The goal was there. The end of a journey which had been planned six years before and far away.

# II  *A Trail through the Forest*

As I burned the last of a dozen leeches off my ankle with a cigarette end, I thought how pleasant it would be to make my next wild life film away from the tropical rain forest. On an island, perhaps, a nice dry one free of these arching, wriggling pests.

That is where the journey to Aldabra began.

Night was beginning to fall rapidly. Everything, including our bedding, was wet. The last burst of a Malayan tropical rainstorm was dripping fatly through gaps in the pandanus leaf roof and, despite the efforts of two skilled aborigine porters, the fire was still only a curling wisp of blue smoke. In the half-light I saw the camp cook sitting on a luminous log which glowed violet with the phosphorescence of decay. He was opening a tin of self-heating soup and had thrown the wrapping paper from the provision box on to the ground. A shiny red spider was moving slowly across an illustrated page. 'Islands of the Garden of Eden', I read.

It was about the Seychelles Islands of the Indian Ocean. The pictures showed granite hills rising from a glittering sea, vanilla and coconut plantations, open forest, long white beaches. It was now dark. I lit the lamp and read on:

'Dotted over 500,000 square miles of the Indian Ocean lie the ninety-two islands and atolls that comprise the archipelago. Although many of these are coral islands, graced only with a few palms and a lagoon, the submarine plateau also supports a group of granite islands, romantically named . . .'

The most remote of all these islands was uninhabited Aldabra. At the time the name meant nothing to me, although its Arab sound rang strangely in a family of French and Portugese titles – Silhouette, Cosmoledo, Mahé, Astove, Praslin. The article was mainly about the last of these with its mysterious Vallée de Mai, the only place in the world where the Coco de Mer tree grows, dropping the world's biggest fruit from a hundred feet, and the sanctuary of the unique black parrot which I had once seen pictured on a Seychelles five cent stamp. As a hot and frustrated wild-life photographer, with ankles so swollen from leech bites I couldn't get my boots on, the thought of this cool, high valley, echoing to the whistle of the black parrot, was enticing. 'Behind the palms is lush undergrowth with bread fruit trees in abundance, mangoes, limes, papaya, bananas and other fruits.' Visions of the Swiss family Robinson.

The soup was almost ready, beside it a leafload of speckled rice with chunks of corned beef. By now the air was full of the syncopated chatter of cicadas and the equally rhythmic croaking of tenor and baritone frogs saluting the recent rainfall. The Seychelles article was carefully folded into a polythene bag, but two thoughts were left outside. 'There are birds as rare as the trees' was one, and the other was about Aldabra: 'The giant tortoise, a prehistoric monster five feet long and as high as a table, breeds happily on the atoll and is in no danger . . .'

The trouble about filming in the rain forest of South East Asia is that you rarely see any animals. There are plenty of signs of life, bird calls in the morning and evening, monkey movements in the high canopy of the trees, and, underfoot the muddy tracks impressed with a fantastic variety of paw and hoofprints. Most of the previous morning we had forced our way along an overgrown river bank following the trail of a herd of elephant. As the river was unmarked on the map and the elephants were moving in the direction we were trying to follow, this was a stroke of luck – but the animals were not far ahead. Water was still oozing into some of the six-inch deep depressions they left conveniently spaced behind them. The porters were nervous. We first noticed this when the straggling file concertinaed and rifles and blowpipes were unslung. Suddenly the silence of the mid-day forest, so unlike the Hollywood concept of interspersed shrieks, whistles and roars, was shattered. A noise like the splintering of a giant match-box came from ahead. We stopped to listen.

'Can't be more than fifty yards away,' our guides said urgently, 'and elephants don't like to be disturbed feeding. Better cut off here.'

We left the trail and started to chop a narrow path through the undergrowth. For the first time that day I felt grateful for the forest wall that shut us out of sight. The giant spiders' webs, under which we ducked whenever there was room, were no longer repulsive; at least they showed there were no big animals immediately ahead. The guide thought it must have been a herd of ten or twelve elephants, yet in four hours of following them, we hadn't seen a single movement or a square foot of grey skin. Tortoises the size of a table lumbering over a coral atoll sounded a much easier proposition. And not nearly so dangerous! If I had known of the hazards Aldabra had to offer I would not have been so complacent.

My interest in wild-life photography, which had eventually led to these hazardous journeys in the Malayan rain forest (on one occasion I found a small pit viper clinging by its jaws to my trousers, but was so weary and sodden I just brushed it off without thinking what might have happened if it had been grown-up) really began in my garden in Singapore. I had enjoyed using a cine-camera since school days and Singapore is the perfect place to practise. It was above all the birds that arrested attention.

Five species of kingfisher were among the visitors to my garden and every evening the brilliant golden oriole could be seen flashing among the trees. This is a bird that always prefers towns and the company of humans to life in the country. And there were innumerable others, from the comic yellow-vented bulbul to tiny sunbirds that used to build their nests right in the window, using the expanded metal screen to support an untidy straw bag. And the white-headed sea eagles that raised a family three years running at the top of an albizia tree just outside my bedroom. It was the eagles that first taught me that the dawn chorus is not necessarily a thing of beauty. Every morning at 5.45 these gigantic birds woke me with a half-hour of raucous screaming and made me sympathize with the London-born cook said to have resigned from her new job in the country because she 'couldn't sleep for the 'ollering of the birds'.

Singapore is one of the best places in the world for nature study on your doorstep and only an hour away by car, in South Jahore, starts one of the largest tracts of uncut rain forest in South East Asia. It was here I made my first film for BBC Television for the 'Adventure' series – at weekends and during holidays.

After leaving Singapore, I formed a film production company in London. This action brought the image of the Indian Ocean islands into sharper focus. It seemed that no-one had yet made a film of the animals and birds of the Seychelles, a Crown Colony which at the time included Aldabra atoll. Research was difficult, very little had been written and what references existed often seemed contradictory. Were the giant tortoises dying out or thriving? Had all the endemic species of birds been exterminated by introduced species from Madagascar, Mauritius and the African mainland? The mystery deepened the further I dug. The difficulty of getting to the Seychelles at all – with one boat a month from East Africa or India and no airfield – made the project all the more challenging. Then, suddenly, I had to abandon the whole idea. An offer to go to Laos, the tiny forgotten kingdom between Thailand and Vietnam, was too attractive to refuse. Aldabra was postponed.

In Vientiane I had little time to think about the Seychelles, although the prospect of oceanic islands teeming with birds and tortoises was more appealing than ever; particularly during the dry season in a landlocked country with dust from the parched rice fields making the sun look like a blood orange. No birds except sparrows were to be seen and hardly a wild animal was left alive within fifty miles of the capital. Every living creature larger than a mouse was shot on sight.

The French *chasseur* instinct, which regards even seagulls as fair game, is here grafted on to the Asian peasant's belief that wild animals are created to be target practice for humans, either because they are good to eat or because they are dangerous. Inevitably, there has been devastation of the fauna of the old Indo-China countries, the more so since firearms are now easily available. This is one of the lesser-known tragedies of the Vietnam conflict and of the 'wars of liberation' that have raged for over twenty years in this region. During the French Colonial times, most of the villagers still hunted with the crossbow.

Around Vientiane and the other towns of Laos almost the only wild animals now seen are those dead, or half-dead, being sold for food in the markets. The range of taste is wide. I rescued and tried to restore to health creatures varying from the scaly anteater, or pangolin, to miniature owls and half-grown pythons. My garden became a small zoo, but some of the animals could not be saved. Baskets of song birds, like the bulbul, are daily on sale in the markets, sometimes already spiked on sticks for a *brochette*. A region that once boasted some of the rarest and most varied fauna in Asia, including the largest wild animal to be discovered in this century, the koupré, a species of wild cattle that twenty years ago moved in herds of hundreds across the savannah forest of North Cambodia and South Laos, is now a pathetically sad place for the zoologist.

These are Buddhist countries and I thought there would therefore be a traditional discipline of conservation and respect for animals; that the priests who walked carefully to avoid crushing an ant would have taught and influenced others by their example. But the only visible effect of this teaching of Buddha today is the horde of homeless and starving pi-dogs that roam the village streets in packs. The doctrine seems to have back-fired. Whereas the mercy killing of these creatures is considered wrong (it is not unusual to see a dog lurching around the dustbin on three legs) the mass slaughter of wild animals seems to raise no priestly anger at all.

During this time in Laos I had hoped to make another wild-life film for television, but on my first expedition in the unmapped north I realized the futility of the effort. I was on holiday in Sayaburi province, splendid country of trackless forest well watered by tributaries of the Mekong River. We had started the journey up the valley on elephant back and the dense forest reminded me of Malaya, but there was a difference. It was not the absolute quiet, it was something else which I could not at first put my finger on. We passed two young Lao hunters carrying rusty shotguns. They stood aside grinning, and as I turned to wave, I saw a squirrel hanging limply over the shoulder of one of the youths; the afternoon's bag. The animal was snow-white, not an albino, but a fairly uncommon species found in this part of the country and a curious contradiction of the camouflage principle; it is one of the very few white creatures that are forest dwellers. I wondered why they were shooting squirrels and not deer or pig, and then suddenly realized what was wrong, in what way this jungle differed from Malaya. There were no animal hoof prints or pug marks on the track ahead.

In the Pahang and Trengganu forests we used to amuse ourselves by trying to work out whether the tiger was following the deer or the tapir, or vice versa. After a week on the trail in North Laos the largest wild animal we had seen was a bamboo rat, not counting an appalling emerald green and grey leech, that stretched fourteen inches up the hindleg of one of the pack elephants.

On our return to the provincial capital, we were invited to dine by the Governor, Prince Ratanapanya, a brother of the King of Laos. His house was right in the centre of the small market town with a fine view of the 4,000-foot hills surrounding it. Coffee was served on the balcony – it was a fine night of full moon. A few pin-points of oil light shone from the windows in the main street and a brighter glow came from a naked electric bulb in front of the Chinese store, fed by one of the few generators in town. The encircling hills were purplish-blue against a lighter sky, with a line of tall trees fretted on the horizon. It was hard to believe that armed bands of Viet Cong and their associate Pathet Lao communists virtually ringed the town, cutting it off from the rest of the country, except by air.

My eyes caught a small light in the forest half way up the mountain. As I watched it spread; other flashes broke out in the darkness around it, but the only sound was the clatter of cicadas and frogs in the swamp behind the house.

'What on earth is that light?' I asked, thinking it might be the Viet Cong.

The Prince did not reply for a moment. He looked worried, distressed. 'I wish I could stop it,' he said, 'but unfortunately we have no money for rangers. This is only the start, now it's the dry season they'll be doing this every night, all over the mountains. Now the Meos have guns, it's much worse.'

'But why are they burning the forest at night?' I knew the mountain-dwelling Meo people, the biggest minority group in Laos, still practised slash-and-burn cultivation, slowly wrecking the primary forest and leaving only rank grass and undergrowth behind when they moved on. But it seemed a curious hour to be working; I must have looked perplexed.

'They are hunting, you see,' the Prince continued, 'probably for tortoises. That's about all there is left. They burn the jungle to drive the tortoises out, then spear or shoot them. They'll kill anything, those people, even a female elephant with a calf. They're destroying all the forest, too.'

The prospects for survival of wild life in Laos are probably not quite so bleak as this experience suggests. The country is about the size of England with a population of under three million. Driven from the vicinity of towns and villages by trigger-happy hunters and fire-raisers, the animals can still find sanctuary in places so remote that man rarely penetrates them.

Inevitably my mind turned again to Aldabra. This uninhabited island would, I felt sure, be offering better protection to its tortoises, the last wild survivors of the giant Indian Ocean species. At the end of 1966, the opportunity came to see for myself. I was at last free to visit the atoll that had been described by one explorer as 'a living natural history museum'.

Moreover, as it turned out, the postponement had made my expedition doubly worthwhile. A threat far greater than that of a few aboriginal hunters hung over the giant tortoise now – indeed over the whole of Aldabra. The film I brought back was to prove useful in the fight to gain a reprieve for one of the last unspoiled islands of the world.

I did not regret waiting for such a chance.

III    *To an Island in Danger*

A<small>T</small> first I couldn't find it on the map. Cosmoledo, the huge atoll seventy miles distant, was prominent, even on a chart of the 'East Ocean' dated 1626. Could Aldabra be that ring of unnamed blobs near the words 'Ila Nova'? What, I wondered, was the origin of the Arabic-sounding name?

Most people I spoke to in London in October 1966 had never heard of the place. 'Isn't that the word magicians use?' I began to agree that there was something magical, mysterious, about this unknown coral island in the 'lost corner' of the Indian Ocean. It was big for an atoll, over seventy miles in circumference, yet uninhabited; none of the records I eventually found credited it with any economic importance. It seemed to have no guano deposits worth exploiting, unlike other islands of the region, and it had not been turned into a coconut plantation. Even at first glance, and from afar, it was an enigma.

It didn't take long to find out the main reason why. Aldabra is almost impossible to reach, unless you happen to own an ocean-going yacht. No ships call there regularly. It is remote from all the shipping lanes and, of course, you cannot go by air. I had early hopes of getting a passage in the schooner belonging to the lessee of the atoll, Mr Harry Savy of Mahé. This vessel made the 700-mile voyage from Port Victoria on Mahé Island, the capital of the Seychelles, about once every two months, to deliver stores and mail to the forty-odd creole labourers working on the atoll and on its nearest neighbour, Assumption Island, and it brought back dried fish and green turtles. But a message from a friend in the Seychelles advised me to look elsewhere for a lift. The schooner was undergoing repairs and no one could say if and when it would sail again. Anyway there might not be room for a passenger.

I must say that later, on my return from Aldabra, when I saw this ancient wooden schooner lying in the clear green water of Victoria Harbour, I felt I had escaped something. It looked top-heavy and far too small to ride out a cyclone – sort of home-made and unpainted. Five members of the Bristol University Expedition had shared a single cabin in the *Argo*, as she was called, the previous year, at a season that was particularly rough. They must have endured acute discomfort in the interests of science. I did not appreciate it at the time, but it was a lucky break that the old lady was out of action when I needed a passage!

As the object of my expedition was to make a film of the rare animals and birds of the whole Seychelles Group, principally those of the granite islands fanning north-east of Mahé, I decided to leave the problem of getting to Aldabra until I reached the area. It must surely be possible to find a fishing boat, perhaps one of the Japanese vessels that now operate in fleets in the Indian Ocean, using the long-line technique for catching tuna, or another inter-island schooner. My friend in Mahé, Frank Sager, was asked to keep his ears open. The difficulty of getting to this mysterious atoll only increased my determination to do so. Meanwhile I began to study the natural history of the other more accessible islands.

There was plenty of interest here too. According to the Bristol Expedition, which had published a series of articles in the magazine *Animals*, several of the rarest birds in the world still survived on these granite mountain tops popping out of the Indian Ocean, a thousand miles from the nearest land. They had discovered that several species, earlier reported extinct, were still to be found, though in dangerously small numbers and usually confined to only one island or even to a small part of an island, where the natural vegetation had not been destroyed and predators were less menacing.

These birds included the Seychelles black paradise flycatcher, which they had seen nesting on La Digue Island exactly ten years after it was said to have died out, and the bare-legged scops owl, now rated by the World Wildlife Fund as one of the birds of the world most in danger. Other rarities included the Seychelles brush warbler of Cousin Island and, scarcest of them all, the Seychelles magpie robin, of which a colony of no more than a dozen or so still clung to existence on Frigate Island.

Aldabra, clearly, did not have a monpoly of zoological interest in the region. The immensely old granite islands, the only ones of this geological form in any ocean, offered a big enough challenge; elusive Aldabra slipped into the background.

With Jeffery Boswall, the producer of the BBC Natural History series 'Look', a television programme on the Seychelles was planned. It was tempting to give it the provisional title of 'The Rarest Bird in the World' in tribute to the splendid magpie robin, whose numbers were so far below the accepted minimum for survival and yet who continued, it seemed, to enjoy the company of man and to frequent, by choice, the gardens and copra-drier of its last island home. With natural optimism and the confidence that always grows greater in direct ratio to distance from the location, I felt sure that television viewers would shortly see the first film of the vanishing land birds of the Seychelles.

There were no big or dangerous animals to offer, of course. All the creatures living on these remote islands, which I later discovered to be quite the most scenically beautiful that I had seen in twenty years of travel, are those whose ancestors must have made landfall under their own steam, so to speak. Or in the case of the smaller invertebrates, insects and amphibians, perhaps as passengers on driftwood or on the feet of birds. But what they lacked in size and 'Daktari-appeal' they made up for, in full measure, by rarity and scientific interest. The origin and evolution of island fauna has been the subject of speculation since the first voyages of discovery and Darwin devoted a whole chapter to it in his *Origin of the Species*. It is a subject that requires further investigation and now, with new techniques available for the study of ecology and behaviour, it is again arousing world-wide interst.

The deeper my research into Seychelles natural history, the more I felt that it was an ample subject on its own, without Aldabra. In any case, Aldabra was an entirely different type of habitat, a relatively new coral atoll, of the uncommon 'uplifted' kind, most unlike these granite outcrops of the central group of islands, whose basic rock was estimated to be 650 million years old, pierced here and there by surface streams of black basalt. The German geologist, Dr Günther Giermann, from the Monaco Oceanographical Institute, who came to Mahé aboard a Soviet research ship during my stay on the island, reckoned that the original basalt now striping the surface at several places, notably in the 'Garden of Eden' valley on Praslin Island, antedated the arrival of life on earth more than 800 million years ago. There was quite enough here to whet the appetite.

I prepared a rough shooting script for a film about the present state of the unique Seychelles wild life, primarily about the endemic species of land birds, their chances of survival and the protective measures being taken and planned. It was also agreed that if, by chance, I should manage to get to Aldabra, which at the time seemed unlikely, we should consider this prospect when it arose. Jeffery Boswall said that the BBC had wanted a film on Aldabra for some time and was pondering ways and means of getting it. He shared my doubts that I would succeed in doing so.

At least I now knew where it was. Two hundred and sixty miles off the northern tip of the huge island of Madagascar and four hundred miles south-east of Mombasa, the main port of departure by sea for the Seychelles. Not enormous distances, when compared to such remote places as Easter Island, Tristan da Cunha or even the Galapagos.

The Aldabra group of three true atolls – Cosmoledo, Astove and Aldabra itself, and one modified atoll, Assumption – is part of that chain of islands stretching for more than a thousand miles from the French-owned Comoros in the south-west to the Seychelles Bank in the north-east, a widely-spaced series of five archipelagos running more or less parallel to the coast of Somalia and Kenya. Between Aldabra and the Seychelles lie the small Farquhar Group and the Amirantes, mere dots in the immensity of the ocean. Somewhere on the latitude of this chain is the northern extremity of the cyclone belt, but it would be a rash sailor who tried to predict accurately where the giant winds like those which periodically lash Mauritius, and the Mascarene Islands to the south, spend their force.

It is, however, known that Mahé itself has endured only one cyclone in the last hundred years. Among the many blessings of the Seychelles is that it lies outside the zone of big winds, a fact which, together with its freedom from malaria and its permanently warm, but never oppressive, climate will certainly strengthen its appeal to tourists when the international airport, about to be built in the lagoon near Victoria, is ready for traffic in the early 1970s.

From the Amirantes southward, storms are frequent and Aldabra is within this danger area. Islands are often cut off from supplies for weeks on end, when landing is impossible even to the expert creole boatmen, and a number of the islands and exposed reefs are better known for the wrecks they have caused than for anything else. The 'sea that leads nowhere' is unmarked on the atlas with the re-assuring dots of shipping lanes. This is not surprising, of course, but in reading early records, I was struck by the way the Portugese and other explorers and traders had always tried to give the area a wide berth, either hugging the coast of Africa, by making the Mozambique Channel, or sweeping north-east from Mauritius. The seas of the 'lost corner' were left for centuries to the pirates and corsairs, a safe refuge from which they preyed with great success on ships trading between Europe and the Far East.

There is hardly an island, it is said, without buried treasure on it; granted only a little has so far been found, but there are still plenty of seekers. One of these is a persistent ex-guardsman on Mahé, who has, with undimmed optimism, been blasting and digging for several million pounds' worth of corsair loot for nearly twenty years! To date he has little to show beyond a few fragments of porcelain, one looking like the base of a jam jar which, I thought irreverently, could have been litter from an eighteenth-century picnic party. Every time he feels like giving up, weird new clues appear to him in the rocks, and the show goes on.

Some have indeed found treasure of the story book kind, handfuls of gold coin in a rotting chest, but they are very cagey about its provenance. Fear of the tax man, or the poorer members of the family, keeps their mouths shut. I suspect that most of the pirates and corsairs, undoubtedly resourceful men, managed to cash rather than cache their loot – one has only to remember the renowned Surcouf, who retired as a wealthy country gentleman to spend his last years in luxury in France.

To the zoologist, each one of these groups of islands is of interest; from the Comoros, where the coelacanth flourishes, through the fantastic sea-bird colonies of the Amirante and Farquhar Islands, with up to three million terns nesting on the tiny platforms of Des Noeufs and Desroches Islands, to the strange land-birds of the granitic Seychelles and the giant tortoises of Aldabra. Few expeditions have traversed this route in the last hundred years, but of these, perhaps the best known are the Percy Sladen Trust Expedition of J. Stanley Gardiner in 1905 and J. C. F. Fryer's visit to Aldabra and some of its neighbouring islands in 1908 to continue its work.

The earliest large collection of flora and fauna from the Aldabra region was brought back for study in 1892 by the American zoologist Dr W. L. Abbott. More recently studies and collections have been made by the Bristol University Expedition to the Seychelles, which paid two visits to Aldabra and whose reports inspired me to follow the same path, and by the pioneer of the aqualung, Commander Jacques Cousteau, in his research ship *Calypso*.

I learned with mounting interest that much of Cousteau's remarkable underwater film 'The Silent World' was shot in the diamond-clear waters around Aldabra and Assumption, a further enticement to me if more was needed. I heard also, from friends in the Seychelles, that Cousteau had tried to lease the atoll for zoological research from the British government shortly after his visit in 1954. It is said that he approached Sir Winston Churchill, who was then Prime Minister, but the request was turned down. At the time the Frenchman was working under the patronage of an international oil company. Could it have been thought he was on to something good? A gusher perhaps?

Another post-war visitor to Aldabra was Dr Ommanney, whose account of a journey across the razor-sharp, honeycombed coral of the atoll, accompanied by a Seychelles government official with the agility of a mountain goat, and a hair-raising voyage in a native pirogue through the Main Channel at ebb tide, made me add a pair of climbing boots and a supply of tough polythene bags to my list of equipment.

One thing I lacked, which all these explorers had in common, with the exception of the Bristol team, whose saga on Harry Savy's *Argo* I have already mentioned, was my own boat in which to make the journey. My wishes were humbler – I would not have minded a cabin below deck in any seaworthy craft. Then the telegram arrived:

'government agrees to your travelling via aldabra on ladyesme leaving mombasa not before fourteenth february please cable if accept.'

The djinn had popped out of the bottle. I accepted with alacrity although I had no idea who 'ladyesme' was. There were ten days left in which to get to the East African port, with everything set for a journey to an atoll, described by an early traveller as 'the most inhospitable place on earth'. What I now needed most was up-to-date information and again I was lucky. Most of the handful of people in England who had been to Aldabra could be contacted.

Roger Gaymer and Malcolm and Mary Penny, of the Bristol Expedition, told me where to look for the biggest concentration of giant tortoises and that there was a population of over 30,000 of these creatures on the atoll. They showed me on the map the best localities for the various kinds of land-birds, most of which were distinct sub-species, and where the frigate and booby colonies were situated. They warned me about the shortage of fresh water and the danger of getting lost only a few yards from camp in a featureless landscape. There were a host of useful tips about creole guides, about how to walk on the eroded coral rock, called in creole French 'champignon', about tides in the vast lagoon and about how to attract the flightless white-throated rail, the last flightless bird of a region once famous for the dodo and the solitaire. They told me that Aldabra was no place for a picnic, but they wished they could come with me all the same. I never forgot their parting words:

'This could be one of the last chances of getting a film record of Aldabra in its natural state; before the bulldozers move in to wreck the place. Let's hope you can get some good publicity for the campaign to save Aldabra.'

Roger Gaymer gave me a copy of *Oryx* with his article 'The Case for Conserving this Coral Atoll'. Until then I had not fully realized the threat that Aldabra faced but, having read his final plea, I resolved to join the battle in any way I could:

'Aldabra needs total protection, combined with facilities for research, so that we can make good use of the unique opportunity it provides. An air base, which would be out of date in fifty years, would leave us with another Assumption, and our descendants would only be able to say, "What an interesting place this must have been".'

Assumption Island, twenty miles away, once boasted a flourishing avifauna, including several unique species, but since the beginning of this century it had been turned into a desert by guano diggers. In the search for this fertilizer, now superseded by chemical substitutes, man had scraped the top off this small island, destroying all its natural vegetation, thus virtually wiping out its wild life. Silent and covered with rank weeds and grasses, Assumption Island was now, according to Gaymer, a grim warning. All the resident sea-birds were exterminated, including the very rare Abbott's booby, as well as three unique land-birds, a rail, a white-eye and a turtle dove.

It seemed that Aldabra was the only island left in this vast expanse of ocean that had not yet been destroyed by man and that it was now in mortal danger from a plan to build an Anglo-American air staging post there. Why had it been left alone? What was it like now? Could I do anything in the fight to save its wild life?

The answer to the first question was becoming clear. Although it was the largest island in the whole chain, counting its huge central lagoon, it was not an hospitable place for the 'naked ape'. One danger was brought home forcefully in a film made by the Bristol Expedition that the BBC showed me. The jagged, razor-sharp surface of Aldabra is pitted with holes up to twenty feet deep, through some of which the sea roars up at high tide. The mouths of these mantraps are sometimes hidden by a tangle of undergrowth; a picture of the carapace of a dead tortoise, gleaming whitely at the bottom of an abyss, stuck in my memory.

Apparently the plans for the airbase, and for a powerful BBC transmitter station on West Island of the atoll, were well advanced; in considerable secrecy, it seemed, for very little had appeared in the press. I learned that a BBC technical team, accompanied by representatives of the Ministry of Defence and the American Air Force, had just returned from an inspection of the island and, from the leader of this expedition, Mr Alan Bosworth, I received a lot of valuable advice on equipment or, more accurately, survival gear.

3. 'Like a cloud of midges', the frigate birds over their breeding colony on Malabar Island. *(The Royal Society)*

4. A female green turtle coming ashore to lay her eggs. Aldabra was once
the Mecca of these reptiles, but due to uncontrolled slaughter in the
past hundred years their numbers have greatly declined.*(The Royal
Society)*

This official expedition had made the voyage in an ocean-going steamer, hired in Mombasa, but had nevertheless been forced by the threat of cyclone 'Angela' to return to East Africa earlier than intended. Several members had narrowly escaped drowning, others had been stranded overnight in the pemphis jungle, covering much of the island, when they tried to make a short journey overland. I heeded carefully Bosworth's warnings.

'Take plenty of plastic sheets and polythene bags,' he stressed, 'and at least two strong pairs of boots. Also a supply of salt tablets, for the heat at mid-day is appalling, with the undergrowth too low to offer shade; it is very easy to get dehydrated and drinking water is to be found at only a few places, miles apart. A supply of insect repellent is also essential and don't forget petrol for an outboard motor and, above all, a good 'panga' for cutting a path through the scrub. Without a compass it's impossible to find your way; some of the land routes have been marked by stone cairns, but the tortoises have a way of knocking these over and even the guides get lost!'

'Just to stay alive on Aldabra is quite an achievement,' Bosworth added. There was one less alarming piece of advice which, as an angler, I found exciting. 'Take along your fishing tackle. You will need lines up to a hundred pounds' weight; big hooks and metal traces.'

Shortly before his expedition left Aldabra, driven away by the threat of mountainous seas and the ominous gathering of black clouds to the south-west, one of the Defence Ministry members had undergone a frightening experience.

Obliged to spend the night in the jungle, because movement in the dark on the spiky honeycombed rock is impossible, the party bedded-down in *Pemphis acidula* scrub and tried to sleep. Suddenly he felt a nip on his cheek. He shied away and saw, clear in the moonlight, a red crab at least two feet broad, waving its claws at him.

Was this an early protest by the threatened fauna of Aldabra against the military plans?

When I heard this story, I was reminded of the reply, by the British delegate to the United Nations Committee on De-colonization, to the Soviet demand that Britain should take early steps to return the government of the Seychelles Islands to its rightful owners, the original inhabitants:

'We have no indication that there is any desire for independence on the part of the giant tortoise.'

The Seychelles Islands were of course uninhabited at the time of the first European colonization in the mid-eighteenth century and there is no evidence that they had ever been lived on by man.

Of all the equipment needed, the most difficult to find were maps and charts. The first hydrographic survey of Aldabra was made by H.M.S. *Fawn* in 1878, and apart from B. H. Baker's geological survey of 1961, little had been done to add to the original information. The search ended with a marine chart, which I started to mark with suggested routes across the atoll and places of zoological interest; a copy of Baker's Geological Sketch Map; and an immense land map, in two halves, which was the most gloriously empty one I had ever seen.

The twenty-one mile, elongated axe-head shape of Aldabra, with its four principal islands encircling a lagoon, was shown in white. Almost innocent of writing, except around the coast, where French names predominated, some of which, I suspected, commemorated corsairs if not pirates. Point Hodoul, at the extreme eastern end for example. And who was the Picard who gave his name to the island in the west? Other names of bays, or 'anses', and sand dunes were homely and told of the relief of creole fishermen at finding food or a landmark – Dune Patates, Anse Maïs, Anse Cèdres, Anse Tamarind. The cèdres' are casuarina trees. Of these island names, I liked best Trou Nenez, which is pure Créole, 'nenez' being the Seychellois word for 'nose', and the intriguing Johnny Channel. Such a robust Anglo-Saxon incursion into an otherwise francophone map would not, I felt sure, have given pleasure to the Gallic purists. It was named, incidentally, after the French vessel *Gionnet* whose wrecked bones can still be seen. 'Johnny' is just a crude Anglicization.

By now I had heard of the German cruiser, *Königsberg*, which, in World War I had taken refuge from its pursuers inside the entrance to Main Channel and remained anchored there for several weeks. Even on the chart, this looked a remarkable achievement and when, later, I saw the tide race and the living coral in this main outlet of the vast lagoon, and was swept out to sea in the current, I could hardly believe that such a feat had been possible. Someone ought to add a German name in tribute to the Aldabra map.

On the eve of my departure for Mombasa to board the boat, which I now knew was called *Lady Esmé* and was skippered by a Captain Sauvage, a reassuring name in such wild waters, I went to the

Natural History Museum to meet Dr C. A. Wright, one of the two scientists who had accompanied the BBC and defence experts to the atoll.

He showed me a photograph that might well have been taken in a Wellsian 'lost world', of seven-foot frigate birds drinking on the wing at a freshwater pool in which a number of giant tortoises wallowed. Dr Wright said that while he was working on snails and other invertebrates in the neighbourhood of Passe Houareau, the east channel, he was kept company for hours on end by a flightless rail; he pinpointed a mushroom island on which I would surely find the rare red-tailed tropic bird. The unique Aldabra fruit bat could, he said, be seen in swarms at Takamaka Grove on South Island, which was also the haunt of many of the land-birds, including the sacred (Abbott's) ibis and the Aldabra turtle dove.

It was obvious that if I could only get to Aldabra, there would be no shortage of subjects to film, and from all accounts the island creatures had little fear of man. I wondered about the butterflies and moths and, as entomology has been one of my interests for a long time and I had recently made a collection of lepidoptera in Laos, which was now at the Museum, I called on Mr Graham Howarth to ask about the insects on Aldabra. Here again the prospects were exciting.

Little collecting had been done on the atoll. In recent years only the French lepidopterist, Legrand, had made any studies there. The British Museum had few specimens from the region. Mr Howarth gave me a net and other equipment and asked me to look out, in particular, for a large white of the *Pierid* family that is known from Aldabra, but is extremely rare. This is a type of butterfly that would be known in less exotic places as a 'cabbage white'. 'Any butterflies or moths from Aldabra will be of interest to us,' he added.

There was no time for more research and, looking back, I doubt if much more information was then available. Early records were scarce and obscure, yielding nevertheless one intriguing mystery. In 1879 a party of forty Norwegian communists, including a number of children, arrived on the island to found a fishing settlement. They seem to have vanished, leaving no trace behind. What happened to their scheme is unknown.

Some of the available reports, made by visiting scientists in the past fifty years, were misleading and contradictory. Not long ago it was suggested that the tortoises were in danger of dying out, yet the Bristol University Expedition, on whose programme was a status investigation of the animal, reckoned a population of over 30,000. Then there were the vanishing goats. A former governor of the Seychelles, Sir William Addis, told me he had seen a number of these creatures on a very short visit in the fifties; others, who had toured the island recently, saw none.

We were approaching Nairobi before I had time to study the last letter from my friend in Mahé who had made the passage arrangements.

He wrote that the *Lady Esmé* was a 160-ton boat, the Seychelles government ferry that normally plied between the populated islands of the central granitic group. She was in Mombasa undergoing repairs and was returning to Mahé via Aldabra to enable an American green turtle expert, Professor Harold Hirth of Utah University, to make a study of the reptile on the atoll and on the adjacent islands as part of a world turtle survey for the FAO. Prof. Hirth had been invited by the Seychelles Government to do this research, because of fears for the survival of the green turtle in a region which, not long ago, was one of its principal breeding grounds.

Also on board would be Mr Guy Lionnet, Director of Agriculture and Fisheries of the Seychelles and the man responsible, as Chairman of the Fauna Conservation Board, for the protection of the wild life of Aldabra.

During the short stop in Nairobi, I rushed into town to order a further supply of colour film for my cine-camera – it would be disastrous to run out. My friend had written that the *Lady Esmé* would be calling at a number of other islands, including the perfect atoll of Astove. The latter had intrigued me for some time, although its chief claim to fame was the number of ships wrecked on its nearly vertical reef. It seems ungracious to say so, particularly as this was my first visit to Kenya, but all I can remember of Nairobi on this hectic day was the bougainvillaea, as a formula-one taxi driver, whose name might have been Stirling Moss, drove me to the city and back. Practically every street seemed aflame with the orange, red and mauve blossoms in unbroken lines and islands. It was quite the most brilliant display of flowers I had seen in any city of the world.

As soon as I had dumped my luggage, now consisting largely of a series of plastic containers, in a Mombasa Hotel, I made at once for the docks. At the gates I enquired the way to the *Lady Esmé* from Seychelles. The police guard glanced in a book and then turned back to me, looking suspicious:

'No ship of that name in port,' he said, indicating by a turn of his head the way out. I thought quickly.
'Are there any ships from the Seychelles at all?'

He hesitated and conferred with a colleague in the hut; without saying a word the second man moved over to my taxi and jumped in beside the driver. There was a rapid conversation and we moved forward into the docks. At least this was the right direction, but from the expression on the policeman's face he might have been about to deport me. The driver turned, grinning:

'One big ship Seychelles, we go.'

Good God, not by the direct route after all this, I prayed.

The taxi stopped alongside a vessel labelled *Southern Skies* which, it turned out, had arrived only that afternoon from Mahé. Several men were working amidships. I hailed them and asked, in French, if they knew where the *Lady Esmé* was.

'She's not here,' one man shouted. My heart missed a beat. He scratched his head and pointed. 'Over in the yacht harbour; she has finished repair, maybe sailing tomorrow. Captain Sauvage is there.'

The *Lady Esmé* was easy to recognize, a typical ferry boat. She looked trim in a new coat of grey paint, but rather high out of the water. Several men in wide straw hats with a black ribbon marked 'Port Department' were lounging on the decks. I was about to ask one of them if the captain was aboard, when a small man in an open-neck white shirt and shorts, with a ruddy tan, blue eyes and curly, grey-blond hair, emerged from the stern awning and stood at the top of the gangway. He waved me aboard without bothering to ask who I was.

The captain and I introduced ourselves. I noticed the extraordinary mixture of races that made up his crew, ranging from flaxen-haired Caucasian types to ebony-black giants. 'They're all Seychellois from Mahé,' explained Captain Sauvage, whose name belied the apologetic manner in which he at once spoke of the accomodation on board.

He explained that we would not be sailing for a few days as neither Lionnet nor the American professor had yet arrived. When I asked him about the route of our voyage he said nothing had yet been decided.

'Everything depends on what this professor plans to do and what Lionnet wants to show him. We'll have to decide when they arrive. Certainly Aldabra, but I don't know about the other islands. I rather hope it won't include Astove – a dangerous place. Sailor's nightmare. I hope you're not in a hurry to get to Mahé?'

Sensing at once that he was, I gave a non-commital answer. I did not mind how long we took getting there. The deadline for the Aldabra film was six months ahead.

Captain Sauvage, who spoke English with a French accent, and fluent French with a curious Seychellois drawl on the first syllable in such words as *tortue, poisson*, told me that the *Lady Esmé* was not allowed to take passengers on a long voyage and that we would have to sign on as crew. Out of the corner of my eye I appraised the 'old man'; aged about fifty, he looked tough and fit and it did not surprise me to learn that, before becoming harbourmaster of the Seychelles, he had skippered tankers in these waters. Just as I was wondering what tasks I might be given, in the rigging perhaps, he asked me whether I preferred whiskey, brandy or gin and how much beer we should take on board for the voyage!

Several times in the course of our conversation, he spoke of the danger of sudden storms and the difficulty of finding an anchorage in the islands. He laughed when I asked which was the calm season.

'Nobody has found one yet,' he said drily. 'Everything depends on luck. I'll try to fall in with the plans of the turtle man, but I must warn him that we may have to leave suddenly at any moment. On Aldabra we'll keep in touch by wireless.' He showed me several small transreceivers of the walkie-talkie type. 'If I call you back, drop everything and come as quick as you can; there's never much time to get away.'

'Do you have a good met. service on the radio in these parts?' I enquired.

The question was irrelevant. The *Lady Esmé* had no ship's radio. I began to understand why Captain Sauvage was so anxious to impress on his 'crew' the need to be alert. The small clouds spearheading a cyclone move swiftly up the horizon. 'Angela' had driven away a much bigger boat three months before, without warning.

In Mombasa it was oppressively hot and there seemed to be no drop in the temperature at night. A group of dusty tortoises in a sunken pit on the hotel terrace kept reminding me of Aldabra. We waited impatiently for the appearance of the rest of the 'crew', but the delay proved useful in several ways.

The problem of getting exposed films back from remote places to a laboratory in England is always a tricky one. It is not so much the means of transport (before now I have despatched them successfully on the first leg by elephant and aborigine runner) but the regulations in newly-independent countries through which they have to pass. Many of these are now highly suspicious of foreign film-makers and not always without cause.

Television teams have the worst reputation. As someone who had worked in the information services of several of the new countries in Asia, I knew that such fears were justified. Visiting directors fall easy prey to the temptation to turn the camera on beggars, slums and ceremonies which have, to the Western eye, a shocking effect. A grossly distorted picture results and this is deeply resented in a country struggling to rid itself of poverty and the relics of barbarism. Often the television team has no idea of the significance of what it is filming and, on a tight schedule, it has no time to find out. It may not even want to be enlightened as this might 'inhibit the creative instinct and truthful reporting', as I was once told.

The so-called 'death houses' of Singapore are a good example of this. Aged and sick Chinese are sent to these institutions by their relatives to spend their last days, with a funeral parlour conveniently located on the ground floor. 'Death houses' used to be on the 'Must' list of every visiting television reporter – they were represented as one of the gruesome horrors of a primitive Chinatown. Such a distorted image of the thriving city, the most advanced in Asia for social services, resulted, in the end in the prime minister, normally tolerant of Western reporters, having to put them out of bounds.

In fact, these 'death houses' are not nearly as grim and callous as they sound. Overcrowding in the poorer parts of Singapore is such that as many as a hundred people may live in a single two-storey shophouse, occupying windowless cubicles hardly bigger than a cupboard, with day-shift and night-shift workers often sharing the same bed in turns. The noise of Mah-jong and children is deafening. For the feeble old people, life can be a misery and families save up to send them to the comparative comfort and quiet of the 'death house'. Nothing is more important to the old-fashioned Chinese than a good and impressive funeral. To have the undertaker and coffin-maker on the spot is re-assuring all round. If the 'dying' recover they return home.

As far as I know this background was never given. Some television teams leave a trail of suspicion and hostility behind them and these tough new regulations for films in transit are their legacy to others.

My films would have to be sent from Mahé through either Kenya or India, since there is no means of sending parcels by air from the Seychelles. In Mombasa I was able to organize, with the help of a local shipping company, a system for customs clearance and forwarding which was nearly delay-proof. Exposed colour film can be ruined in a matter of hours if left lying around in a tropical customs shed.

These negotiations introduced me to Tony Bentley-Buckle, Chairman of Southern Lines, at whose house in a green suburb of the town I met another recent traveller to Aldabra. He had stayed a fortnight on the island collecting shells; although unable to move far from the settlement on West Island he had some useful tips.

'Watch out for the moray eels, they are even more aggressive than usual,' he said.

We admired the colour of his 8-mm. film and he told us the light on Aldabra is so brilliant 'you won't believe your exposure meter'. His close-ups of the birds, notably a striking scarlet and yellow cardinal, were the most convincing proof of their tameness I had so far seen. There was a shot of a red-tailed tropic bird on her nest taken at less than two feet. She refused to budge and show off her magnificent red tail feathers. The bird's aristocratic face bore, it seemed to me after three brandies, a scornful look. I dislike the whimsy of animals being made to act like humans on film, but I could have sworn that bird was thinking: 'What the devil are these two-legged tortoises bothering me for? Why can't they leave us alone as they have for the last 50,000 years?'

I was in full agreement with the sentiment.

Next day, as I was marking my map with new information, there came a knock at the door and in walked a stocky fair-haired man. It was Lionnet, the leader of our expedition. He was clutching a copy of the *Percy Sladen Trust Expedition Report* of 1911 and told me we would be sailing in a few days. I warmed to him at once when he proved to be a keen entomologist; in all my travels in wild places I have always found 'bug hunters' to be the best company. Perhaps it is because they can never be in a hurry and it is always, in my experience, the byways and the unforeseen halts that lead to the best discoveries and the adventure.

The soft-spoken government servant, equally at home in French and English – it occurred to me then what a rich source of bi-lingual talent the Seychelles would be if Britain ever joined the Common Market – had only once before been to Aldabra and then only for a fleeting look at Settlement Island. He was as keen as I to see the whole atoll and to prolong our stay. We resolved to talk the captain round.

The American Professor Hirth was due next day. He was coming from Aden, where he had been studying the status of the green turtle on the south Arabian coast. Lionnet was sure he would want to see all the breeding grounds of the turtle in the region, which he would be visiting for the first time. He would certainly want to inspect all the beaches on the seventy-mile rim of Aldabra and this could not be done properly from the sea. A complete tour of the atoll! Exactly what I had hoped for. It was the height of the egg-laying season for green turtles.

Guy Lionnet had been Director of Agriculture and Fisheries in the Seychelles for many years. As an official of the government he had to speak guardedly about the plans for Aldabra. As we chatted over a glass of iced East African beer, and laughed at the story of the land crab attacking the man from the Defence Ministry, I tried to detect in his humorous face his own feelings about saving Aldabra from the destruction that threatened it. Although he was obviously the type who would want to see for himself first, I got the impression, not so much from what he said as what he omitted to say, that he would prove a champion in the atoll's defence. And it turned out to be correct.

Harold Hirth flew in next morning from Arabia and was recommended to a hotel in town favoured by American visitors. The air-conditioning promptly broke down. This made him as anxious as we were to get to sea as quickly as possible, out of the steam-bath of Mombasa.

He seemed surprisingly young to be a professor – with a blond crewcut and the deep tan of the desert he looked more like a student. I had not realized until then that in the United States you do not have to be the head of a university faculty to earn this title. It is sufficient to be responsible for the tuition of a small group of students. But after a few minutes' conversation I realized we would have a dedicated expert on board, a man whose whole interest was centred on one reptile, the green turtle.

Hirth was the deputy and assistant of the renowned authority, Prof. Archie Carr of Florida University, whom I had heard mentioned by Tom Harrisson when, a few years before, I was staying on his turtle island reserve off the coast of Sarawak. Between them, Carr and Harrisson had made remarkable discoveries in their research into the habits and distribution of the green turtle, and I was to learn much more about these matters during the weeks ahead.

The American seemed to be travelling light. After months in wild places seeking the beaches where turtles breed, his equipment had been reduced to two haversacks, one containing turtle tags, which are clipped to one of the creature's front flippers and allow records to be kept of its fantastic voyaging, a small camera and a notebook. I thought with dismay of all the heavy equipment, including a massive tripod, long-focus lenses, and tape recorders, which I would be struggling to carry round the islands, equipment that could be damaged in an instant, with no chance of repair or replacement, by an unexpected wave on the reef or a fall on the honeycomb coral. But it was too late to change careers. We left next morning.

The East African coast soon disappeared in the midday haze. Then there was nothing, just the empty sea of the South Indian Ocean. The journey would take two and a half days, and the first land sighted should be Aldabra. Captain Sauvage was studying the charts:

'I don't want to arrive at Astove Island by accident,' he said emphatically. '*That's* a place to avoid.' The coxswain, standing next to him at the wheel, an angular Seychellois of about sixty, smiled wryly.

We were lucky with the weather. The sea was so calm, disturbed only by a lazy swell, that the tracks of flying fishes, radiating from the bows, traced silver lines as the winged blue fish took off and landed. There was nothing to do but laze under the awning and read again Fryer's reports on Aldabra. At the time, though published half a century before, they were still the best guide. The skipper gave his new and inexperienced crew no duties; anyway none of them carried union cards.

I discovered that the Seychellois creole sailors could understand French, spoken slowly, without abstract words. This was a pleasant surprise as I had always believed that Créole was a very distant relation, disliked by French purists. Traffic in the other direction was more difficult and, until one learned a few key Créole words – such as '*comme-il-a*' for 'now', '*lisières*' for 'eyes' or '*buldu*' for 'girl friend', to quote a few useful examples – the comprehension gap yawned. As I spoke French, the sailors evidently assumed I understood the local Créole, for this language is spoken fluently by the old Seychelles residents of French origin. Nevertheless, contact could be made. I set out to learn all about Aldabra and its adjacent islands from the first-hand knowledge of the sailors. The cabin steward, whom I tried first, had never before left Mahé, so that was no good. He advised me to try the deck hands.

To my amazement it drew a blank too. Not one of the twenty-odd Seychellois on board had ever been to Aldabra. Two had anchored briefly off the settlement on West Island, but no one had been inland, crossed the lagoon or seen the east end of the atoll, the strange flat land, or 'platin', where the world's last surviving population of the giant Indian Ocean tortoises roamed.

The nearer we got, the more mysterious and remote Aldabra became.

# IV   *A Living Natural History Museum*

WHAT had caused this tremendous outcry in defence of an atoll that no one had bothered much about before? Why did it arise so so suddenly? Above all, what was so important about Aldabra?

These were the questions I had been studying from the moment I had learned, through Roger Gaymer's article in *Oryx*, of the threat to turn the atoll into an Anglo-American military airfield and the site for a radio transmitting station. At first glance there were certain puzzling features. Why, for example, had there been no similar protest when other oceanic islands like Gan, Bikini or Christmas Island had been flattened to make military airfields or testing grounds? Was it simply that the cold war was hotter then and the pleas of conservationists would have seemed frivolous at a time of crisis? This may have been a factor, but it explained neither the vehemence of the conservation case, nor the level at which the battle to save Aldabra was being waged on both sides of the Atlantic Ocean.

Before leaving London I knew that the Royal Society itself, the oldest and most distinguished scientific body in the world, was leading the campaign and that its counterpart in the United States, the American National Academy of Sciences, was in support. It was, as far as I was aware, almost unprecedented for the Royal Society to take up such a cause in its own name. The unanimity of scientists on the question was striking.

This had been demonstrated at a conference, called by the Royal Society in London five weeks earlier, which had been attended by representatives of leading international and British scientific and conservation organizations in Britain, the American National Academy, and the Smithsonian Institution (the National Museum). It had considered a report on Aldabra which had been prepared by Dr D. R. Stoddart of Cambridge following his visit to the atoll with the Ministry of Defence-BBC Expedition two months before. The one that had been curtailed by cyclone Angela.

Dr Stoddart, who had joined the expedition at the request of the Royal Society, with Dr C. A. Wright of the Natural History Museum, was charged primarily to make recommendations for a 'crash programme' of research and conservation in view of the impending threat to build a military airfield on the island. To suggest how something could be saved from the wreck, so to speak. This he did, but a crucial paragraph of his report read:

'A very strong case can be made for preserving Aldabra from any development whatsoever, on purely ecological grounds, as a total ecosystem which could form an unspoiled island laboratory with unique and quite irreplaceable characteristics. This case will undoubtedly be presented in the strongest terms by many organizations . . .'

The conference reaction to this report was immediate and urgent. There was complete agreement on the scientific importance of Aldabra and support for the Royal Society's case for its total preservation. A recommendation that a nature reserve and research station be established as soon as possible was passed and, most significant of all, there was general agreement that to build a military airfield on the atoll would be a 'biological disaster of the first magnitude'. Coming from a body of eminent scientists, aware of the arguments of the military planners, strong words indeed.

This was the situation when I left England in the middle of February, but I had also heard that the Royal Society intended to make public its concern before the end of the month. Until this time, little had appeared in the press about the possible use of Aldabra for defence purposes.

In retrospect, I think this must have been intentional on the part of the military planners. There was a veil of secrecy about the early defence moves which could not be attributed entirely to security needs. It is true that, as far back as 1964, newspapers in Britain had carried reports of plans to build island staging posts in the Indian Ocean and that, in April 1965, *The Times* named Aldabra, Diego Garcia and the Cocos Keeling Islands as possible sites. There were further press reports in 1965 and 1966, but none of these were specific, nor was there any suggestion of urgency. Certainly there was no hint that detailed planning for one site, Aldabra, had already begun.

It was not until the middle of 1966, when the Royal Society got wind of the proposed reconnaissance of the atoll by BBC transmitter engineers, that the danger signals were seen outside Whitehall. When the facts of the Aldabra affair become known it will, I think, be established that it was the presence of the two independent scientists, Dr Stoddart and Dr Wright, on this expedition that first turned the tide to avert disaster.

What, in fact, would the disaster have been? What did the world stand to lose by the disturbance, if not the total destruction, of Aldabra?

In short, the loss of a unique natural wonder, one of the few islands in any ocean that remained relatively unspoiled by man – the violation of a 'living natural history museum'. Dr Stoddart's report and the Bristol University Expedition of 1964–65 catalogued the most important treasures of the museum.

Aldabra was the last home of the giant Indian Ocean tortoise – a creature once widespread in the region that had been exterminated in the wild state everywhere else. It was the breeding-ground for a vast number of sea-birds, including the frigate bird of seven-foot wingspan, the red-footed booby and the red-tailed tropic bird. Aldabra alone of the Indian Ocean atolls had never been mined for guano and therefore retained most of its original vegetation; among the 170 species of plant so far identified, no less than eighteen were unique. Many of its land-birds were distinct species or sub-species

forming links in evolutionary series which extend from Madagascar
and the Comoros north-eastwards through the scattered chain of
islands to the Seychelles.

Aldabra was an elevated atoll, raised fifteen to twenty feet out of
the sea, unlike the sea-level atolls found elsewhere in the Indian
and Pacific Oceans; consequently its range of habitats was much
more varied. It was also close to continental land – Madagascar and
Africa – and had therefore had unusual opportunities for colonization
by plants and animals but, since it was at the same time an oceanic
island, these immigrants had, in isolation, sometimes evolved into
distinct species.

Insects were known to be three times more numerous on Aldabra
than on any other Indian Ocean atoll. In the most obvious group, the
butterflies and moths, tentative studies had so far revealed that nearly
a quarter were endemic, that is, restricted to the atoll. The atoll also
claimed endemic crustaceans, freshwater fish and a distinct form of
fruit bat.

On Aldabra alone, in a region once famous for the extinct dodo, a
flightless bird survived.

Among the Indian Ocean islands, Aldabra alone had a largely
intact ecosystem, a community of plants and animals almost undisturbed by human interference. Its vegetation had not been
cleared for coconut planting nor its land devastated by guano
diggers. Because it had been spared large-scale human settlement,
there were few weeds, its waters were free of pollution and man's
escort of predators, cats, dogs and rats, had not wrought havoc on
its defenceless wild life.

These salient features of the 'uniqueness' of Aldabra were clearly
brought out in Dr Stoddart's memorandum on the atoll prepared for
the Royal Society. It also stressed that scientific studies on Aldabra
had so far been only superficial and that vastly more important opportunities for research lay ahead if the atoll could be spared development, particularly in the field of evolutionary theory and the processes
of colonization by plants and animals.

Such basic ecological principles as the working of population
control mechanisms in a natural environment, where evolutionary
pressures and their results are not hidden under a mass of man-made
disturbance, could be investigated on an intact Aldabra. There were
few other places left where such opportunities existed.

The two words that so often prefaced items on the catalogue of Aldabra's riches began to conjure up a picture by themselves – Aldabra alone. The island that had been ignored and avoided by man.

One estimate of the age of this platform of eroded limestone, the remains of a coral reef that once flourished on top of a submerged volcano, gave it as 50,000 years. Give or take twenty thousand, it was still a puzzle why man should so suddenly have become interested ·in it.

Its early history is obscure and there are few references to it, except in ships' logs, before the middle of the last century. Even the origin of its name, believed to be a corruption of the Arabic word 'Al-Khadra' – 'the green' is a mystery. It was probably given by Arab sailors trading between Zanzibar and the Comoros in the Middle Ages. On Pilestrina's map of Madagascar dated 1511, the atoll is called 'Alhadara', a Portugese phonetic version of this name. Professor Hirth maintained that it was well-known as a green turtle breeding base as far back as Greek classical times, but there is no record of any attempt at settlement before the atoll became part of the British Colony of Mauritius in 1814 during the Napoleonic Wars and even nineteenth-century accounts are few and often contra-dictory.

Perhaps it was the forbidding coastline and the sight of wild seas bursting through the honeycombed cliffs, to reappear in great spouts far inland, that deterred sailors from trying to land, but it is now clear that many descriptions were largely conjectural, repeating the mistakes of earlier travellers. In those days 'good timber for spars' and a fresh water supply were the first things to be sought on an island. Aldabra was falsely credited with having both.

Following the hydrographic survey made by Commander Wharton in H.M.S. *Fawn*, a number of scientists did carry out investigations on the atoll over the next forty years and several of them, notably Abbott in 1892, Voeltzkow in 1895 and H. P. Thomasset, Dupont and Fryer in the first decade of this century, brought back collections of flora and fauna. But earlier visits, such as those of Lazare Picault in 1742 and Nicolaus de Morphy a decade later, seem to have been fleeting and threw little light on Aldabra. The survey ship, H.M.S. *Fawn* reported that the atoll was uninhabited when it called there in 1878.

However, a few years earlier, news had reached England of a plan

5.  Probably the rarest bird in the world today: the Seychelles magpie robin of Frigate Island. About a dozen still survive on this privately-owned island. Not long ago they were common. *(The Author)*

6. A Seychelles bird, reported to be extinct, found feeding her young long after the obituary. A small colony of the Seychelles black paradise flycatcher still flourishes on La Digue Island. (*The Author*)

to establish a wood-cutting industry on this remote outpost of the Colony of Mauritius. This had resulted in a protest that first turned the spotlight of world attention on Aldabra, for among the group of naturalists who sent a letter expressing their concern to the Governor of Mauritius was Charles Darwin himself.

This letter of 1874 marks the start of active conservation of the tortoises. It expressed concern over 'the imminent extinction of the Gigantic Land Tortoises of the Mascarenes in the only locality where the last remains of this animal form are known to exist in a state of nature' and went on:

'The rescue and protection of these animals is recommended less on account of their utility . . . than on account of the great scientific interest attached to them. With the exception of a similar tortoise in the Galapagos Islands (now also fast disappearing), that of the Mascarenes is the only surviving link reminding us of those still more gigantic forms which once inhabited the continent of India in a past geological age . . . . It flourished with the Dodo and Solitaire, and while it is a matter of lasting regret that not even a few individuals of these curious birds should have had the chance of surviving the lawless and disturbed conditions of past centuries, it is confidently hoped that the present Government and people . . . will find a means of saving the last examples of (their) contemporary.'

The woodcutting project was abandoned, but the letter did far more than this. It drew attention for the first time to the shameful fact that an animal, which until recently had been thriving on many islands of the South Indian Ocean, had been practically wiped out by the rapacity of man. Unfortunately the tortoise was good to eat, and in the days before refrigeration it offered, with the green turtle, the most convenient supply of fresh meat to ships at sea. Both reptiles are hardy and remain alive for long periods, even lying on their backs, without water, and in the sun.

Despite the appeal of Darwin and his friends and the subsequent legislation, few positive steps were taken by the Mauritius government to protect the tortoises of Aldabra. Indeed, from 1888 onwards, the atoll was commercially leased for the exploitation of its timber, green turtles and fish at what amounted to a peppercorn rent. The first lessee was Jules Cauvin of Mahé. He built the first settlement near West Channel and tried planting coconuts, fortunately without much success. His successor was a certain James Spurs, reckoned by the government to be 'a lover of nature and an observant man' who was 'unlikely to kill the goose that lays the golden eggs'.

It must soon have become clear, even to the Seychelles officials who read his reports every year, that his love did not extend to the green turtles, for Spurs proposed to limit his catch to 12,000 of these reptiles a year! As he was paying only £35 annually in rent for Aldabra, he seems to have been on to a good thing. Spurs did, however, respect the tortoises and even tried to repopulate West Island, before moving the settlement there to its present site.

In 1900, the lease passed to a commercial company who concentrated on the fishing rather than on timber extraction and who, once again, tried to plant coconuts. Again they were beaten by the 'intractible' terrain and occasional cyclonic winds. Aldabra seemed to be winning its battle for survival, but in 1904 came a lessee whose ruthless exploitation of the turtles practically exterminated them, M. D'Emmerez de Charmoy, who employed 'nature lover' James Spurs as his manager.

This was probably Aldabra's darkest hour, but the dangers inherent in the system of leasing the island to exploiters, with supervision well-nigh impossible, continued until 1945. Then Aldabra had ten years in which to lick its wounds. These had been confined largely to the extreme western tip of the atoll and to the surrounding waters where the green turtle was the main victim.

For some unexplained reason, probably the loss of young naturalists in World War I, scientific interest in Aldabra seems to have lapsed after Fryer's last expedition in 1909, and between than and 1953, only the biologist, Vesey-FitzGerald, is known to have made any studies there. He was interested in the land-birds and the plants.

Aldabra had become part of the Crown Colony of the Seychelles at the time of the latter's separation from the administration of Mauritius in 1903, and it was the Seychelles government who restarted the system of commercial leasing in 1955, with a thirty-year grant to Mr Harry Savy of Mahé, the present lessee, from whom I now carried a letter in my pocket addressed to the manager of the settlement.

When one considers what might have been the consequences of leasing an island so remote from the eye of the landlord and so inaccessible, that control or restraint was impossible to exercise, it was remarkable, by all accounts, how little damage Aldabra had sustained during these seventy years of exploitation. I was beginning to suspect that most of the credit for this astonishing survival belonged to the atoll itself and that it had its own strong defences. Very soon I was able to confirm this on the spot.

The extent of damage and interference caused by the lessees, apart from the slaughter of the green turtle, seemed to be limited to the building of a settlement for up to a hundred creole labourers at the western extremity of the atoll, and to the introduction of domestic fowls, cats and dogs, some of which had become feral, mainly in this area. There were reports of a few cats and rats running wild in other parts of the atoll, and goats, herbivorous competitors of the giant tortoise, were known to have been introduced by Spurs when he was lessee in 1890. Beside the coconuts, which had not prospered, and some tiny plots of maize, cotton and sisal around the settlement, there were only a few introduced plants and pantropical weeds to compete with the natural vegetation. In general, disturbance was confined to Picard Island and to the scattered landing beaches or 'anses' in other parts of the atoll, where tall casuarina trees, waving high above the pemphis scrub, indicated the passage of man. These were almost certainly planted by the early lessees.

A French naturalist, Dupont, spent two months on Aldabra in 1906 and made a fantastic recommendation which, mercifully, was never acted upon – that rabbits, hares and cattle should be brought in to augment food supplies. If they had survived, which is doubtful where goats find it difficult, the competition for a limited food supply might well have wiped out the tortoise population.

On the whole Aldabra had defended its independence well, a fact noted by all recent visitors. In the past fourteen years, since the visit of an Italian Zoological Expedition in 1953, a greater number of scientists had carried out researches there than ever before.

Cousteau went in 1954 to study crustacea and marine biota and, in 1957, the Yale Seychelles Expedition paid a visit. Other studies were made by individuals of the lepidoptera, the green snail, the tortoises and birds, as well as of the geology of the atoll, during this period, which also saw the first commercial fisheries survey under the leadership of J. F. G. Wheeler.

Most of the post-war visitors published papers which advanced knowledge of Aldabran flora and fauna within scientific circles, but it was left to the two most recent expeditions, those of Bristol University in 1964–65 and of Stoddart and Wright in 1966 to focus worldwide attention on Aldabra as a whole. Both assessed the extent of human interference and the effect that it had had on indigenous wild life and vegetation and came to the conclusion that Aldabra's ecosystem was relatively undisturbed. It was this, the atoll's whole complex natural community of plants and animals interacting together, that gave Aldabra its unique scientific importance and made it deserving of total protection.

Greatly increased urgency was attached to their reports because of a political decision that had recently been made. This, the greatest threat Aldabra had known, was just visible on the horizon at the time of the Bristol visit. When Stoddart and Wright were there, it was overhead.

I well remember my surprise when I read in a local newspaper in Laos in 1965 that Great Britain had just created a new colony. Moreover, that a Socialist administration had done it. My Asian colleagues were equally taken aback at the bald announcement of the 'British Indian Ocean Territory' created at a time when the old Empire was being dismantled with almost indecent, if not imprudent, haste. I had to wait weeks for a copy of Hansard to find out more.

The new colony was to consist of four islands – Farquhar, Desroches, Aldabra and the Chagos archipelago – to be acquired from Mauritius and the Seychelles and, in the case of two of them, from private Seychellois owners. The Colonial Secretary explained in the House of Commons that it was intended that the islands of BIOT should be available for the construction of defence facilities by the British and the United States Governments. Nothing more specific and it was apparent that Government wished to say nothing that could arouse the anxiety or the ire of independent Afro-Asian states with Indian Ocean frontiers. The United States had paid two-thirds of the purchase price and was prepared to pay half the cost of any base that was built.

The obscurity surrounding the conception and birth of this political anachronism was so great that it does not seem to have alerted the conservationists and the fact that it straddled such a vast area of ocean, and offered four alternative sites, may have contributed to the complacency. The naturalists may also have believed that no government would contemplate the conversion of Aldabra into a military base. They had a right to expect that the scientific case for sparing an atoll which Darwin himself had championed nearly a century before would be taken into account and that expert advice had been sought even before the new colony was created. But as the curtain of secrecy slowly lifted, the worst fears were realized.

To the dismay of the conservationists it became obvious that, far from sparing Aldabra and developing the other three parts of BIOT, all of which were comparatively valueless to science, it was Aldabra alone that was to be bulldozed and levelled and dammed. The atoll was to be the strategic key of the new Anglo-American colony. Studying the plans now, it is hard to believe that Aldabra was not its justification, the other islands merely a blind.

They envisaged an airfield with a 4,500-metre runway and staging post buildings for airforce personnel at the east end of South Island; a dam across the main channel to give harbour facilities for 20,000-ton tankers at the west end and a linking road between the harbour and the airfield running the length of Polymnie and Middle Islands and crossing the East Channel by a bridge or causeway. The BBC Transmitter Station was to be located near the present settlement on Picard Island. The latter project was said to be independent of the defence plan, in the sense that it could go ahead even if this were scrapped.

More than the magnitude of the scheme, which would directly cover a third of the land area of the atoll, it was the siting of the various installations that gave cause for greatest alarm. The site chosen for the airfield was precisely where the giant tortoises congregated in largest numbers – on the smooth 'platin' zone of South Island. The link road would pass right through the frigate and booby colonies of Middle Island, the biggest of their kind in the South Indian Ocean, and the home of the flightless rail. Damming the main channel would alter the whole character of the lagoon and, by restricting water circulation, would destroy conditions for great flocks of wading-birds which feed on the drying flats.

The view of BBC engineers was that their transmitter station would have no more effect on the ecology of the atoll than did the existing settlement, but the generators needed to run it would need great quantities of fuel. Although scientists appreciated the BBC's assurance that every precaution would be taken to prevent accidents and to minimize disturbance of wild life, the dangers were all too apparent.

★　　　★　　　★　　　★　　　★　　　★　　　★

As we lay offshore that morning, waiting to cross the reef, the situation was that no firm decision had yet been taken to go ahead with either project. This had come from the Minister himself, but there were alarming indications that all they awaited was a final nod and the rubber stamp. Defence members of the recent expedition were not engaged on a preliminary reconnaissance of the atoll to find out whether it was suitable for an airfield. They were further along the road and working on practical problems, the last to be solved before construction started. The reconnaissance had already been done five years before. A pile of bleached turtle and tortoise bones at the old R.A.F. camp-site at Anse Maïs was said to be a silent reminder of it.

I looked across the shining water at Aldabra. The sun was now high and the mist had vanished. The line of the reef was no longer clear, marked now only by oily waves instead of breakers. The white beach below its fringe of coconuts and casuarinas had shrunk.

As I watched, eight small black figures started rolling a pirogue down the sand to the water's edge. A large grey shark circled idly round the *Lady Esmé*.

'He's at least forty feet under,' said a voice behind me. Captain Sauvage peered down. 'There are a lot of those around, but don't worry, you'll make it all right. They're good boatmen, these chaps, they have to be.'

I hoped he was right. I wanted to see for myself the 'living museum' of Aldabra. This could be the last chance.

# v  *Raised Atoll Ahead*

THE manager of Aldabra was called Archangel Michael – a slim, wiry, coffee-coloured young man with a big grin. He clambered aboard the *Lady Esmé* at the head of his darker oarsmen, most of whom had a physique that would not have been out of place in weight-lifting finals at the Olympic Games. If this is what a fish diet does for you, I thought, then the sooner we start the better. The labourers exchanged ribald greetings with our creole crew; we were the first boat to arrive in three months and news from Mahé, the home of most of the Aldabra labourers, was given in rapid Créole which I found impossible to follow. Few of the labourers are allowed to take their wives and children to the atoll so they wanted news of their families. Since in the Seychelles practically everyone is related, this was freely available.

When a packet of mail had been handed over, Captain Sauvage introduced the manager and I gave Mr Archangel my letter of

introduction from Harry Savy. He thanked me in English, although
he was obviously more at home in French, and said he had heard of
my coming and had been expecting me for a week. This good news
was almost miraculous, although it did not strike me so at the time,
in the hubbub and excitement of loading the pirogue and general
celebration. How could he have been warned, with no ships calling
and no wireless in the settlement?

Long ago it would have puzzled me, but the working of the 'bush
telegraph', even over water, is something I now take for granted. And
anyway there was no time to marvel at the Aldabra Information
Service. Two huge labourers were in my cabin passing my equipment out on deck and I went over to take charge of the most delicate
items. One of the creoles sidled over with a secretive look. 'Cognac,'
he whispered. A half-bottle was handy, so I gave it to him with a
glass. Sweating and gleaming like rain-soaked iron, he put the bottle
to his mouth, swallowed several inches without pause, wiped his
mouth and the bottle top with his hand, belched quietly and smiled,
'*Moi pas boire longtemps*'.

The black pirogue with its elegant curved bows accommodated
Lionnet, Hirth, myself and all our gear comfortably. Sauvage leant
over the side:

'Radio me every morning and evening at six-thirty. I'll be tuned
in,' he shouted. 'Good luck. If I call you back, come as fast as you
can.'

No precise date had been fixed for our return. Everything depended
on the tides and the weather and how long it took Hirth to inspect the
beaches of the atoll. Barring accidents, we hoped to be back on
Picard Island within ten days, but it was difficult to estimate the
time it would take to make a journey that, as far as we knew, had
never been attempted before – the seventy-mile circumference of
Aldabra mainly on foot.

As we approached the reef, I marvelled at the incredible clarity of
the water, a brilliance heightened by an escort of mackerel that had
been scavenging around the stern of the *Lady Esmé*. These were like
no mackerel I had ever seen before, bright blue with canary-yellow
tails. Watching and trying to film these fish, I hardly noticed it
when we passed over a gap in the reef; there was a sudden change
in the intensity of the light and the colour of the water turned to
pale green. A triangular fin, followed immediately by two more,

broke the surface ahead; sharks seemed to be massing to oppose our landing. It was surprising that Archangel Michael at the tiller looked so unconcerned. I turned to ask about sharks and dangerous fish generally, when he said, '*Pas requins; gros poissons de sable*'. I made a note not to be taken in by 'fools' sharks' in future, a complacent attitude I had reason to regret later.

The pirogue was behind the crest of a roller leading out to the beach; with no warning at all, waves fit for surf-riding had grown out of the glass-calm sea. I tightened the polythene bags over my cameras and tape-recorder. But there was no need to worry. A creole, with the agility of a spider, leapt on to the locker in the bows of the rowing boat and shouted directions to the helmsman. A few ugly rocks mottled the sandy bottom as a large wave carried us in, until with a soft thud we hit the beach. The oarsmen jumped overboard together and struggled to keep the boat pointing straight inshore. This is the danger moment. If the boat is allowed to swing in the wash, a capsize is inevitable. A human chain rushed the luggage ashore and stacked it at the top of the beach.

The last leg of the journey to Aldabra, the sailors' nightmare, had proved as easy as landing for a Sunday picnic on a holiday beach.

Here there were no signs of the dreaded 'champignon' rock, said to cut boots to pieces in a few days, nor of the *Pemphis acidula* scrub that had been the despair of explorers in the past. Behind a fringe of casuarinas and a few coconuts and fruit trees were the houses of the settlement labourers, square white boxes of coral rock or wood. There were a few larger buildings scattered over the sandy plateau behind the beach and we were immediatèly led to one of these. It was not exactly the Grand Hotel Imperial, Aldabra Plage, just a two-room wooden bungalow with a balcony front and rear. But it was far better accommodation than I had expected to find, equipped with beds and a great number of wooden chairs, frames for the mosquito nets and two large tables. I discovered later that chairs are a status symbol in the Seychelles, your social rating being assessed by the number you can cram into your living-room, presumably indicating the wide circle of your friends and relations.

The air-conditioning was first class. Big windows fitted with shutters looked out in all directions and the front balcony hung over the lip of the beach.

It would have been a nice place to spend a few days, although I did not fancy swimming among the '*gros poissons*', but we had decided to take advantage of the fine weather and get started to the interior without delay.

Our first destination was to be Anse Maïs, a few miles south of the settlement beyond the west channel of the lagoon where, among other things, the Bristol Expedition had discovered a nest of the Aldabran kestrel two years before. There was a small beach and several others in the vicinity which Hirth wanted to inspect for turtles. This part of the journey would be done by boat and we decided to leave the next morning. Fortunately we had a good supply of petrol for the outboard motors, because the settlement stocks were low.

By now a number of the workers had congregated around the rear balcony of our resthouse, and, standing in the background, were a few women and small children. Mr Archangel introduced me to his wife, who was holding a small girl by the hand and carrying a fat baby in her arms. She said she had been a schoolteacher in Mahé and, in good French, told me about life on the atoll. She was longing to get home when her husband's tour ended in a few months, but added that life was not too bad on Aldabra. Food and water were plentiful and the manager's house was comfortable. She pointed to a white building with red shutters on the far side of a wide sandy expanse. It could have been described as the village green if there had been more grass on it.

There was, of course, no school – only six children on the island, not counting the babies, she said. She added that her main anxiety was about medical attention if someone developed a serious illness or had a bad accident. The only medicines were a few things like aspirin and laxatives that the manager had in his store. Not for the first time, I realized that this was the real snag about living on the paradise, tropical island of story books. What happened if you got appendicitis, for example? The answer was obvious. The prospect to a mother like Mrs Archangel Michael would have been less alarming if the Aldabra settlement had had wireless communication with the Seychelles, but it had none. Nevertheless, all the Aldabrans I saw that first morning looked remarkably healthy and robust.

The maps, including the huge, empty white affair, were now out on the balcony table. It was exciting to hear the men talk familiarly of place names that, until then, had been exotic exclamations on the bald map of an atoll as unattainable as a mirage. I could tell by his face that Harold Hirth felt the same way. Powerful black fingers followed the inscriptions letter by letter and, when the name was read aloud, it was greeted with delighted cries:

'*Dune Jean-Louis. Quantités tortues.*'

'*Takamaka! Anglais Oiseaux content.*'

This last announcement meant, I learned later, that 'Mr English Birds' – the immediate Créole nickname for me – would be pleased by the number of birds at Takamaka Grove. Harold Hirth was given the descriptive name of '*Anglais Tortues*' which, I thought, for an American professor, he took with praiseworthy calm and lack of protest. He did not mind being called 'Mr Tortoise', but I suspect the English attribution may have stuck in his gullet!

More confusing was the use of the French word 'tortue' to describe both turtle and tortoise; this sometimes led to misunderstanding. That the French have no specific word for turtle, other than 'tortoise of the sea', struck me as a curious omission. Another surprising discovery I made at this time was the absence of a French word for 'shallow'.

The creoles bought us all sorts of fresh food to supplement our supplies, mainly rice and tins of meat in varying shades of pink, sugar, coffee and salt. I began to have some sympathy for minor disturbance of the ecosystem of Aldabra by the introduction of chickens and the planting of food crops round the settlement! In return, they welcomed cigarettes, which were obviously scarce, beer and sweets, particularly the latter. As I had so often found in wild places, all the adults enjoyed sucking sweets. They had no inhibitions about it, nor fear of the calory intake and how it might affect the waistline; and everyone on the atoll smoked when they had the chance.

Archangel Michael was leaning over the map. I caught sight of several jagged white scars above his breastbone, looking quite new. He seemed to guess what I was wondering.

'We had a bad accident last month,' he said turning down the corners of his mouth. 'One man was killed. We don't know whether he was drowned or battered to death on the cliff. There was a piece of champignon stuck in his head when we got the body back. Deep in.'

'Where did it happen?' I asked.

'We were fishing off the south coast. A storm blew up suddenly and we tried to make land in one of the small anses. Got over the reef all right, but then a big wave turned us over. We were three. Two of us managed to reach the shore, but the other man disappeared. I thought we would all be killed. Climbing up the overhanging cliff was terrible The rocks were sharp like knives and the sea kept banging me against them. The other man was badly cut up – his hands and chest. I was lucky to get away with this.' But he was fit again and anxious to go with us.

From my reading of recent accounts of Aldabra, notably that of the Bristol University published in *Animals*, a copy of which I carried with me, I was particularly intrigued by one bird – the flamingo. Was it a local breeding species? Why had its numbers declined from a reported thousand at the turn of the century to the latest estimate of fifty? Since the end of World War II, it had been sighted only once by a visiting naturalist. In fact Roger Gaymer's report of 1965 was the first indication for many years that the flamingo still existed on Aldabra. Most of the settlement workers who were not out fishing had now assembled round our balcony and an active discussion about bird colonies was in progress. I decided to ask the question uppermost in my mind.

'Where do you see the flamingo?'

This was greeted by several blank looks, a few sage shakings of the head and some laughtèr. An old man spoke up:

'*Moi pas voir. Flamants longtemps aller.*'

The others, including the manager, seemed to agree with this statement, from which I understood that no one had seen the flamingoes – they had gone away.

'Is there no one here who travelled with the young Englishman two years ago?' I continued.

Several people cried 'Laporte' and a boy dashed away to re-appear a moment or two later accompanied by a thin, middle-aged man. There was something odd about his walk that struck me at once, high-stepping with the body bent slightly forward from the waist. It was not until much later that I realized this came from walking across the 'champignon' coral, where the foot had to be placed with extreme care and every movement is a balancing act.

Laporte had spent over twenty years on Aldabra. He was immediately bombarded with questions by the other creoles. In several I caught the word '*flamant*'. He spoke in a soft voice, diffidently, but when he pointed to places on the map, there was no hesitation. He said he knew the beaches where turtles came up to lay; he had marked some of the tracks to them with stone cairns. Although he was older than the other men, he looked sinewy and alert. We must all have been hoping for the same thing, but it was Guy Lionnet who put it into words.

'Could he come with us as a guide?' he asked the manager. There was a brief consultation. Laporte had been suffering from a sore foot, but it was now all right. He could. I noticed his bright eyes light up with pleasure but, in retrospect, I think it must have been at the thought of his fee rather than the excitement of the journey.

He had seen the flamingoes about a year before, but 'far away and in a difficult place'. From the expression on his face I suspected this was an understatement. He imitated the wing movements of a flamingo at take-off which caused an outburst of laughter, but I could tell the old man was respected. When he started again, about the tides in the lagoon, the bystanders were immediately silent. My fears that he might be like the guides one had so often suffered in Asia evaporated. Unlike the latter, he admitted there were some creatures he had not seen, the nightjar for instance.

There was still time to make a tour of the settlement before nightfall. During our conference I had seen several strange birds, including the brilliant scarlet and yellow cock cardinal, the size of a sparrow, flying around the house. Obviously a number of the unique Aldabran species of land-birds, one of my main interests on the expedition, still survived on Picard Island despite the presence of humans.

The creoles, I observed, took no notice of them. It was too soon to say that the birds were respected, but certainly they showed little fear of man. I had counted more than a dozen cardinals and sunbirds during our noisy conference on the terrace and, on two occasions, a cardinal had perched on the handrail a few feet away from us. Several sunbirds, one of them a splendid male, whose metallic blue-green helmet and breast shone in the afternoon sun, darted about in a casuarina tree. Both of these are distinct Aldabran sub-species, and albeit common and too small to be worth eating, their presence right in the heart of the village made me impatient to see what other endemic land-birds could still be seen in the only part of the atoll inhabited by man. There were a lot to look out for.

Of the sixteen land-bird species known to be breeding residents, the great majority are unique to Aldabra. They include a tiny kestrel, the only bird of prey, a coucal, a red turtle dove, a blue pigeon, a nightjar, a white-eye and a drongo among the smaller birds, in addition to the cardinal and sunbird I had already seen. Not counting the flamingo, which had a large question mark over his head at the time of my visit, there were two larger birds with distinctive characteristics – the sacred ibis and a dimorphic egret which appears in three forms, white, sooty grey and piebald.

And, of course, there was the white-throated rail, the only flightless bird surviving in the Western Indian Ocean. This bird, which had already become a symbol of Aldabra in my mind, had never been reported from the settlement island, so I didn't expect to see it that day. I hoped to do so later, probably on Middle Island. By all accounts, the rail, one of which I had seen stuffed in the London Natural History Museum, was a trusting bird with an over-developed sense of curiosity. It must have lost the power of flight since coming to Aldabra – it just gave up flying.

A number of other land-birds, the pied crow, two species of heron and the Madagascar bulbul also breed on the atoll, but are not thought to differ from those found elsewhere in the Malagasy region. Nothing is more remarkable about Aldabra than its astonishing variety of land-birds, so many of which are unique. Knowledge of them is far from complete and I felt sure that new discoveries would soon be made.

As Laporte and I set off down the sandy track that led through the settlement, I glanced out to sea. A slight wind was rising and the *Lady Esmé* was rolling at anchor beyond the reef. Suddenly a black shape broke the surface fifty yards from shore, then two flippers thrashed the water and half a carapace rolled over. Then another head appeared. I called out to Harold but he was already on the rest-house balcony. It was a pair of green turtles mating. They remained visible for several minutes and I was so interested in watching them, I paid no attention to a pirogue that had left the beach hurriedly with four fishermen aboard, one standing in the bows. Harold told me about it later. If I had followed their movements I would have witnessed an action that accounts more than anything else for the decline of the green turtle in this part of the world.

In the middle of the settlement were several larger buildings including one that puzzled me at first. This was a low, square construction of coral blocks with an inverted roof of corrugated iron forming a shallow 'V'. Looking under the eaves I found it was half full of water. This was one of two reservoirs for the settlement fed entirely by rainwater. Most of it is caught on the roof, but several conduits led from the gutters of neighbouring houses to supplement the direct fall. The rainy season had just ended, and by this ingenious means, the inhabitants were assured of a good supply during the dry months ahead.

On the sea-shore was a substantial boat-shed where several crafts-men were at work repairing an old pirogue and building another. For this work they were using wood of the takamaka tree which grows on the atoll and which, they said, was best for withstanding hard knocks on the coral. The manager's two-storey house overlooked this vital centre of activity and behind it were two other buildings, larger and more solidly built than the rest.

Archangel Michael had now joined us and he explained that the first was the church – I had missed the small wooden cross on the gable – and the other, the gaol. A nice juxtaposition of heaven and hell. Hell had three doors all of which stood open.

'Do you have a policeman on the island?' I enquired.

'No, I am responsible for all discipline,' explained A. M., 'but we have a very good lot of men now. I haven't used the gaol for months. It's usually for drunkenness.'

I wondered how one could get drunk without a pub or wine store for hundreds of miles and then I remembered the Tamil toddy collectors of Singapore reeling merrily after a day in the palm trees collecting fruit for that delicious drink. There must be ample oppor-tunity for making a three-star alcoholic tipple on exotic Aldabra!

'The church is used once a year for Mass,' the manager said. 'A priest comes from Mahé in the *Argo*, Mr Savy's boat.'

'When is he next due?'

'He should have come in December but we had bad luck. Every-thing was ready for him and sure enough the *Argo* arrived off the reef. But the weather was so bad he couldn't land. They hung about for three days, but it was no use. Now I suppose we'll have to wait another year.'

In my imagination I could see the portly bearded figure of the French priest, robes blowing in the wind, trying desperately to meet his little flock with the savage Aldabra tide-race barring his path. He had braved seven sea-sick days in a wooden tub only to meet this mighty obstacle within sight of the church. The manager's bald account had something of the pathos of a Greek tragedy. I felt sure, however, that the mere sight of this hardy man of God, a white dot in an ocean of heaving blue, must have given comfort to the settlement folk, clad in their Sunday best. Most Seychellois creoles are devout Catholics and, somewhat irreverently, I thought they cannot have had much to confess. 'I killed an ibis. I was very hungry and it tastes like duck,' or 'I got drunk on rice wine which I brewed myself and had such a hangover I couldn't work properly next day at turtling'. The little church, bare as a board, still looked spotlessly clean.

From a window I saw a flash of scarlet in a tree a few yards away and immediately grabbed my tripod and camera. A male cardinal was helping to build a nest. It was no more than eight feet from the ground, an untidy hanging dome of straw, typical of weaver-bird construction, on the outside of the tree with no attempt at concealment. The balcony of a labourer's house was so near that a man with a long reach could have touched the nest. It was in full sunlight and the striking colours of the bird's breeding plumage made the whole activity ridiculously conspicuous. An old man was repairing a fishing net at the foot of the tree.

Here I was, filming a bird that is found nowhere else in the world, at a distance of ten feet (I could have got nearer but the angle would have been wrong) with several chattering humans watching. Although I had been told that many of the land-birds were tame, I never expected such a photographer's dream as this, and right in the middle of the settlement too. It was like a studio set-up with the cardinal an efficient member of Equity; I filmed a hundred feet of the bird at work and it scarcely looked up as I moved on.

It was clear that the cardinals, at least, were safe; the villagers just ignored them, although on one occasion I saw a handful of rice thrown to birds hovering round the door of a hut.

The sunbirds, too, were in no danger. Within half an hour, a trio of small boys who had joined the party showed me four nests of this tiny bird within a quarter of a mile of the settlement. The nests were even more conspicuous than the cardinal's, hanging only two or three feet from the ground on small trees. A hide was unnecessary. It was enough to remain quietly in front of the nest for a few minutes to see

7. The extreme eastern tip of Aldabra Atoll. Jagged 'champignon' rock crowned with pemphis scrub at Pointe Hodoul. *(The Author)*

8.  In Creole the distinct species of Aldabran white-eye is called 'oiseau lunettes' – the spectacles bird. *(The Royal Society)*

the bird, with slender scimitar beak often gripping an insect, fluttering in and out to feed her young.

If the birds were as tame as this in the settlement, surely in the hinterland which had never been inhabited by man they might be even more approachable! Mulling over these euphoric thoughts, something warned me to beware of snags, not to be too optimistic. I was glad later that this cautionary voice had spoken. The relatively civilized surroundings of Picard Island give the newcomer no idea of the monstrous difficulties ahead.

Beyond the vegetable and sisal garden, I had glimpsed the notorious pemphis scrub, a mass of grotesquely distorted branches thinly coated with light green leaf, forming a wall of vegetation eight feet high. But I had no need to challenge it yet; quite enough of interest could be observed on the sandy plateau flanking the beach. As for the dreaded 'champignon' rock, I had so far seen none.

On this first walk I learned a salutary lesson. Do not express too much interest in seeing the birds! I had been reading the stone inscriptions in a small graveyard at the northern end of the village. One of the graves was larger than the rest and had Chinese writing on the tablet. It fascinated me to find the ubiquitous Chinese even on remote Aldabra and I had just been told that it was the tomb of a sea-slug collector, an employee of an earlier lessee, when there was a sudden commotion and a loud squawking behind me. I turned to find a creole boy clutching a young coucal and proudly asking me to photograph it.

The bird was still very speckly, awaiting its adult plumage; it had obviously just left the nest. I took a quick snap and told the boy to release it and that I wanted to photograph animals in the wild. He put on a rather pained look but this vanished in the general laughter as the coucal, none the worse for wear, tunnelled into the undergrowth like a rabbit and disappeared from sight. This curious habit of a bird which is by no means flightless, is something I observed several times later.

The coucal, a relative of the cuckoo, was the rarest bird I had so far seen and I was just thinking it would probably be my last prize of the day when Archangel Michael clutched my arm and pointed. Twenty yards away, staring at us, was a bird silhouetted sharply against the sky. Its long, thick-forked tail was unmistakable and I recognized with a thrill the Aldabran drongo, the most distinct of all the native land-birds. Unfortunately it was too far away to film but I was assured that it could often be seen in this area. I watched to see how it reacted to the presence of humans. Although it did not come close to investigate us, it was definitely in no hurry to fly away. At the time I didn't know it, but the drongo is the most aggressive of Aldabran birds and will attack human invaders near a nest.

The manager said it would be easy to recognize the spot, it was on the land 'the radio men had chosen'. He ran a short way into the undergrowth and opening the branches, pointed to a red and white post. There was a rough clearing marked with several more posts. So this was the site selected two months earlier by the BBC engineers for the proposed transmitter station. There had been so much else to think about and see that afternoon that I had forgotten about it. The threat to Aldabra, now being opposed in faraway London, came back with a jolt as I looked at these silent posts in a clearing that was already beginning to disappear.

The creoles pointed out where the buildings would be, generators here, transmitters there, offices this side. I suspected some intelligent guesswork and the suspicion turned to certainty when they gave me the date on which building work would start and, finally, the number of local staff to be engaged at vast salaries to run the station. All this excited discussion around the evidence of the posts made the project seem certain and near so that the only consolation I could feel was that the site lay practically within the settlement boundary. The buildings would not entail much more destruction, but of course this was only the beginning.

For a number of years, in several countries, I had been intimately concerned with the selection of land for radio transmitter stations. (Once, in Laos, in association with Soviet Russian and American experts at the same time – a unique project.) It was not the small site required for the control and office buildings that mattered but the much larger area needed for the aerials. Where was this going to be? And how and where would the necessary supplies of diesel oil be landed on an island that had baulked even the parish priest on his annual visit? Although I was far from being a qualified conservationist, it was obvious what one of the consequences of building a jetty would be. Easy immigration for rats.

This gloomy speculation was cut short by a new sound. We were now approaching the north end of the beach and above the hissing of the waves on the sand, an echoing boom could be heard. I ran through the casuarina fringe to investigate. It was almost high tide and the wind had risen. I could see the end of the beach, the beginning of the real Aldabra. It was an awesome sight. I understood at once why sailors had given this elevated atoll a wide berth, how easily it could have claimed the life of a fisherman two months before.

A grey cliff crowned with a thatch of confused scrub rose from fifteen to twenty feet out of the sea. The rock was porous and jagged and large orange and blue crabs could be seen scuttling from one cavity to another above the waves. It looked like a wall of pummice with here and there coral formations embedded in it, the blades and points of rock so sharp they were almost painful to look at. Even more striking than the texture of the rock was the concave shape of the cliff. If a giant with a gouge had worked on it, he could not have done a neater job. Erosion by the sea had made the overhanging lip of land so thin and brittle it looked dangerous to stand on. The limit of the overhang protruded at least eight feet over the waves now scouring the curved wall beneath. I watched fascinated as one wave, sizzling up the concave wall, fell on the back of the following wave. It would be impossible to land even on a calm day. As the waves retreated I noticed that even the rock at the base of the cliff, which would be under water except at low tide, was jagged and pot-holed offering no place for a would-be climber to stand while he sought a way to the top.

Archangel was at my side.

'How did you do it? Climb up that?' I asked, unable to take my eyes off the coral wall.

He was silent for a moment and his hand moved involuntarily to his chest.

'We were lucky. It was very high water, big waves too. When I was carried in I was able to grab the overhang and haul myself up. For several seconds I was hanging in space, then another wave came and I was over. I don't remember much after that. The other man who got himself ashore was fifty yards away. His hands were cut to ribbons. I bandaged them with a shirt.'

The sun was beginning to set and the scooped-out cliff looked black and sinister. We turned towards the settlement and a few small lights began to appear among the palm trees.

Guy Lionnet had now made detailed plans for the start of our

journey. We would leave in mid-morning by boat for Anse Maïs, the
clearing on South Island, spend at least one night there and look at
the nearby coves. We would take nine men in two boats for the anti-
clockwise circuit of the atoll, a journey of something like eighty miles,
with detours. He had found it hard to estimate how long it would
take, but the portable radio sets meant we would remain in close
contact with the *Lady Esmé* and in theory, we could return by the
direct route through the lagoon in less than thirty hours from any
part of the atoll.

Captain Sauvage had said that if the weather remained fair he
might try to bring the ship round to Cinq Cases at the eastern extremity of Aldabra to see how we were progressing, but he had never
tried to anchor on this windswept coast before and could promise
nothing. Enough food for ten days and a supply of drinking water,
fuel for the outboard motors, canvas shelters and ground-sheets,
cooking utensils, and some useful medical stores had already been
stacked for loading.

A very efficient cook and houseboy had now taken over our creature
comforts in the resthouse and a dinner featuring some tasty but nameless meat was now served with the panache of a French restaurant. It
was the *Lady Esmé* cuisine all over again. As in Indo-China, here was
this valuable legacy of French rule, excellent cooking and a civilized
approach to a meal, which persists in such widely scattered places as
Vietnam and the South Indian Ocean Islands. I had enjoyed '*coq
(jungle) au vin*' in the savannah forests of Cambodia, '*crêpes Suzette
flambées*' in the unmapped jungle hills of North Laos. The present
repast was well up to Gallic standards, and was washed down by a
bottle of red wine. Harold, who had been roughing it on the Arabian
coast for long hot months, looked overwhelmed. Implicit in this
French belief in the importance of eating well, no matter the circumstances, is a sentiment I strongly share: 'Any fool can be uncomfortable in the jungle'. On this occasion there were useful by-products.

The white table cloth that had appeared as a matter of course was
exactly the surface we needed for the moth-catching session on the
programme for after dinner. When the meal had been cleared, Guy
Lionnet placed a pressure lamp on the centre of the table and we
waited for the assembly of night-flying insects. Already pleasantly
surprised by the absence of mosquitoes, which we reckoned would be
a pest away from the settlement, we wondered whether moths would

prove as scarce. Aldabran insects had been little studied in the past and only the French entomologist, Legrand, had done any recent researches in the field of lepidoptera. Both Guy and I were deeply interested and I was supposed to be collecting what I could for the British Museum. It may seem odd to some people with a dislike of 'things that go bump in the night', but we sat poised around the table with all the expectant excitement of a theatre audience at a first night.

Earliest arrivals were flying ants and other small bugs outside our field of study. Then slowly, like ghosts, the moths materialized. We didn't know what to expect. Several years before, I had been mothing in the Malayan mountains with the inventor of the celebrated 'Robinson mothtrap'. We had been literally bombarded by giant Sphingidae (hawk moths) for hours on end and he had told me of occasions in England when the mothtrap had assembled as many as ten thousand insects in one night. I remembered one very exciting incident well. We were on Maxwell Hill near Taiping. He had set up the lamp and I had vanished into the bathroom for a moment. Suddenly there was a tremendous bang on the wooden outside wall.

'What on earth is that?' I cried, thinking there had been an accident. It sounded like a cannon ball.

'Come and see,' yelled Robinson with, to my relief, no sound of panic in his voice. At that time Taiping was in an area infested with communist bandits.

We had really hit the jackpot. Lying on its back, struggling to turn over, was the largest beetle I had ever seen. Black and shiny and almost round, it was the size of a substantial bun, a big handful.

But we didn't attract anything like that among the early arrivals on Aldabra. These were all small grey or brown, light-bodied noctuids, mostly of the genus Geometridae. We boxed a dozen or so in the first half-hour and gradually a few larger species made their appearance. A watching group of smiling creoles must have thought we had gone berserk – something in the wine – as we scrambled over the balcony, balancing on chairs and packing cases, catching these undistinguished-looking insects with whoops of joy. Around nine o'clock the supply of new arrivals dried up and we were just about to give up. For no particular reason, apart from Micawberish optimism, I said to Guy Lionnet, 'I am sure if we wait a bit longer something larger will turn up'.

And I had hardly finished speaking before a shadow crossed the lamp – a moth, much bigger than the others we had caught, landed on the far end of the table. I approached it stealthily and, at the second attempt, managed to get it into the glass-topped box. Triumphant moment. At first sight, the moth was as dull and drab as the others, not that this is any indication of its importance to a collector, but when it moved its body, two round eyes glared up from the hindwings. It was unlike any insect we had seen earlier.

At this time we knew almost nothing about the moths of Aldabra. They were much less numerous than I had anticipated and even Guy was surprised at their scarcity. It could be seasonal, of course, but he thought that one or two of the species we had caught might be new and I felt he was right. Already a Seychelles moth bore his name, attributed by the finder, Legrand.

I looked out at the dark settlement before turning in for an early night. Ours was the only light visible and the moon was hidden by a clump of palm trees. Nothing stirred, there was no sound above the crashing of waves on the beach and the distant thunder on the reef. A brief shower earlier in the evening was causing a trickle of water to plop into the reservoir from the gutter. There were about sixty people sleeping on Aldabra that night, all tucked away in one small corner of its north-west tip.

The labourers who live here are employed by the lessee of the atoll, mainly to catch and dry fish – I had seen great quantities being sun-dried that afternoon ready for shipment – and to exploit the green turtle. The extraction of timber is another occupation though of less importance than it used to be and, under his lease, Mr Savy is allowed to export a few giant tortoises each year. Some of these are sold to zoos, others find their way into the hands of old Seychellois families in Mahé who like roast tortoise on the menu for a wedding banquet.

Nearly all the labourers are black creoles recruited in Mahé on a two-year contract for service either on Aldabra or Assumption Island, which is leased jointly with the atoll. The basic wage of the labourer is so low that I could hardly believe I had heard right when I was first told – the average amounts to £2 (or less than five dollars) a month. Even in a region where both wages and the cost of living are low, this seemed to me incredible. Admittedly there is nowhere to spend money, no shop or club for the workers, but without the prospect of a substantial nest-egg at the end, I would have thought it difficult to recruit men to serve, separated from their families, on an island so remote from all civilized amenities. The pressure of over-crowding and unemployment in the Seychelles, aggravated by a very high birth-rate and religious attitudes to family planning, must be the explanation.

The basic wage can be supplemented by small bonuses earned from spare-time fishing and from catching giant tortoises within the quota. I believe it is five rupees for a tortoise delivered to the settlement pound. Since the average weight of an adult is around two hundred pounds and transporting it over the champignon must be quite a problem, this looked like 7s 6d or 90 cents well-earned.

The labourers I spoke to said they would much rather be on Aldabra than on Assumption Island, which made me wonder what the terms and conditions of service on the latter could be like. In both places there are, of course, a number of side benefits and basic foods are supplied free, or at very low cost. As this is deducted from the wages, the cut price was almost inevitable. To an outsider, the rewards to the Aldabra labour force seemed pathetically small com-pared, for example, to the wages now earned by rubber tappers in Asia, but there must have been compensations or invisible attractions for Mr Savy never had difficulty in recruitment.

Under Article 17 of the lease of Aldabra, not more than two hundred people may be resident on the atoll without the permission of the Seychelles government. Even counting our party as temporary residents, there were many less than that tonight.

Most of the creoles never moved far from Picard Island. Earlier that evening, Guy had discussed with the manager the question of porters and guides. Naturally he preferred to have men who had already travelled widely on the atoll, especially those with first-hand knowledge of the tracks and pools at the remote eastern end between Cinq Cases and Anse Cèdres, the area said to be densely populated with tortoises and reported to have the greatest variety of bird life. But he was disappointed.

We were suprised to learn that no one, except Laporte, knew the east of Aldabra at all. 'They never go there, it's dangerous and drink-ing water is hard to find and anyway, we have no work in that part,' explained Archangel, adding that he had never seen it himself. He asked if he could come along and we were delighted to agree.

As I climbed under the mosquito net in my well-ventilated room at the 'Hotel Aldabra', I started to think of all the things that could go wrong – the loss of my cameras in a capsize, colour film wrecked by the blistering sun, falling into a twenty-foot hole in the champignon. Then I gave it up. So, next day we would be setting out for the unknown. At least we would all be in the same boat; bar one, of course.

As it turned out, we were lucky Laporte's foot had healed in time.

# VI Journey on a Porcupine's Back

I WOKE soon after dawn and went quickly on to the balcony to look at the sky. There were a few thin lines of cloud on the horizon, no wind at all. It was a perfect summer day. I could hardly believe our luck. Were all these stories about the wild Aldabra weather merely designed to drive visitors away?

With the tide still a long way out, a broad expanse of greyish sand crossed by several ridges of rock was revealed below the steeply-shelving beach, and stalking majestically across these flats was a grey heron, busy fishing in the pools. It moved jerkily, occasionally in film slow-motion, then darting forward a pace or two to be perfectly reflected in the shallow water. Its dark silhouette against the silver background was so arresting that I did not for a while notice other shore birds feeding on the mud; a flock of crab plovers skittering about as if they had lost something, and two egrets of the dark variety. A more peaceful scene it would have been hard to imagine. Motionless above it, anchored in the deep blue water beyond the reef, was the *Lady Esmé*, our watchdog and escape route.

The idea that we might need to leave in a hurry seemed fantastic on a morning like this.

There were two hours to spare before the tide would be right for our journey to the south, so we set off together on foot to sèe the green turtle pound at the mouth of West Channel, a mile away. The track led through a part of the settlement I had not so far visited.

There were the same little wood huts with the occupants coming out to smile as we passed, the same fringe of casuarinas above the beach, but somehow it looked different here. A lot of timber was lying about; suddenly I saw what was wrong. Very few of the coconut trees were standing. Healthy young palms were sprawled in all directions on both sides of the track. One of the porters explained that they had been blown down in 'the big wind' a few months earlier. Probably the path of cyclone Angela.

The devastated coconut plantation had now given way to sand dunes dotted with 'bois d'amande' bushes. It was getting very hot and there was little shade. Both Guy and I were hopefully carrying butterfly nets; we had seen very few insects in the village but here they were more plentiful. If we had been expecting to see strikingly new shapes and colours, we would have been disappointed, for on the wing the butterflies looked exactly like those commonly seen on the Asian mainland and in East Africa. Without difficulty we netted several Danaids and a number of small grass yellows which, at first sight, did not seem to differ from those I used to see in thousands all over Malaya. They were worth keeping all the same, for sub-specific identification is not something that can be undertaken in the field with sweat misting your sunglasses. The general impression, however, was that the lepidoptera of Picard Island were not remarkable either in quantity or variety.

On the outskirts of the village there were several mounds of litter. I always look carefully at these in a new place – they can tell you a lot and occasionally they yield treasure. Some of my best finds of Ming porcelain had been made in rubbish dumps in Johore; fragments dug up in the vegetable patch and thrown on the heap, but it is about eating habits they are most informative. Here there was immediate confirmation that some of the wild birds of Aldabra were taken for the pot. Sticking out of the mounds were the gaunt black wings of several frigate birds and a number of heads. When they tire of fish, the creoles enjoy a breast of frigate for a change. This I knew from a gruesome photograph Roger Gaymer had shown me before I left England, but it was still quite a shock to see this evidence. I looked up. There, as usual, were the black dots – two frigates wheeling gracefully in the blue thermals 2,000 feet above the midden.

Half a mile further on, we came to the West Channel, one of three main entrances to the vast Aldabra lagoon, but much shallower and more cluttered with islands than the other two. The scene could not have been less like that described by travellers who had passed through its jaws in a storm.

Tiny ripples broke the surface and flopped lazily on the talc-soft sand. My companions were already crossing on foot and I noticed the water barely reached their knees. They were making for a palis-saded enclosure on a big island. The sun was higher now, shining across the lagoon from the east. Silhouetted against the pale water were a number of objects that I can only describe as giant mushrooms – champignons. The French word to describe the eroded coral rock, as seen in these undercut islets that grew out of the pass, could not have been more apt.

Some were hardly larger than a round banquetting table with the single 'leg' so thin and eroded that it could barely support the circular top. Others were much larger, in an earlier stage of solution by the tides, and resembled warships with the superstructure replaced by coarse vegetation. These 'mushrooms' are all that is left of the atoll rim in this sector. At some point in the distant past the sea breached Aldabra's wall of coral and the roaring currents speedily in a geological time-scale did the rest. We were to experience these currents later that day. One mushroom I saw had already collapsed, its centre post no longer able to bear the weight, and would soon become dust on the channel bed. There are few other places in the world where these extraordinary relics of sea erosion appear so dramatic.

Looking down the channel my eye was caught by what appeared to be a pair of small coracles under the bushes at the back of the beach. I went closer to investigate. A black and white pied crow, one of the few land-birds not native to the atoll, flew away in noisy panic. The smell warned me that the objects were not what I had thought. They were upturned and empty carapaces of two green turtles which, judging by the red interior of the shells, had only recently been killed.

A hail came from the far shore. The rest of the party had reached the turtle pound and were calling me over. The American professor was in a state of great excitement.

'You must film this, ' he said to me the moment I had clambered over the open fence of palm trunks that formed three sides of the pound. 'I have never seen so many male turtles in my life. As you know, the males never come ashore of their own accord. This is a unique opportunity. These are all males.' As he said this, he gave a mighty heave and another turtle fell over on its back with a wet thud, flapping furiously.

Apart from the six huge beasts that Harold Hirth had already turned over, helped by Laporte, for it is not an easy job for one man to flip over 250 pounds of reluctant turtle, there were six more idly swimming round the pound. They were circling the fence of stout tree trunks, obviously trying to find a gap. Harold was busy measuring the overturned turtles with a huge pair of wooden calipers and making notes in his diary. He was obviously too busy to be interrupted. I decided to pick his brains later.

The male turtle can be recognized not only by the sex organs but also by the greater length of his tail and the presence of two powerful claws on the fore flippers. These are used for gripping the female during the mating act, which takes place while swimming in the water, as we had seen the previous afternoon. As this was the close season for turtles, no females could be caught, hence the all-male population of the pound. Without looking up from his labours, Harold told me to stand clear of the flipper hooks; these could inflict a nasty wound. It seemed that one of his associates working on the turtles of South Arabia, had been badly gashed by an amorous male who presumably mistook him for a female turtle! It seemed a bit undiscriminating to me, but it is no use being wise after the event, so I took two paces backward.

After the first few seconds of angry flapping the turtles did not seem to mind the American professor's gentle attentions and quietly allowed their vital statistics to be recorded. I learned that these males, which looked healthy and fat, were just about average size and weight, probably youngsters. Harold had measured much larger ones near Aden and in Costa Rica, but he seemed reassured just the same. The green turtle Mecca was clearly attracting its pilgrims still.

Bearing in mind what I had been told about the creature's claws, I was amazed on turning round to find Captain Sauvage, who had accompanied us on this tour of the settlement, swimming on a turtle's back. He was clutching its shell on each side of the neck and making a fast and exhilarating circuit of the pound. Luckily for him, perhaps, the creature could not dive as the water was too shallow and its speed was restricted by the limits of the fence which enclosed an area of about a quarter of an acre. I realized at that moment that the people of the Seychelles probably understand turtles better than anyone on earth, but it wasn't until later that I learned the reason why.

When Harold had finished his measuring and righted the turtles, a more difficult job than turning them over, we prepared to leave. The tide was rising fast. The turtles lumbered clumsily across the wet sand, but as soon as they reached water they became as graceful and swift as eels. We climbed over the pound wall and left them, several heads with large luminous eyes poking above the water, watching our departure with interest. I could not help feeling sad that these creatures would never be free again. They were awaiting shipment to Mahé, under agonizing conditions.

The water in the channel was now deeper and reached waist height as we waded back. The current into the lagoon was growing stronger, too, and the carpet of green weeds on the sandy bottom, still visible as if through glass, waved horizontally to the east. There was no coral to be seen and few fish, except for some small eel-like creatures striped sky-blue and black.

'No wonder the turtles come here,' remarked Harold over his shoulder. I looked around for clues but could see none. At that time I knew very little about the green turtle.

'This is good turtle grass. Some of the best I've seen. It's their favourite food.' The American stopped for a moment and looked down at the waving fronds; we were crossing a patch of pale green grass that resembled a submarine lawn. The more I heard about the green turtle, the more I marvelled at man's folly in killing it so ruthlessly. Its meat is delicious, as I now knew, and it grazed on fields that needed no farmer's attention. I hoped that we would discover on our tour of the atoll that here, at least, it was still thriving. I dismissed the memory of those two drying shells on the beach. Harold had told me that there were records of as many as 400 females a night coming up to lay on one beach in this favourite corner of the

Indian Ocean. Surely such a vast population could not have been decimated in fifty years.

A scene of tremendous activity greeted us as we got back to the settlement beach. Half the population of the island was crowded around two black boats lying just above the waveline, one of which was being fitted with an outboard motor. The second and smaller boat had the curved and elegant lines of a typical Seychelles rowing pirogue, the standard craft of all inshore fishermen of the islands. Two big coils of rope and several drums of petrol or drinking water were being loaded. Most of the porters who were to accompany us were wrapping in canvas an assortment of cooking vessels, tins of food and a sack of rice. All of them, I noticed, were barefoot but I guessed they must have shoes wrapped in their personal kit. From what I had heard of the champignon, even a fakir could not walk on it unshod! Archangel Michael, who had gone ahead from the turtle pound, called out that we must go quickly, the wind was strengthening and there was no time to lose. As he spoke a heavy wave hit the bows of the motor-boat and four men strained to keep it upright and bow-on to the sea.

In a matter of minutes we were aboard, surrounded by haversacks, butterfly nets, cameras, first-aid kits, tape recorders, a killing bottle, collecting boxes, compasses, maps, mosquito nets, several glass floats filled with drinking water, turtle measuring gear and two vast packages, which Guy said contained a tent and all our food and camp kit. I thought no human being could possibly carry it all across a bowling green, far less a 'porcupine's back' of coral blades and spikes interspersed with yawning cavities twenty feet deep. But the porters looked happy enough and we were off.

With a mighty heave and loud cries of mixed joy and alarm, the crew, all of whom were still ashore, launched the heavy boat through a big wave on to the calmer water behind and leapt in from all sides, grabbing the oars in one split-second movement as they landed. While Archangel Michael leaned on the tiller and shouted directions, they rowed like devils. In a few seconds we were well afloat and moving fast. I was so fascinated watching this skilful manoeuvre from a seat in the bows that I did not look round until, suddenly, all the rowers shipped their oars and gripped the side of the boat. A green roller with a curving lip was about to crash down on us. Seen from my angle, it looked like the end of the expedition before it had begun. A perfect surf rider's wave from Waikiki, I remember thinking, in the inconsequent way one does when faced with certain disaster. For a second there was dead silence in the boat, then I found myself catapulted forward on to a mound of haversacks, nice and soft. We seemed to be almost vertical in the water. There was a tremendous crash and, to my surprise, we were on the level again. Oars were unshipped and the crew started rowing smoothly on a calm sea. Aldabra settlement was still there.

Several more humps came, but each one was smaller than the last. When the breakers had been passed, oars were shipped again and the engine started. The slender pirogue had caught up and a line was thrown to it. Archangel gave the signal for full ahead and, with the pirogue in tow, we started cruising easily down the coast, still on the landward side of the fringing reef.

My fellow explorers looked a bit shaken but the creoles were unconcerned. Perhaps departures from the beach were always like this. Suprisingly, very little water had been shipped, the delicate equipment had been well-stowed and hardly a drop glistened on their polythene wrappings. All systems were working.

The voyage began to acquire some of the holiday mood of a picnic party. A creole in the pirogue behind started to sing, and the sun shone on water of such clarity that the colours of fish could be seen thirty feet down. Two trawl lines were thrown overboard armed with enormous hooks, as a white booby skimmed the sea ahead, rigid as a small white aeroplane. Then came the sound of another motorboat and, turning round, I saw the dinghy of the *Lady Esmé* overtaking us, going like a speedboat. At the tiller the bright red face of Captain Sauvage shone like a beacon. He came level with us and slowed to our speed.

'You ought to try fishing,' he shouted over the roar of two engines. 'Look!' and he dived into the bottom of the dinghy and held up two fish for us to admire. 'Caught these in the first five minutes.'

'What are they?' I roared.

He stood up in the boat holding the two fish high in each hand. One was a giant barracuda, the other a kingfish. As he drew them up they looked endless, quite the biggest fish I had ever seen caught on a handline.

'I'm going to try again. Good luck. And don't forget to call me up tonight.' Sauvage swung the dinghy in a tight arc and vanished in a cloud of spray.

As we approached the first mouth of West Channel, I noticed without paying too much attention, that Archangel changed course until we were making out to sea. This time the waves took us completely by surprise. One moment the boat was moving smoothly through a calm sea, the next it was bucking like a wild horse in ten-foot waves that came from all directions. We were drenched as green water crashed over the sides. All hands started baling. It was amazing. We were suddenly in the centre of a maelstrom and the horizon had disappeared. As a great shower of spray blanketted the boat, I heard Harold's voice in my ear:

'How much did you say your equipment cost?'

I could not help laughing and wondering at the same time if the insurance company would pay up. The end had come so suddenly. Would anyone believe my account of the 'circumstances of the loss', a capsize in a mill pond? We had been discussing earlier the economics of wild-life filming which is by no means a short cut to fortune. I suppose my equipment was worth about £2,000 (nearly 5,000 dollars). Everything on board seemed to be afloat and the camera I was using streamed with salt water, the fastest destroyer of all. As the slightly hysterical laughter subsided, so did the sea, as suddenly as it had risen, and the way ahead was calm and blue.

'It's always a bit bumpy at the entrance to the pass,' said Archangel with memorable understatement. We had lost the pirogue – it had cast the tow-rope during the 'big dipper' ride – and we now circled to pick it up. The four men were still in it and the songster had started on another shanty. It was again obvious that nothing unusual had happened to ruffle their calm. Huge white smiles broke out on the shining faces as the tow was renewed.

I pulled my cameras out of the forward locker, which was still awash, and opened the plastic covers to inspect the damage. There was none. For the first, but certainly not the last, time I felt a sense of overwhelming gratitude to the inventor of polythene bags and to Mr Tupper, whose air-tight sandwich boxes held all my film stock.

A number of small coves began to break the grey cliffs to our left. From the map I recognized two of these as Anse Anglais (what peripatetic Englishman had left his mark here?) and Anse Badamier, though at this distance I was unable to spot any badamier trees near the tiny beach. (The badamier tree was, I knew, one of the favourites for boat building in the Seychelles.) Then we started to turn towards

9. The sacred ibis was once so tame that it poked in people's shoes for food. It is still curious and unafraid and will investigate any visitor. The largest colony is near Takamaka Pool on South Island. (*The Royal Society*)

10. China blue eyes are one of the distinguishing characteristics of the
Aldabran sub-species of the sacred ibis. *(The Royal Society)*

the shore and a larger bay, screened by sharply overhung cliffs, came into view. At the back of this inlet was a very steep bank of sand on which the waves were breaking noisily.

It was Anse Maïs, our destination. The landing looked tricky, but such was my new admiration for the skill of our black boatmen I had no anxiety about making it dry. The engine was cut and we were carried in on the rollers. Bump, crew overboard, four men rushed to hold the bows steady and with incredible speed the mound of equipment was formed by a human chain on the dry sand above. We set foot for the first time on South Island, the huge sickle of land which encircles almost two-thirds of the Aldabra lagoon, one of the last unspoiled wild life sanctuaries in the world. It was a thrilling moment.

'We are now in the nature reserve,' announced Guy Lionnet as we waded ashore through the warm water.

I had not realized until then that a large part of Aldabra was already protected by law. Apparently South Island was named in the commercial lease concluded between the Seychelles government and Mr Harry Savy as a place where there could be no human settlement, where all animal life must be protected, where no new animal or plant might be introduced and where no resources, apart from mangrove wood, might be exploited. These clauses, which bound the lessee to respect South Island, had been inserted in the Aldabra lease when it was renewed after a ten-year lapse in 1955. They were new ones and credit for them belonged largely to Commander Cousteau, the French marine biologist. The year before he had visited Aldabra in the research ship *Calypso* and, as we have already heard, had tried in London to lease the island himself as a 'wild life reserve and tropical research centre almost uncontaminated by man'. Though he did not succeed, the publicity he gave the island led to protective measures. In a very short time we would know whether they had been effective.

The sight that greeted us on breasting the ridge of rank grass above the beach was quite unexpected. Instead of dense scrub, a sandy parkland dotted with bushes and some large trees, including a grove of healthy coconut palms, stretched several hundred yards in all directions. It was a perfect place to camp. My first reaction was to keep it a secret if I ever wrote about Aldabra. Anse Maïs (Corn Bay) looked exactly like a desirable building site in the Bahamas of the kind that gladdens the eye of smog-weary businessmen dreaming of retirement in the sun. I did not know at the time that it was a a unique place on a unique island, that in the whole of the atoll there was nothing else quite like it.

We pitched our tent a hundred yards behind the beach and started immediately to explore. How far did this parkland extend? There was no need to worry about an invasion of property developers. A short walk showed that we were hemmed in on all sides. The landward approaches to the anse, except for a narrow strip stretching southward down the coast and leading to another small bay, were closed by a wall of the thickest scrub I had so far seen. This grew in a tangled mass of grey roots straight out of a bed of champignon rock. Some of the roots disappeared into deep clefts. There was no sign of earth. It looked completely impassable. The wall of pemphis and champignon began so abruptly that it looked as if a giant bulldozer had been at work and that levelling had been stopped suddenly.

The coastal defences were even more formidable. Near the limits of the bay it was like walking on hollow land. I edged a little way across the spiky rock to see over the cliff top. It was high tide and the platform echoed to a hollow boom. A wave crashed in and, to my surprise, the loudest noise, a sort of explosion, came from behind me followed by a shower of spray. I turned quickly to see a waterspout falling back into a ragged hole twenty feet from the cliff. When the next wave came, I glanced along the shore. Jets of water were spurting up through the hollow rock at half a dozen other points. This was no place to go exploring at night. It looked dangerous enough in the daytime. But there was something horribly fascinating about the deadly coastline.

As the sea sizzled back over the pitted rock, huge grey-green and orange crabs, mottled with black, rushed out of the holes and darted for refuge to other holes nearby. They seemed to be playing a game, waiting for a wave until the last second, then vanishing deep into the grey honeycomb. They were bigger and more colourful than any coral crabs I had ever seen. A fall from the clifftop would have been certain death although it was only fifteen feet. I imagined the crabs were looking at me hungrily. In the bright afternoon sun the scene was strikingly beautiful – a sort of technicolour nightmare.

It was a relief to return to the slabs of flaggy rock that led to the grassland; some of these were loosely balanced and rang noisily as they fell back into place. I picked up a slab and dropped it on another.

It made a noise exactly like bathroom porcelain, putting the lid back on the cistern. This must be the type of rock called 'platin' in Créole and which Fryer said was composed mainly of coral fragments of reef debris and a few shells 'weathering into large flat slabs'. He considered this to be a 'back reef' deposit, formed as a reef flat and subsequently uplifted, but Dr Stoddart's recent studies showed that the platin rock probably had a more complex history, that it had undergone considerable vertical erosion. Stoddart found that the character of the platin surface is highly variable and generally weathers by 'spalling or exfoliation of large but thin slabs of rock, which ring musically when walked over'. My musical return journey to camp made me sure I had hit the right geological formation.

Like just about everything else on Aldabra, this platin is still something of a mystery. According to Stoddart, the processes causing the weathering into thin slabs are not yet fully understood, and the flatness of its surface and its height above sea level are further problems to be solved.

Platin meant a lot to us. You might say that it was our ambition to reach the platin. This was not only to give our feet a rest on its smooth, open surfaces but because the large areas of platin at the eastern end of South Island were supposed to harbour the biggest concentration of giant tortoises and rare birds. There would be days of hard slogging before we could possibly reach this goal, so it was comforting to be introduced to even these few small pieces at the outset. Proof that the stuff existed.

I was just thinking this when I turned a corner and found my way barred by an angry crab, standing in the centre of the track waving both claws. It was unlike those I had seen playing above the sea, larger and pink-coloured as if it had already been par-boiled. Feeling confident in my climbing boots, I advanced slowly on Horatius. He held his ground until I was only a few inches away then sidled round me still poised for the attack. My intrusion was deeply resented. He was the first of tens of thousands of similar crabs we encountered on our tour of Aldabra and by no means the largest. Indeed he was just a baby, albeit twelve inches from claw to claw, compared to some of the fearsome characters we met later.

It may have been because I was watching my step so carefully, eyes glued to the ground, but thus far I had seen very few land-birds. A dark shape darting around the top of a fat bush gave itself away, by an unmusical chattering, as a bulbul, one of the few Aldabran land-birds that are probably not distinctive. Suddenly the sun caught its orange beak and confirmed the identification. A pied crow had flown overhead and two sunbirds had been over to look at me as I stood on the cliff. Anse Maïs was the place where the Bristol team had made one of their most interesting discoveries, the nest of the rare Aldabran kestrel. I would now concentrate on the birds. It was only five o'clock and there was an hour or more of daylight left.

The first thing I noticed was mysterious; every bush seemed to be alive. There was almost no wind, yet there was undoubtedly move-ment in them. With camera at the ready, I took up a strategic position under cover and watched. After a minute or two a small greenish bird poked its beak out of the foliage and darted back. Too quick. I crept nearer, keeping close to the ground. Now I could see some of the branches in silhouette and several more birds fluttering around inside the bush. One emerged in full sunlight and turned its head to nibble at a flower. This action made it immediately recognizable. It was, to my delight, an 'oiseau lunettes' or 'spectacles bird', the pleasing Creole name for the white-eye. A small flock of these tiny green birds was vibrating inside the bush, but as no individual kept still for more than a second or two they proved hard to photograph. The clear white ring round the eyes gave them a comic, intellectual look and after a while I realized what else had given me the feeling that the undergrowth was alive. The white-eyes kept up an almost continuous low twittering that sounded more like insects.

These birds are a distinct Aldabran sub-species and we discovered that they are common all over the island but more particularly in woodland. One of the most charming scenes I witnessed anywhere on the atoll was a pair of 'oiseaux lunettes' courting, sitting side by side on a branch preening each other. Jeffery Boswall told me later, when he was viewing my film for BBC television, that they were, in fact, 'clumping', and my fondness for these round green birds in-creased further. Whoever invented that word deserves a medal. White-eyes visited every one of our camps and often used to watch us bathing in the rock pools, but I never got a good photo of one despite hundreds of attempts. No one did.

While I was struggling to get them in focus, two large black and white ibis flew over the clearing, their long curved beaks making them easy to identify. I hoped they would land and inspect us but is was just an aerial reconnaissance. Dr Abbott, who spent three months on the atoll in 1892, said they were so tame they would poke in people's shoes for food. I wondered if they still had no fear of man. We would know soon enough. This was too far west for the ibis and I had not really expected to see them at Anse Maïs. The main breeding colony was said to be at Takamaka Grove which we would reach, if all went well, in three or four days. Though I had no evidence, I suspected the reason they no longer frequented this end of the atoll was that the creoles ate them. By all accounts they would be an easy target and they tasted like duck.

The sun was setting when I returned to camp but it was not yet mosquito time. According to all reports, Anse Maïs was infested with them, and although I was already covered with aerosol insecticide I wanted to make sure that the final refuge of a mosquito net was ready. There was said to be no malaria on Aldabra, but there were other fevers and I had always been attractive meat to insects. Long before, I had discovered that a hungry mosquite will bite through clothes if they are tight against the skin and that dark socks are a powerful magnet. Explorers should wear light colours. I found out something else, too, that never failed to bring on the worst feelings of envy. Mosquitoes are choosy.

Several traumatic experiences stuck in the memory. Taking tea in the house of a friend in Kuala Lumpur one afternoon, in daylight mark you, I was so plagued by a cloud of Anopheles that they were even biting my face, usually a secondary target. About to sympathize with my host and hostess, who were very lightly clad in beachwear, I noticed to my shocked surprise that they were right outside the line of fire, not a single mosquito near them. The cloud was mine alone! Even worse was one night on an island off Singapore. We were sleeping in a Malay fisherman's hut; should I say trying to sleep, for rest was out of the question. The mosquitoes and sand flies were appalling and unfortunately we had no nets. I had covered myself with all the clothing I could find, but still they found a way through. Smoking, which is sometimes a protection, was of no use. They were obviously addicts. At 2 a.m. I got up to take a walk and switched on a flashlight. There, stretched out on the bamboo floor, dressed in nothing more than a sarong which exposed vast areas of naked flesh to all night-flying creatures, was my friend, fast asleep. Uncharitable thoughts came to mind. In the course of these involuntary researches

I have made an interesting discovery – if you have reddish hair you are lucky, mosquitoes will not find you so tasty.

The camp was a bustle of activity. On the advice of Archangel, our tent had been moved away from a tree that looked too dead to be safe in a high wind, and out of range of falling coconuts. The latter is an important precaution and easy to overlook unless you have seen the consequences, like the Japanese sentry with a fractured skull I remembered during the war in the Far East. A lamp had been lit, standing on a white sheet to attract moths for our collection. Several pots were steaming in small holes in a champignon outcrop which made a convenient cooking range. The reassuring ghostly gleam of mosquito nets rose above the camp beds. Guy was sitting half under his, fiddling with the radio transreceiver:

'Allo, allo *Lady Esmé*. Calling *Lady Esmé* from Anse Maïs.'

Switch over, loud crackling. He tried again.

Harold was studying the map with Laporte, working on a route to likely turtle beaches nearby for an early morning inspection. I was just thinking how well the expedition had begun when Guy said he could not raise the ship. It was now well after the agreed calling time. I tried, but with no better luck. We thought that the captain, who had after all seen us earlier in the afternoon, had perhaps decided to waive the radio contact while we were on the west end of the atoll or, maybe, he was still too busy catching barracuda. It never occurred to us that the equipment might be to blame!

Archangel called me. It was still quite light and as I approached he was sitting on a small mound, laughing. Suddenly he swung round jerkily and emitted a low grunt. Then I saw what was happening; his seat was a giant tortoise which now lumbered slowly away, neck extended, carrying its burden.

'This is a small one,' he said. 'There are some much bigger over there.' He pointed in the direction the tortoise was taking him. From under a dense clump of bushes four tortoises were now fanning out over the grass.

'During the day they hide, ' continued Archangel. 'Get into the bushes away from the sun. Look. Now they're all coming out.'

Sure enough, the grey domes of tortoises were emerging from the undergrowth all round the clearing, some apparently making straight for our camp. They all looked at a distance like smooth stones, closing, as in some Edgar Allen Poe fantasy, on the human intruders.

I went up to a big fellow about four feet from stem to stern and at least knee-high, who had stopped facing me. When I was about a yard away he pivotted quickly in a half-turn to the left, withdrew his head and let out a short, hissing grunt. With a clatter of carapace on stone, he then turned right round with his back to me, and sank to the ground in a resigned sort of way. I waited to see what would happen. Aftèr about a minute I saw his horny beak peering round the side of the shell. We exchanged glances, then he hoisted himself on curiously long legs and steered away. In the bush ahead an even larger tortoise was cropping leaves that were almost out of his reach and again I marvelled at the length of the sinewy grey neck. To reach the leaves he was half-balanced on the back of another tortoise which appeared to be asleep. Suddenly the underdog lurched aside and the giant fell to the ground with a dull thud.

This first sudden encounter with the giant Indian Ocean tortoise I shall always remember most vividly. To be face to face with an animal that belonged to the age of the dinosaur, that had survived here and nowhere else, was impressive enough. But something more made the encounter memorable. I think *Testudo gigantea* made me feel small. This monstrous version of the pet tortoise is so like his small relations, in appearance and habits, that everything seemed out of proportion. The illusion was increased by the strange vegetation and the half-light, not to mention the docility of the tortoises. These colossal 'pets' had no particular fear of man. They reacted to his approach as they might to a feral goat. Although it was too dark to start filming, I realized that here at last was the easiest subject that any nature photographer could hope for and even this brief introduction had shown that there would be no want of action. Several things already intrigued me. Where were the babies? I had seen only adults so far. Why did some of the tortoises have dents on the back of their shells, as if they had been hit by something? Where did they get water to drink? The questions piled up as I made my way back to the light and towards the smell of cooking, to the camp of trespassers in a prehistorical world.

So few moths had been drawn to the light that tonight for a change we used the white cloth as a dining table. The temperature had dropped to somewhere in the seventies and a slight breeze was blowing in from the sea. There was no sound but the breaking of waves on the beach and cliff ramparts and the occasional bursts of rapid

Creole and laughter from the porters around their small fire, which sent a column of grey smoke spiralling among the dark plam trees. Something was missing. My mind was so full of tortoises I had forgotten the mosquitoes. There were none!

It seemed almost too good to be true. Not one of us had been bitten and there was no buzzing in the ears to warn of impending attack. Anse Maïs was supposed to be one of the worst places on Aldabra, yet here we were, just at the end of the rainy season, when breeding conditions should be ideal, sitting in the open, at night, unmolested. I was quite prepared to accept this phenomenon at its face value with no probing at all; just to pray that the insects had vanished from the whole atoll. No one would mourn the disappearance of this species of wild life.

Our cook, resplendent in a black trilby hat which he treated with as much care as I did my cameras, showed on this first night that he knew his craft well. The corned beef and rice was seasoned with unknown herbs and served with the aplomb of *haute cuisine*. It had followed a soup which tasted like turtle but which probably came from a less exotic container, and the whole was rounded off with a good cheese. I began to understand why the bundle of camp gear was so enormous. As if reading my thoughts, Guy remarked that later on we would be having more fresh food. Shocked silence. 'I mean fish and crab and things like that,' he explained.

Although the cook had not been more than a year on the island, he had a lot of information about it, derived mainly from his cousin who had spent ten years on Aldabra since the last war. He was better-educated than the others and seemed to have quite an interest in wild life. I commented that I had been impressed by the number of shore-birds on the mud flats in front of the settlement that morning and asked if there were always that many. He nodded his head before answering and looked around.

'Twenty years ago there were many, many more. Thousands of them every morning. Now there are only a few. Why, in the old days – twenty years ago – the men used to complain they made so much noise at dawn they couldn't sleep. Those thousands of birds on the beach used to wake them every day.'

He did not say as much but he obviously meant that many had been killed for food. I wondered how so few humans (the population of the settlement rarely exceeded fifty) who were well-supplied with fish and frigate breasts, not to mention their livestock, could manage to eat so much in such a comparatively short time? Yet what he had told me rang true. Such graphic details as the dawn chorus would hardly be invented, but was it not more likely that the birds had been frightened away, had moved elsewhere?

As I crawled under my mosquito net and took up a comfortable position on the new camp-bed I had bought in Mombasa (which creaked horribly), I hoped we would encounter the displaced flocks of shore birds on some new refuge. The thought of a dawn chorus did not bother me at all. The only thing that did was the prospect of a robber crab climbing up the net, and waking to find its claws clamping a few inches from my nose.

This had happened to one of the Bristol explorers. I tucked the net as tightly as I could under the sheets. When I told Guy what I was doing, he chuckled loudly. Crabs always made him laugh.

In the middle of the night, or so it seemed, I heard the American get up. Laporte was standing outside the tent with a torch waiting to lead him to the turtle beaches in time to catch the females before they returned to the sea after laying. I wished him luck and decided to remain awake to record the morning bird song. Several of the Aldabran land-birds were said to have good, if not particularly musical, voices. The tape recorder worked well, apparently undamaged by sea water.

Dawn was still an hour or two away but the stars and a quarter-moon made it light enough to see. I went outside and was greeted by a cool breeze, refreshing after the stuffy tent. The white starlight cast shadows of the palm trees across the clearing. I looked around for the tortoises which had encircled us the night before but there was no sign of them. Presumably they slept under the bushes; or were they grazing further afield?

Someone in London had warned me not to go walking on Aldabra at night because of the deep holes, often masked by pemphis thicket or fallen branches, and the danger of walking without warning on razor-sharp rocks, but this sector of Anse Maïs was generally smooth and sandy. I slipped on my boots and, armed with a torch, strolled down to the beach.

The sea was calmer now and waves barely a foot high were breaking in showers of phosphorescence on the white sand. It was high water and the beach shelved so steeply that only a yard or so above the waves it was quite dry and powdery. Dozens of hermit crabs were on the move, from giants occupying shells as big as a fist to tiny creatures smaller than a walnut – minicrabs, bungalow dwellers. They covered the sand with a tracery of double dotted lines, reminding me of the tracks made by monitor lizards without the central groove left by the tail.

I looked out to sea and was not surprised to find it empty. From this point, five miles south of the settlement anchorage and slightly to the east of it, the *Lady Esmé* would be out of sight and the arc of vision was further restricted by the cliffs flanking the bay. Not for the last time on Aldabra I had the strongest 'end of the world' feeling of utter remoteness. It was not unpleasant. The fact that we were out of radio contact with our ship accentuated it. A world war could have broken out and we would know nothing of it for days, or even weeks. My train of thought was broken.

Creeping around the north arm of the anse and about a mile out to sea were the lights of a ship. They moved slowly across my line of vision and disappeared to the south. I wondered why the *Lady Esmé* was cruising at this time of night and why she was so well lit. It could have been my imagination but the silhouette did not seem quite right. The deckline appeared broken where it should not have been. Yet what other ship could conceivably be in these waters, so near to land? The nearest shipping lanes were hundreds of miles away. It was mystifying and, in a subtle way, sinister. Could they be poachers? Then why the lights?

Dawn was beginning to show as I got back to the tent and, as if on cue, five loud notes in a falling cadence broke the silence. After a few seconds they came again. Hurriedly I switched on the recorder. It was unmistakably the Aldabra coucal. Malcolm Penny had imitated this call for me when I saw him in London. It was unlike any bird song I had heard before and from that moment it became for me the signature tune of Aldabra. The coucal belongs to the same family as the cuckoo and its call is quite as distinctive. It was a kind of summons to wake up in the morning and later, when we heard it in even remoter parts of the atoll, it sounded like an invitation to venture deeper into the unknown; a familiar and enticing voice.

Harold returned while we were having breakfast of coffee and local bread, raised by the heat of the sun. He was exhausted and, I could tell at a glance, disappointed. Having visited four beaches on the 'Mecca of the Green Turtle' his total count of laying females, at the height of the breeding season, was one. This he had turned over after she had finished laying, tagged, measured and then released. Harold Hirth was a man of few words, but I knew from what he had told me earlier that he was expecting to find several reptiles on each of the small beaches from Anse Tamarind to Anse Badamier.

Perhaps it was too near the settlement and fishing grounds. Arch-angel tried to cheer him up: 'The beaches near Dune Jean Louis are much better. You will see a *quantité* of turtles laying there.' Laporte nodded his head in agreement, but I thought I saw doubt on the faces of the other creoles who were listening.

I had not yet learned to suspect the word *quantité*; it suggested a multitude but, as we were soon to find out, its meaning in Creole is elastic, anything from 'several' to 'hordes'. One *quantité* turned out to be a small flock of four birds.

At the next high tide, we would enter the lagoon and start our journey around the atoll. More question marks than ever now hung over the land to the east.

# VII   *Last of the Giants*

I<small>N</small> the darkness all I could see were the glowing cigarette ends from the pirogue behind; it was as black and silent as a commando raid, even the outboard motor sounded muffled. No one spoke.

We were now clear of the West Channel and moving south-eastward through the calm lagoon, waiting for the first show of dawn. The passage of the channel at full tide had been uneventful. I looked out for the champignon islets in the darkness and had difficulty in spotting them. Their stems were now covered and only a slight roughening on the surface of the dark sea gave them away. A powerful current had swept the two boats effortlessly through the pass, but as there had been quite a lot of swerving and two men had remained on look-out in the bows shouting instructions to the helm, I guessed there must have been hazards, albeit invisible. It was only when the two men sat down, their peaked caps silhouetted against the slowly lightening sky, that I realized we must be through and safe on the vast lake behind.

The Aldabra lagoon, one of the largest in the world, is over sixteen miles long and up to five miles wide. I strained to see land, but, apart from the low coastline to our right, could find nothing. What I was looking for in particular was Ile Esprit, one of the two main islands enclosed within the lagoon and a prime geological puzzle.

Ile Esprit was said to be fifteen feet higher, on its central ridge, than any other solid rock of the atoll. According to Fryer, who made a close study of it in 1908, it was of particular importance in assessing the age and origins of Aldabra. Towards the centre of the island he found a series of 'grotesque, upstanding pillars and walls, varying up to fifteen feet in height and standing on brown conglomerate rock', unlike any other formation. A number of theories have been advanced to account for the anomaly of Ile Esprit but all have left a number of geological problems unanswered. In his paper published in the *Smithsonian Atoll Research Bulletin* of November 1967, Stoddart thought it possible that the original uplift of the atoll was not less than thirty feet and that Esprit is the last remnant of a widespread lagoon fill. But there remained the problem of 'the horizontal bevelling of the marginal cliff tops at about fifteen feet'. What process of erosion or submarine upheaval had caused this island to tower above the rest?

A pale yellow ball of sun, streaked with long grey clouds, was now rising above the horizon. We were, of course, out of earshot of the birds' dawn chorus but the boatmen made up for it. A duet in resonant bass started between a calypso singer in our boat and another, distinguishable as a huge white grin, in the sharp bows of the pirogue in tow. The lagoon, unruffled by the smallest wave, was slowly turning silver-grey. As it lightened, the outline of Ile Esprit materialized on the port side, first a broken line of trees which, in the gloom, appeared to be growing out of the water, then the dark mass of the central ridge where Fryer had established his camp nearly sixty years before.

François the creole helmsman tapped me on the shoulder:

'There are many *(quantité)* cattle birds and running birds. You take photos very good.'

He indicated the size of both birds and moved his neck sinuously. I could tell at once that he was referring to one of the two species of egret that occur on Aldabra, either the cattle egret or the dimorphic little egret, and to the flightless white-throated rail. The second piece of intelligence was particularly interesting for it confirmed something I had learned in Mombasa. My shell-collector friend had told me that he had seen the rail on Esprit during an afternoon's visit a few months before.

I was beginning to find it quite easy to understand our creole guides who invariably made up for a lack of English and French words with vivid mime. It was remarkable too, how well they were able to imitate bird calls, a skill I had often admired among simple villagers and one which, in South East Asia, had a practical application. Sad to relate, it indicated not a nature-lover but a hunter. The skill was used very effectively in the chase to attract birds within range. Many types of bird will come close to investigate if the right call is given. The technique is now widely used by recordists and cameramen as well, not only for birds but for mammals. I remembered how David Attenborough had used it with striking success in Madagascar. By playing back the animal's voice, tape-recorded the day before, he had managed to film a remarkable sequence of the big indris lemur there.

I would like to have landed on Ile Esprit but there was no time. Our destination, Dune Jean Louis on the south coast, was still over ten miles away, and Harold was anxious to start his turtle investigations on the promising beaches in that area while the good weather lasted. As Aldabra's tallest rocks vanished astern, I shared the feeling that this small island with the ghostly name (actually a corruption of the French word 'surprise') might one day provide the key to Aldabra's origin.

We were now travelling due east with the sun, clear of cloud obstruction, full in our eyes. Although it was only just after seven o'clock the heat was already intense and we were grateful for the slight breeze. I looked overboard for signs of life on the sea-bed. In the settlement there had been stories of fantastic marine life in the lagoon – giant worms ten feet long, the water black with rays at certain seasons. I suspected that some of these were embroidered for our benefit, but there had been too much detail for them to be dismissed as pure invention. It was, therefore, with surprise and some disappointment that I scanned, clear through the water at a depth of some fifteen to twenty feet, a sandy and quite lifeless bed. There was no coral or weed and, after a quarter of an hour, I had counted only two small fish. No one had bothered to put a fishing line overboard; the bottom seemed to be level and quite free of rocks.

I had been told that the lagoon as well as the outer ocean was slowly eating Aldabra's rocky rim, eroding with its vanguard of mangroves the narrow rampart of dry land, which was already breached in four places. The processes that are causing this slow death of the atoll are not yet fully understood, but later that morning I was to get an idea of one way in which the demolition is effected. For the moment, however, there was nothing to see but the smooth dead layer of muddy sand, presumably the drowned remains of a coral platform that once rose above the sea.

It was a relief to turn suddenly towards the shore, making straight for a mushroom whose stem was just beginning to show. Not a word had been spoken. The swerve seemed almost instinctive. Something warned me to get my camera ready. When we were about a hundred yards away, the jagged flat top of the islet suddenly exploded. What I had taken to be rock pinnacles took wing and turned out to be a flock of about a hundred noddy terns. They scattered in all directions, and one flight came straight for our boat, like a dive-bombing attack. A bird flew so close above my head, squeaking loudly, that I could easily have caught it without rising from my seat. The reconnaissance party circled the two boats several times and then, as if satisfied that we were mere humans, flew back to the mushroom and landed again.

Archangel cut the engine and we drifted to within a few feet of a circular coral platform standing a yard or so above the water. A score of noddies, braver than the rest, held their ground and as we circled the rock followed our movement, their elegant pale grey heads swivelling to keep us firmly in view. The pirogue had by now cast the tow rope and had rowed to the far side of the islet. I still had no idea of what was happening.

A number of birds were sitting in holes on the pitted surface and some were standing guard above a single egg or fluffy chick, perched on the sharp needles. I estimated there were between forty and fifty nests in a space hardly bigger than two billiard tables. There was no vegetation on the rock but the noddies had upholstered some of the nesting holes with dried weeds and small sticks. In my diary I noted the date – March 2nd.

I thought we had approached just to have a close look at the colony and was so busy filming that I did not at first notice one of the labourers who had clambered on to the ledge. The spiky surface looked brittle and quite impossible to walk over. I nearly dropped my camera in the water with amazement when I saw that the creole, stepping from pinnacle to pinnacle like a circumspect spider, was barefoot. He was gathering eggs. When he had collected two handfuls he returned swiftly to the rowing boat.

The grey noddy tern is not, of course, confined to Aldabra and protected; indeed it is one of the commoner sea-birds of the tropical zone but, nevertheless, I was taken aback to see this robbery of their eggs done so openly. Guy did not look nearly so surprised.

'That's our breakfast,' he said, turning to me. 'They don't see anything wrong in taking a few eggs; they believe the terns will lay again to replace the egg that's been taken, but I'll tell them we don't want any more.'

I knew that the Seychellois were tremendous eaters of sea-birds' eggs consuming well over a million, mainly of the sooty tern, in a good season. The scale of the industry was enormous. In 1930, for example, one island in the Amirante group produced five million eggs for sale in Mahé and as barrelled yolk for export. Until 1933 there were no restrictions on the cropping of eggs. Then a close season was introduced, for it had become obvious that the uncontrolled and inefficiently-managed industry was seriously damaging the tern populations. There was a lot of wastage in the packaging and handling of the eggs and to ensure that only fresh eggs were shipped the collectors used to smash those laid between the visits of boats. Since the war two experts, the Hon M. W. Ridley (now Lord Ridley) and Lord Richard Percy had, at the request of the Colonial Office, carried out surveys of the industry and made recommendations for its control to the Seychelles government. Many of these had been accepted and were now in force, but custom dies hard and there was good money in the business. The main bird islands are now patrolled by the police, no easy task in such wild and inaccessible places, and the export of egg yolk was finally prohibited in 1952.

One of the difficulties in bringing order to the industry and in reducing it to a scale that would not endanger the breeding colonies was the very size of the tern population, visible for all to see. How could a simple people be made to understand the need for control and conservation? The Ridley-Percy Report gave examples of the decrease in numbers before the advent of protective legislation; it noted that little Bird Island alone produced well over 10,000 cases of 750 eggs every year before 1890 and only 200 cases in 1954; that

11. Lomatophyllum in bloom on South Island. At least ten per cent of the flora of the atoll is unique. *(The Royal Society)*

12. The scarce Aldabran kestrel, one of the smallest birds of prey on earth. Its diet consists mainly of lizards. *(The Royal Society)*

five million pairs of sooty terns nested on Desnoeufs Island in 1931 compared with less than a quarter of a million in 1955.

The experts also investigated the ability of the terns to replace an egg that had been smashed or taken. They discovered that the birds are not the 'inexhaustible laying machines' they are sometimes thought to be. Admittedly the birds often relay, but the replacement is by no means 100 per cent. Other factors intrude and Ridley and Percy also found that the noddy tern takes much longer than the sooty tern to relay after losing its first egg. The latter takes an average of fourteen days and will sometimes lay again even when it loses a chick.

One consolation we felt as we left the islet, carrying the breakfast eggs, was that this breeding platform was unlikely to be disturbed again before the noddies had had time to repair the damage. It was in a part of the lagoon not often visited by the labourers.

For the next hour we hugged the coast, marked by low mangroves. At a point which appeared to me quite featureless, Archangel, who was now at the tiller, swung the motor boat towards the land. We entered a channel in the mangroves. My experience of this strange aquatic tree had led me to expect nothing like this. The mangrove forests I had penetrated often before grew out of stinking grey mud which turned to black ooze at knee depth. They were gloomy and well-nigh impenetrable. This swamp was bright and clean looking, not at all like the sinister haunts of snake and crocodile I was used to. The mangrove trees looked fresh and spring-green and the mud in which they grew was white. It was a blindingly brilliant scene under the hot sun with the water suddenly turned to milk, opaque and chalky. As the channel grew narrower it became impossible to estimate its depth. Archangel continued to steer hesitantly with the engine at half speed. We seemed to be crossing the atoll rim and I remembered that Fryer, in his last report on Aldabra in 1909, had forecast that the next channel would probably be formed at this point on the south coast.

I was feeling lazy in the burning heat and hoped that the erosion had made good progress since his visit. This was seeing Aldabra in tourist luxury, but the cruise was not to last for long. We grounded softly in the white mud and two men jumped overboard. From then on it was careful poling until we reached an inlet flanked by slabs of platin. A clearly marked path led through open champignon country covered with sparse scrub not more than four feet high, with here and there a larger bush or gnarled tree. From the landing place we could already see the sand hills of Dune Jean Louis, the highest ground of the whole atoll, rising fifty feet above sea-level and crowned with bushes and grass.

Archangel led the way through the mangrove. The mud was sticky. The warm water swirled even whiter with our footsteps, but the going was easier than expected. One got the impression that there was a rock bed under the mangrove mud; even my fifteen stone never went deeper than a foot or so into the white glue. Guy, who was up front, stopped and waved to me to come over to where he was standing.

He was on the lip of a muddy pool gazing at three tortoises, two adults and a juvenile, who were floundering about in the mud buried to half-way up their shells. For a moment I thought they might have fallen in and were in difficulties, then I caught sight of another, lying placidly in the pool regarding us with sleepy eyes. He was obviously contented. The creatures were just enjoying a mud bath, one way of keeping cool. This supposition was confirmed when another tortoise, which already bore a tidemark of mud on its carapace and body, came out of the bushes behind and slid gently into the ooze. They reminded me of nothing so much as water buffalo enjoying their daily wallow in a rice field, or the happy hippopotamus which is allowed to get nice and dirty in the Plymouth Zoo.

We were still in the mangrove belt but on the edge of the rocky rim and more and more outcrops of champignon were beginning to obstruct our progress. I looked closely at one of these which was standing clear of the mud and which revealed a cavity underneath; it was supported by a series of small pillars – mangrove shoots. The brown shoots were prising up the heavy slab of rock with the strength of their growth. In the same area I found several more examples of this undermining of rock by mangroves. It was a vivid illustration of the slow destruction of an atoll from within.

A well-worn track opened up as soon as we reached dry land, but it was still necessary to walk with care to avoid sudden holes, masked by a tangle of undergrowth, that yawned on either side. I peered into some of the larger ones and found they all had water in them. The openings were generally about six feet across but several of the larger chasms became wider with depth. Perfect man-traps!

Several times we had to skirt a giant tortoise which had settled confortably on the path. As we approached, it pivoted smartly, emitting an irritated hiss, and veered away to make room. Once again I noticed that some of them had nasty dents on the back of the shell, right in the centre where it starts to slope down. It looked almost as if they had been hit hard with the end of a pole, although who could have done this and for what reason it was difficult to imagine. Perhaps it was more likely they had suffered the wound, which did not seem to bother them, by a fall on the sharp rock, but then, why were they all in exactly the same place? It was a mystery I never solved.

As we reached the top of a slight incline, the track widened out and we were presented with a magnificent view: the line of the south coast now visible for a distance of several miles in both directions, rolling grassland behind a series of beaches separated by low, undercut cliffs. The tide was out and beyond the sand there was a wide expanse of rust-coloured rocks, which I took to be coral, dotted with pools left by the retreating sea. Across the deep blue of the empty ocean, a line of white breakers marked the course of the reef half a mile from the shore. To our right, facing south west, the sand dunes rose steeply. The land in front of them as far as the cliff edge was open and undulating, looking rather like a golf course. Behind them, reaching to the distant horizon, was a jungle of pemphis scrub, grey-green and featureless, the most forbidding landscape I had ever seen.

We made straight for a broken-down fisherman's hut a few yards from the beach, dumped our baggage and sat down to a very late breakfast of fried terns' eggs. It was so hot outside that I felt the eggs would have cooked without a fire. Fortunately, we had brought plenty of drinking water and some stronger liquids, for there was no sign of a well. Although the rainy season had only just ended, the vegetation already looked parched. It would have been nice to have a swim but the tide was too low.

From the shelter of the hut I planned an exploration route. Harold was walking to Trou Nenez five miles away to make a survey of the beaches and Guy intended to hunt for butterflies at the back of the dunes. I wanted to observe the tortoises and find land-birds to film. On the walk from the lagoon I had seen several pairs of sacred ibis overhead and I hoped to meet them for the first time on the ground. But for the moment there was very little sign of life and even the giant tortoises had disappeared. It was nearly mid-day and I supposed every living creature with any sense would be sheltering from the sun. As far as I knew there were no mad dogs on the atoll and I was the only Englishman.

A curious construction of wood and old iron standing in a depression immediately behind the largest beach, a few hundred yards away, had caught my attention. Guy Lionnet had muttered something about 'calipee' but the word meant nothing to me at the time. It would be the first thing to investigate. There was something about the way he occasionally looked at it that made me think it was an object he had not wished to see. The memory of the mystery ship at Anse Maïs returned. Could there be any connection? I had discussed the ship with Guy but he had no idea what it could be.

Reinforced by a bowl of hot coffee (how I missed tea, the world's finest drink on an expedition), I set out across the burning grass with Laporte, carrying cameras, a tripod, tape recorder, binoculars, a butterfly net and a flask of water. We made straight for the ugly erection in the hollow which at first sight seemed to be surrounded by heaps of pale grey slate.

'*Tortues*' explained Laporte, as we came nearer. I thought he was referring to the tortoise I now saw sheltering under the rusty corrugated-iron roof. He picked up one of the grey objects and showed it to me. The penny dropped. These were dried sections of a turtle's carapace, the contraption was a primitive boiler for oil extraction and for preparing calipee, the cartilage of the belly shell of the green turtle – the source of turtle soup. Two rusty iron bowls lay nearby. The ground for yards around was littered with grey turtle bones and there was another massive heap of them in a hollow not far away. It was impossible to tell how long they had been there but the boiler itself was certainly in working order. It was a green turtle graveyard and the giant tortoise sheltering in its midst served only to heighten the sense of desolation. If I had known then what I have since learned about the appalling waste the extraction of calipee entails, I would have found this slaughter-house even more depressing. But there was too much else of interest to linger.

Apart from the sheltering tortoise the only movement around the deserted boiler was of an army of hermit crabs, some of which were themselves seeking shelter under the tortoise. There must have been tens of thousands of these crabs on the grassland, crawling far from the sea. I wondered what they could be finding to eat. Could it be tortoise droppings?

Quite suddenly I felt we were being watched. It was a strange sensation in such an open and lonely place. I looked around. Nothing moved except the crabs, even our camp was out of sight. Both the sky and the land were empty of life. But the feeling persisted. I picked up my binoculars and examined the trees on the sand dune overlooking the hollow. At the far end of the highest dune a post was sticking up. It seemed to have something perched on top. Just as I focused on it, a bird took off and vanished over a *tournefortia* bush. It was too far away to identify.

Having no other immediate quarry I hurried towards the spot, hoping the bird would not return before I had got into a position. The best vantage point was in a sand gully a few yards below. Quickly I threw myself down but as quickly jumped up again – the sand was furnace hot. I stirred it up to bring cooler grains to the surface and tried again. It was just bearable but I knew it would cool off gradually. Now I was taking the full heat of the sun on my back. The bird had not yet re-appeared. I waited and watched, slowly incinerating. Ah, the joys of wild-life filming!

But it was worth it. One moment the top of the post was empty, the next it was crowned by a bird with rich brown wings and a grey-white breast, spotted and streaked with black. It showed its profile to tear at a small lizard held firmly in one claw, and revealed the curved beak of a bird of prey. The Aldabran kestrel, one of the rarest of the atoll's endemic land-birds and among the smallest birds of prey in the world. I think it had seen me but was not disturbed by my presence. For the next hour I was able to watch it hunting successfully for lizards and having a series of meals. There was no sign of a mate. An accurate count has not yet been attempted of this bird and observing it in this exposed position, I thought how easy it would be to over-estimate its numbers. Kestrels everywhere make themselves con-spicuous and an easy target for a catapult. I was delighted to get a film sequence of it and now began to feel that a television feature was beginning to take shape.

Rising from my cramped position, I did not realize how time had passed. It was nearly four o'clock and the sun was less fierce. I climbed to the summit of a dune from which there was a perfect view of the coast to the south west for several miles. In the distance a tall clump of pandanus probably marked Anse Aux Vacois, one of the turtle beaches Harold planned to inspect. There were the same rolling dunes I had noticed before but now there was a difference – they were no longer empty, lifeless. The tortoises had emerged from the shade. Like shiny brown stones on the golf course, the huge reptiles dotted the grassland and low scrub. At this distance they looked motionless but through binoculars the long extended necks could be made out, showing they were on the move. Without changing my position I counted nearly 150, widely scattered. They did not seem to wander in groups, preferring probably to keep to their own bit of pasture. It was an astonishing sight, these monsters of a past age quietly grazing in their own peaceful sanctuary, the last wild home left to them by man.

There was a cracking noise behind me and I turned to see a leviathan of a tortoise lurching from under a fallen tree. The moment I moved he retracted and half turned. To give him a chance to go about his business, I remained motionless until he had jacked himself up again on his powerful pillar legs and had started downhill on the sand. When I followed, he increased his pace; I had no idea giant tortoises could move so fast. His black and wrinkled hind legs were so like those of an elephant that I could well understand how the tortoise earned the early scientific name of *Testudo elefantina*.

It may be because of my fondness for elephants, but I felt drawn to this huge chap. He evoked memories of the elephants I had ridden in Laos and of the first time I tried to hire one.

'What kind of elephant do you want, a slow or a fast elephant?' the headman asked.

'What is the difference?'

'In the cost of hiring,' he explained, 'slow elephants are more expensive.'

I was mystified, and thought I had heard wrong.

'Why is that?' I felt bound to ask.

He gave me a look which seemed to cast doubt on my basic education.

'Why? Well because they take longer to get there.'

Which classification did lumbering Joe belong to, I wondered, as I followed him over the sand. In Laos one of the highest compliments you could pay to a woman was to say she walked like an elephant. Although I never tried the gambit myself, I can see what they meant.

The elephant is indeed graceful, almost dainty, in its walk. But old Joe did not quite merit this elephantine tribute, his walk was entirely functional. Nothing artistic about it. He moved more like a tank, giving the impression that he was happy to be moving at all. It is, when you think about it, quite an achievement to raise and carry 300 pounds of solid flesh and shell over such uneven and hazardous ground.

There are early records of Indian Ocean tortoises weighing as much as 800 pounds, but whether these giants lived on Aldabra or on one of the other islands of the ocean, perhaps better supplied with fattening food, is not clear. We saw no animal on the atoll of more than about half this size, though later, on Cousin Island in the Seychelles granitic group which once had flourishing populations, the owner, Mrs Jumeau, introduced me to several tortoises which were larger than any we found on Aldabra, and they were only twenty years old. In his paper on giant tortoises published in the *Journal of the Zoological Society of London*, Roger Gaymer noted that males continue growing for five years longer than females and the actual size achieved is probably due to local differences in food and water supply. He also found that growth in captivity is twice as fast as growth in the wild for the first ten years.

Mrs Jumeau's reptiles were grazing in lush pasture and, in a sense, were in captivity. They also occupied a territory which, in the wild, would have supported a much larger population. The origin of these Cousin tortoises, which were brought to the island as babies by her late husband, is uncertain and it is now thought possible that they may be the last survivors of the Seychelles sub-species. The tortoise reaches maturity at 20–25 years. Gaymer gave interesting examples of their rate of growth. One animal grew from 23 pounds to 441 pounds in 15 years, another increased its weight 12 times in only 7 years. An Indian Ocean tortoise, kept in Ceylon, starting at just over a pound achieved a weight of 220 pounds in 19 years. Their size also increases rapidly in the early years of growth. Eight tortoises measured in the 1930s had an overall length increase at the rate of 7·2 centimetres a year for eight years.

As my friend continued to lumber downhill, I wondered how old he was. The longevity of tortoises is something that has intrigued man, with his promise of three score years and ten, for centuries. The Chinese regard them as the symbol of long life. A hundred years is quite a modest life-span for a giant tortoise. I understand that up to 150 years is a reasonable expectation for these monsters, and further research might well show some of them live very much longer. Certain famous individuals suggest this is so.

A conversation I had in 1950 with the King of Tonga, when he was a Crown Prince and a student at Sydney University, had remained vividly in my mind. I had asked him if there were any historical monuments, similar to the Easter Island stone heads, on Tonga.

'We have eyes still living that saw Captain Cook,' he replied in a deep bass voice that fitted his giant 6 ft. 7 in. frame.

I knew that Cook in his Pacific travels had been twice to Tonga which, because of the warm-hearted reception he always received there, he had named the Friendly Islands, but his last visit was in 1774. A rapid calculation – that was exactly 176 years ago. I thought the oldest man in the world was only 130-odd, a Soviet Armenian. Prince Tui chuckled at my surprise.

'The tortoise he gave to my ancestor is still alive. You would be interested if he could talk.'

This eminent tortoise, about whose great age there can be no doubt, was called Tu Imalalia. He was later in life accorded chieftain's rank and given his own apartments in the royal palace. Not only was he old, but he was tough too. Tu Imalalia had survived the loss of an eye, two forest fires, being run over and being kicked by a horse which fractured his shell. He could reasonably have claimed to be the oldest living creature on earth, but there were rival claimants.

Until recently there was a giant tortoise on St Helena which was adult at the time Napoleon was in exile there. Sad to say, this comparative youngster as famous tortoises go fell off a cliff and was killed a few years back. He was far too active to die of old age. Another celebrity in the longevity stakes is Marion's tortoise in the Seychelles, known to be at least 152 years old. Among the scores of giants I could now see, cropping the grass on these silent dunes, there could easily be, I reflected, several older than the United States of America itself, who had seen the ships of France flying the blue Bourbon flag in the days before the Revolution, or a contemporary of Dr Johnson or even of Isaac Newton.

These musings were interrupted by a hoarse bark that seemed to come from somewhere a long way away, down by the beach. Several tortoises were strolling about, one of them clambering on the back of another of smaller size. As I watched, the big one on top stuck his neck out and emitted the same echoing sound I had heard before. I was seeing the mating act for the first time. The female was unwilling and lurched away whenever she got the chance. I did not want to disturb them, so I approached carefully in a wide detour, camera held ready. But the male spotted me and at once slipped back to earth. I never succeeded in getting close enough to a mating pair to record this noisy prehistoric union and eventually gave up the attempt in the interests of population growth. The creatures were obviously modest and it seemed all wrong that I, a human intruder, should interfere with their married happiness.

Already at Anse Maïs I had noted that there were no young about. From pictures the Bristol University team had taken I was aware that the baby giant was tiny, that it could be cupped in a man's hand. These surprisingly small offspring hatched from eggs and we had already searched in vain for them. Guy Lionnet was particularly keen to obtain a few for his tortoise enclosure in the Mahé Botanical Gardens. It was not until several days later, in the vicinity of Takamaka Grove, that we eventually found several babies and the reason they were so scarce was at once apparent. They are agile and move with remarkable speed and cunning. I had heard that the eggs were laid in sheltered patches of sand and earth, deep in the undergrowth; and that the small tortoises stayed most of the time under cover. Although the adult tortoise on Aldabra has no predators except man, to fear, the young could obviously be preyed on by large birds, crabs, rats and the few feral dogs and cats known to be at large on the islands. But two important factors aided their survival – a rapid rate of growth to the size which made them at the least indigestible and their ability to hide quickly.

We had striking evidence of this gift when one of two baby tortoises Guy had at last managed to capture escaped from a cardboard box. Although the loss was discovered only a minute or two after the tortoise had absconded we never found it again. We were in the platin country and there was only sparse vegetation to hide under. Six of us searched for a quarter of an hour but the creature had vanished. Although we were disappointed it was good to know that the tortoise had a few tricks up its shell. It went to explain how an animal with no offensive mechanism can have survived for so long.

Adult males will sometimes fight over a female, banging each other's armour plate and snapping, but this seems to be untypical behaviour. Confronted by a glamorous 'bird' what else could they do? If tortoises subscribe to the belief that 'only the brave deserve the fair' they must at least put up a show. Just to be defensive, stop, collapse on their belly shell and withdraw all moving parts, would hardly be sufficient when faced by a rival. Although I never witnessed one, I understand such combats can be prolonged and noisy and always produce an outright winner.

How does one distinguish the sex of a giant tortoise? The full-grown male is bigger than the female but this is, of course, no help when faced by an assorted mass of varying sizes sheltering under a tree and looking like brown buns on a baker's tray. Guy told me that the plastron or belly shell of the male is concave to help in copulation but, in fact, the plastron is concave in both sexes. Roger Gaymer points out, however, that the plastron of the large males is indeed more deeply concave, also that they have a longer tail and a lower appearance to the carapace, but he says that the sexing of small tortoises is impossible. The creole labourers, on the other hand, encounter no such difficulty. When I put the same question to them, there was no hesitation. Male tortoises have tails pointing to the left, females to the right. I liked this simple rule, scientifically accurate or not. And we certainly could not argue with it.

From fossil remains it is known that tortoises and turtles – chelonians – have existed for more than 250 million years. They come in all sizes, from the small 'pet' tortoise found in Greece to a giant with a shell almost eight feet long whose remains were unearthed in Lower Pliocene deposits in India. Until about 200 years ago, the giant varieties abounded on at least thirty islands of the Indian Ocean, although they had been exterminated on the Continents by natural enemies long before. Early travellers, such as François Leguat in 1691, reported carpets of several thousand huge tortoises on islands like Rodriguez. In the peace and seclusion of these oceanic sanctuaries, a lethargic vegetarian fossil had managed to survive well into historical times. Yet by 1835, at the time when Darwin was working on his theory of evolution, the giant tortoise was extinct in the wild in all but two of its ancient homes, Galapagos and Aldabra. What had happened?

Man was entirely to blame. In the Pacific the tortoises were slaughtered mainly for the fine oil they contained – a big one could yield as much as three gallons.

In the Indian Ocean they were hunted and killed for their tasty meat. This direct slaughter by man reduced the populations, but the work of destruction was speeded by the domestic animals he introduced in both tortoise habitats. Goats, cattle and horses competed for the limited supplies of green fodder and, being more nimble, beat the slow tortoise to it. More aggressive animals like pigs, dogs and cats attacked their soft-shelled young and ate their eggs whilst man's accompanying horde of rats added drastically to the slaughter. The giant tortoise was unused to predators. It was meeting competition and facing aggression for the first time in millions of years. The outcome was a foregone conclusion. In the space of less than one hundred and fifty years it was wiped out in all but these two remote island groups.

To make matters worse, most of the island habitats had been ruined irretrievably. Tortoise food plants had been cut down, the natural forest and scrub levelled for coconut plantations. In the Indian Ocean, some of the scattered survivors were transported to inhabited islands and kept in semi-domestic conditions, awaiting slaughter for a wedding feast. The taste for tortoise meat among the French planters and creoles persisted long after the reptile had been exterminated on every accessible island. Indeed it continues to this day.

The fate of this most inoffensive of animals is the climax of a grisly story of human folly and greed. Sensibly protected, the tasty giant, which for more than a century had offered sailors a convenient supply of fresh meat at sea in the days before refrigeration, could have remained a source of protein in a region where it is lacking. But it was not to be. Darwin found a desert of destruction.

By the middle of the nineteenth century, there were giant tortoises only on the two oases, with some semi-domestic herds on other islands of the Seychelles and Mascarenes. The principal difference between the Pacific and Indian Ocean survivors was that whereas the Galapagos tortoises generally remained on their original islands, where they had evolved different characteristics, the Indian Ocean tortoises had been transported freely from island to island by the shippers, and had become thoroughly mixed. In this region, Aldabra alone was believed to have retained its original variety. For Darwin's purpose, therefore, the Galapagos tortoises were of greatest interest and it was indeed the study of their distinct island forms that contributed to his theory on the origin of species.

At the moment of its greatest danger, the giant tortoise had suddenly become of unparalleled scientific importance, yet steps were not immediately taken to protect the few that survived. In the Galapagos they continued to be hunted by 'oil prospectors' from Ecuador and, as we already know, Darwin himself had to intercede for Aldabra to prevent the establishment of a wood-cutting industry there which would have sealed the fate of the Indian Ocean subspecies in its wild state. The tortoises still had a long time to wait before man came to their aid.

Active conservation of the Aldabra tortoises was begun not by the British government, whose ultimate responsibility the atoll was, but by private philanthropy. Even after the appeal by Darwin and other naturalists, the leasing of exploitation rights continued without legislation to save the tortoises, until in 1900 the zoologist, Lord Rothschild, took the initiative. He agreed to pay half the lessee's annual rent if the tortoises were 'rigidly protected'. The first to sign this agreement were Messrs Baty, Bergne and Co., and their successors on Aldabra followed suit. There is no doubt that this far-seeing action by an eminent scientist was of crucial importance in saving the reptile from extinction. Above all it brought home to the Seychelles people, in a way they could understand, the worldwide importance of the few wild tortoise survivors in their remote backyard.

For some unexplained reason, however, the local government still dragged its heels. Although the giant tortoise could have been scheduled in the Wild Birds and Animals (Protection) Ordinance of 1906, it was not. The first protective legislation did not come until 1961, almost ninety years after Darwin's plea. Then, under the Customs Management Ordinance, the export of giant tortoises from the Seychelles was, for the first time, prohibited without written authorization. But there is still, apparently, no law forbidding the removal of tortoises from Aldabra to any other island within the Seychelles group, nor the killing of tortoises on the atoll, although the governor has powers to 'make regulations for the protection of wild animals' and there are further safeguards for the tortoises embodied in the terms of the Aldabra lease itself. In this, as we have read, the lessee is required to 'protect and not to interfere with' the tortoises.

In fairness it must also be said that since Aldabra came under British Administration from the Seychelles more than fifty years ago, large numbers of tortoises have not been taken from the atoll. Even without legislation they have had protection. Government and public opinion were at last on their side and the procession of visiting naturalists greatly helped to promote a new concern for a remarkable wild life legacy.

The smoother parts of Aldabra today present an astonishing sight. At mid-day you can see tortoises stacked two deep in the shadow of trees and large bushes, often as many as sixty under a single shelter. It is probably true to say that there are tortoises around every fresh water pool of South Island, and after the rainy season there are hundreds of these where the shade of the large trees gives shelter from the blistering sun. At the cooler times of day, early morning and around four o'clock in the afternoon, the spectacle is even more fantastic. The tortoises are dispersed and feeding and you cannot walk more than a few yards without seeing one. The low scrub is intersected by well-worn tortoise tracks, the creatures browse on water weed in every stretch of shallow water, dot the sand dunes like pepper and are even to be seen on the beaches. A convenient rounded seat for the weary explorer is always at hand and, if you rest long enough, it may well start moving in the direction you want to go!

The biggest concourse of tortoises is at the east end of South Island, on the wide expanse of platin land that is the feature of this part of the atoll, but around Cinq Cases, the principal beach at the east end of Aldabra, they are equally numerous. Another popular resort is Takamaka Grove three miles from Dune Jean Louis, which boasts several fresh water pools and big shady trees.

In 1965, the Bristol Expedition reckoned there were 30,000 tortoises on South Island and another 3,000 on Malabar or Middle Island. They stressed, however, that as the time available to them was so short, this must be regarded as a rough estimate. The figure was greeted with amazement even in the nearby Seychelles, and delighted international scientists who had gained the impression from several pessimistic reports published in the past thirty years that the giant tortoise was in danger of extinction.

But if this news of a vast and flourishing community came as a pleasant surprise to a world more accustomed to hearing of the disappearance of wild life, the latest information on the tortoise population obtained by the Royal Society Expedition that is on the atoll as I write, will be no less than staggering. This gives a total of 80,000 animals plus or minus 20,000. Even the wildest optimist would not have dared, a few years ago, to suggest that up to 100,000 of these gigantic creatures had managed to survive on the forgotten atoll. The importance of Aldabra as a 'living museum' stands out even more clearly when one compares this colossal population to the maximum of 3,000 giant tortoises left on the Galapagos Islands.

A few tortoises are undoubtedly still taken for food by the settlement labourers. The lessee, Mr Savy, is allowed to export a small number each year to zoos and similar institutions (a quota which, I understand, he has not used fully for a long time). The treacherous terrain takes its toll of both adults and young, and there are probably tortoise diseases which will, in due course, be studied. But despite all these hostile factors, the tortoise population is undoubtedly on the increase. This is the best conservation news for a long time.

Walking round the atoll it is easy to get the impression that the mortality rate is high, as it probably is among the juveniles. There are no porcupines to devour the dead white shells and these are particularly outstanding against the uniform grey and green. I saw these hollow shells in a variety of places – often where they told their own story. The shell of the tortoise that got wedged in the champignon rock trying to reach shelter and was burned to death by the sun; the shell at the bottom of a fifteen-foot hole. One was wedged under a fallen branch and another, under a pile of driftwood, was probably that of an animal caught on the beach that could find no exit and no adequate shelter. Then you see the mystery skeletons, the ones with a wound on the back of the carapace. Death is very visible on Aldabra and there are many ways in which even a tortoise can meet it.

Several times, particularly on the edge of the mangrove swamps, we saw animals apparently in difficulties and whenever possible we tried to give them a leg up or a heave. This high champignon rock with its gothic pinnacles, an appalling obstacle for a man, is quite impassable to a tortoise, and the biggest number of skeletons I saw was on the edge of this spiky wilderness. They were invariably trapped in holes, some quite shallow and barely larger than the creature's shell. Most of these tortoise-traps were overgrown with vegetation and it looked very much as if the tortoise had been trying to feed off it, had slipped and fallen in.

The signs of a desperate search for food were everywhere. Most trees and large bushes had a crop-line as if grazed by a herd of tiny cows. Tortoises resting underneath often reared up on the back of another to reach the green leaves, extending their necks a foot or more. This was the end of the rainy season when the vegetation was relatively luxuriant, and yet I often saw several converging on a single small plant on the stony plain. This may, of course, have been a prized delicacy but, dare I say it, I sometimes felt that the place was over-crowded, that Aldabra was not an ideal home. It just happened to be the only one man had left them.

When I mention this to ecologists, they smile sympathetically and speak of the balance of nature. Jeffery Boswall was particularly courteous when I voiced these heretical views – not in the film com-mentary, of course, but in private conversation – but I could sense he thought I was talking through my hat. I probably was. Nature has many ways of adjusting animal population in a limited habitat. Although the land rim of Aldabra is being slowly eaten away by the sea and the lagoon, it will be a long time a'dying.

But there is no doubt that the tortoises are either hungry or just plain greedy. At every camp we had scavengers who would come right into the tents searching for scraps. Paper was a favourite snack and several nibbled at bits of meat. I thought they would draw the line at tinfoil, but far from it. A special friend of mine at Dune Jean Louis, who featured prominently in my television film, filched a packet of cigarettes when no one was looking and devoured it with obvious relish, cellophane, tobacco, cardboard, tinfoil and all. Roger Gaymer told me that one of their visitors got through a boxful of vitamin pills and a tin of green paint!

It was easy to feed them by hand, even with ordinary leaves plucked from branches above their reach. The horny head would dart forward and cut a tall parabola from the extended leaf, provided the donor kept quiet and still. I wondered if tortoises were deaf, as water monitors are, because they were never disturbed by loud conversation whereas the slightest movement caused them to retract and pivot away with a mild hiss.

After a short stay on Aldabra, you grow very fond of the tortoises.

They are perfect company if you like peace and quiet but not un-broken solitude. They are friendly and call on you but never overstay their welcome. Their siesta time is the same as yours. Their slow movement and occasional noises, clattering carapace, the quiet hiss, a rare throaty roar, is comforting in a moon landscape that is often so silent you can hear the grass grow. The thunder of the reef is always there but after a time it only accentuates the burning stillness of the land and you notice it no more.

We had been walking for hours along the east coast. It was mid-day and there was no shade. Whenever the going seemed about to improve, more outcrops of reef rock barred our way. Even the patches of sand, seen from afar, proved a delusion, just thin coatings on razor blades of champignon. I saw a solitaty tree ahead wobbling in the heat haze. I had never felt so exhausted or so thirsty. My camera weighed half-a-ton and I felt like dropping it in a rock pit to join the whitened tortoise skeletons.

'Do we stop here?' I croaked to Laporte, who walked like a chamois just ahead of me. He turned and I was glad in a way to see that he too glistened with sweat and dried salt.

'No. Better trees further on. *Petite distance!*' he said and tried to smile.

Under the tree was an unbroken lumpy carpet of giant tortoises, grey-brown in the shade. Motionless, filling every inch of the circle of shadow. It was all I could do to skirt the tree. I wanted to flop down, out of the sun, on the rolling bed of tortoise shells. But Guy was ahead and carried the drinking water. I staggered on behind Laporte. As he passed the solitary tree, his long knife flashed and several branches of green leaves fell to the sand.

'*Pour les tortues*' he said without breaking his stride. The action and the words seemed almost automatic. He did not do it to impress me, we were both far too exhausted. In any case I was 'Anglais oiseaux' not 'Anglais tortues'.

I had not forgotten that.

13. Even the giant tortoises find the going difficult on Aldabra. They avoid as much as possible the coastal reef rock, razor-sharp and potholed and exposed to a blistering sun. *(The Royal Society)*

14. A red-footed booby among the lagoon mangroves. The slave of the frigates, the booby is nevertheless their harmonious neighbour. (*Roger Gaymer*)

*East to Takamaka*

'THEY must have swum here,' said the American professor as we sat around a camp table of driftwood that evening at Dune Jean Louis. We were talking about the tortoises, of course, over cans of the best tinned beer I had ever drunk. Although we had tried to keep the cans cool, they exploded with a violent report and showers of delicious spray when pierced. The residue was like nectar.

It was about six o'clock and a cool breeze was blowing from the sea. Again there were no mosquitoes and the beds had been set up without nets. Sounds of cooking came from a canvas shelter the porters had erected in the lee of a rock nearby. We had all had a good day. Harold was pleased with the turtle beaches he had found and planned to visit all of them again during the night. Guy had caught a number of new butterflies, including several *Precis* similar to what are called 'blue pansies' in Malaysia, and a black and white Danaid which we had not seen before. I had filmed the kestrel, a flock of sacred ibis and many co-operative tortoises doing what comes naturally. Half-a-dozen pairs of tortoise eyes watched us casually as we sat drinking. They seemed to be waiting for something. All the odd litter around the camp had already been removed by these reptilian vacuum cleaners. The conversation had inevitably turned to them.

'It's the only way they could have come. Probably from Madagascar or the African mainland. Let's try an experiment.'

A medium-sized tortoise was already on the beach sniffing at flotsam. I reckoned he was a 250 pounder. The high-domed and lumpy shell, so unlike the smooth streamlined carapace of the green turtle, did not make the animal look at all buoyant, while the pillar hind legs that had earlier put me in mind of an elephant, and the fat fore legs ending in blunt claws were scarcely those of a swimmer. Was it fair to try the experiment? Well, if elephants can swim so well, why not this namesake? The American had no doubt at all, so we went ahead, with every safeguard for the unsuspecting tortoise.

The sea was choppy as two black weight-lifters hoisted the animal fore and aft and carried it twenty yards out. Harold joined them while Guy and I took up strategic positions on the flanks to guide the swimmer towards the beach. The tortoise was lowered gently into the water with no signs of protest. The long neck arched up; he was afloat. To my amazement less than half the shell was submerged. For a few moments the tortoise made no effort to swim. It bobbed around in the small waves, head held high above the spray. I noticed its legs already extended. As if it had decided that the demonstration of its buoyancy was now over and the crazy human beings could pack up and go home, suddenly it started paddling resolutely towards the shore.

We burst into applause. It was a splendid sight, as if a chapter of Aldabra's ancient history was being re-enacted for us. So this was how the atoll's mighty and venerable inhabitants first arrived, hungry and exhausted, after probably weeks at sea. How long, I wondered, did the first one have to wait for the arrival of a mate? Or perhaps she was a female ready to lay her eggs. The speculation was cut short as the tortoise reached the shallow water. It started to walk ashore and then was washed out of its depth again by a retreating wave. This happened four times. I would have liked to have given it a hand but this would have spoiled the experiment. A larger wave approached and carried the reptile further in than before. It rolled about in an undignified way and then dug its foreflippers deep into the wet sand. The waves retreated and the tortoise was safe on dry land. With shining black carapace and no backward glance it walked straight to the lip of the beach and vanished over the top to where the grass grew.

I was thinking that the giant tortoise must be the easiest wild animal in the world to film. If you make a mistake the first time, you have only to put the actor back at the same starting point and the whole performance is repeated. No Union trouble, no overtime payments. All you need is time – plenty of it. Tortoises take several minutes to decide that you are not dangerous, just a nuisance. And time was a commodity we were always short of. I mention this only because I was never satisfied with any sequence I shot on Aldabra. I would like to have spent three times as long on every one of them, but we had far to go and there was no means of telling how long the fine weather would last. The sea was beginning to roughen ominously and Archangel kept pointing to the bank of clouds forming slowly in the east. But it is still true to say that Dune Jean Louis, away from the champignon, was the ideal wild life film location, and its friendly 'camp-follower' tortoises, the perfect performers. I thought it impossible that any wild animal could be less camera-shy, but I was soon proved wrong.

Something was moving at the back of the tent when we returned. Its silhouette against the setting sun darted swiftly behind a pile of haversacks and I got a glimpse of a snake-like neck. To catch it in the sun I made a wide detour, silent in the sand, with camera held ready, but there was no need for the cautious approach. Several times that afternoon I had seen a small flock of sacred ibis flying low over the dunes and landing near our camp to forage in the grass around the outcrops and from a distance I observed that when they were disturbed by the approach of a human – twice it was Guy with a camera – they waited till he came within about twenty feet, then took off to return to earth a short distance away. I was in no hurry to film them because I knew we would see many more at Takamaka Grove and near the platin pools at the east end of the island, but the sight that greeted me now was too good to miss. The eight black-and-white birds were inspecting our baggage, completely ignoring a creole sleeping a few feet away. Their white bodies, terminating in a flourish of shiny black feathers, were duck size, standing on tall but sturdy legs and surmounted by a black reptilian neck. But it was the head that arrested attention. It seemed to be all beak, perhaps a foot in length, down-curving and strong, above which china blue eyes shone like an aquamarine in the the black skin. One bird, which I later learned was a juvenile, had a white neck and head and looked scruffier than the others.

The ibis were behaving exactly as the American ornithologist, Abbott, had described three-quarters of a century before. They spotted me at once, the blue eyes gave a cursory glance but they were too busy to bother. One was pecking on a discarded tin of spam, another had taken what looked like a piece of fried egg. I wished I had been wearing shoes for Abbott had told how they were so tame they would approach to probe in them. Climbing boots were not so convenient. The birds gleaned around the baggage for several more minutes and then scuttled away, disturbed by the noisy arrival of a porter. But they did not seem alarmed. They had run past me and, when I turned, I found they had stopped only a few yards away and were looking back.

The sacred ibis is the most striking of the endemic land-birds of Aldabra. Most early explorers commented on its tameness and inquisitiveness. It illustrated how the birds of Aldabra were un-afraid of man or, perhaps it would be more accurate to say, ignorant of man, but I had been told by people who had visited Aldabra recently that the ibis had become more cautious. Although still curious it now kept its distance. As the settlement labourers were known to kill some for food, presumably when the manager wasn't looking, and when they were thoroughly sick of a fish diet, it was not surprising that they had become less tame. I was therefore delighted at this first close encounter.

One danger with birds as forthcoming as the sacred ibis is that they very easily give the impression that they are more common than they are. I suspect it is in fact one of the rarest birds of the atoll and deserves the strictest protection. Only one or two large nesting sites are known, and the Bristol Expedition had made an observation which gives cause for concern. They found twenty-one nests containing in all forty eggs. Despite minimal disturbance, five days later all the eggs had vanished. In 1909, Fryer had found a similar colony of ibis nests built close together in several small trees. Here two of the eggs were destroyed, apparently by clumsy birds trampling on other nests as they tried to gain access to their own. As the birds are good to eat and the easiest target for stick or stone (fortunately there are no guns in the Aldabra settlement) they would probably be one of the first to join the dodo if the island were developed as a military base.

It is a distinct Aldabran sub-species, bearing the name *abbotti*. Related to the Madagascar sacred ibis, it differs in several ways. I had already remarked two of them – the almost white neck of the juvenile and the extraordinary china-blue eyes, which look glamorous in a colour photograph.

Meeting these tame birds made me impatient to go further east, to Takamaka Grove and the platin country at the tip of the atoll. Two magnets were pulling strongly. Aldabra's dodo, the flightless rail, and, though I did not like to mention it too often, the mysterious flamingo. Every time I mentioned the 'flamant' there were polite smiles and head waggings. I was told repeatedly they were very shy, that most recent expeditions had searched in vain for them, that they frequented a part of the island no one visited. In twenty years they had been sighted only twice, the last time by the 'jeune Anglais' (Roger Gaymer) and then only on his second visit.

I had no means of checking these stories, but the fact that Guy Lionnet, the man responsible for the South Island nature reserve, seemed to agree, gave them a convincing ring. He advised me not to be too optimistic. I promised. But the flamingoes at once became an obsession. Far from wanting to abandon the search, I became more determined than ever to find them and to make the first film record. They were by far the biggest land-birds on the atoll and the most brilliantly coloured. How could a flight of flamingoes, with carmine and black wings outspread, escape detection? More sinister thoughts entered my mind. Did the creoles really know their habitat and wish to keep it secret because they hunted and ate them? This might explain the extraordinary decline in numbers from a reported thousand at the turn of the century to the latest estimate of fifty. Above all, were they an Aldabran sub-species or just birds of passage from Africa or Madagascar? On our last evening at Dune Jean Louis I decided to make the search for the flamingo my number one priority. The first requirement was to go east before the wet season pools dried out.

Harold Hirth, too, was impatient to move on. After the disillusion of Anse Maïs he had hoped to find and tag at least a dozen female green turtles on the beaches of the south coast. He had been told in the settlement that Dune Jean Louis was the best place to look, that a *quantité* of turtles came up to lay every night, but after inspecting every possible landing place, some of them twice in one night, he returned to camp exhausted and disconsolate. The total count on these miles of sand was two. It was still too early to give up hope but, by the way he spoke, I knew he no longer expected much from he historical Mecca of the reptile. The prospects for tagging and eventual research into turtle behaviour were fading fast. It would have to be an estimate of the chances of the turtle's survival. There were said to be a few small sandy inlets to the east of the dunes, so he and Guy decided to undertake the walk along the trackless reef rock and to join me later at Takamaka Grove. I would go through the lagoon with the baggage and approach the grove through the mangrove forest.

My journey, mainly by boat, ended once again with a cautious paddling through milky channels of the swamp. For a camp-site we chose a clump of bois d'amande trees that threw a lacework of shade on slabs of grey rock already burning like a Bombay pavement although it was barely ten o'clock. A shallow pond nearby was apparently to serve as a reservoir, kitchen sink and bathroom, judging by the immediate actions of the creoles. Archangel pointed out a small circle of blackened stones which showed that other nameless travellers had used the place before.

Behind a screen of spindly trees a few yards away, I found several deep pools of brackish water, and in one of them, taking care not to overbalance into a bottomless abyss, I bathed and shaved, watched by a pair of twittering white-eyes. Unlike Guy, I did not care to grow a beard, it was hot enough without one. My own inclination in wild places is to try and defeat the lack of mod-cons, and although I would not go as far as the eccentric planters of Somerset Maugham and change for dinner in solitary splendour, I always find it a pleasant challenge to maintain certain standards whatever the obstacles.

Above all, you must have a well laid-out camp. It can so quickly turn into a chaotic barnyard, even if you are lucky and have a team of porters as we did. Then it is miserably uncomfortable ('Who put all the matches in the milk?' 'Those aren't salt tablets, they're aspirin' 'Pass the sauce! don't be a clot, that's oil for the outboard' 'You're sitting on the biscuits') and equipment is bound to get lost and damaged. Take my cine-film for example; I had over 6,000 feet of colour stock in 100-foot cans. If one of these tins had been left lying in the sun for, say, ten minutes it would have been ruined. And if you have bug hunters with you carrying killing bottles, 90 per cent ammonia and cyanide, a touch of high drama can be added to the bedlam.

The walkers were not expected for an hour or two, so while the equipment was being carried from the boats a mile away, I decided to do some exploring. The country was open beyond our copse, a wasteland of ashen rock dotted with low scrub and here and there a dead tree turning silver in the sun, the crazy outline of a screw pine. It was a bewildering cross between champignon and platin.

Picking my way carefully and jumping from one hot slab of rock to another, I avoided most of the razors and needles that were already making mincemeat of my boots. As usual the loosely-balanced slabs rang like porcelain, but they never cracked. Angry land crabs glared from black boot-button eyes. I noted carefully the shape and disposition of the trees surrounding our camp while it was still in sight, then I set out in pursuit of a bulbul singing, if that is the right word to describe its atonal screams and gargles, in a patch of pemphis a short distance ahead. I followed it, and several of its mates, as they bustled around in the tangle of branches.

The bulbul, which looks like a faded and unkempt English blackbird, is one of the very few Aldabran land-birds that may not be peculiar to the atoll. At first sight, it is indistinguishable from the Madagascar species, but some ornithologists believe further study may show it has undergone evolutionary changes here, where it is a common breeding-bird, and that it may deserve to join the formidable list of local sub-species. The bulbul has the usual 'dull-grey, rare-island-bird' colour (as a naturalist once put it to me) and its most notable features are a bright orange beak and a tufted head as if it had forgotten to comb its hair. They showed no fear of me and hopped to within a few feet of the camera, while to other birds they behaved aggressively. I watched them drive away, with fierce calls and dive-bomb tactics, a white or fairy tern and two comoro blue pigeons. These elegant pigeons, dark blue with white head and shoulders, have eyes framed in brilliant red, looking like a blood spot on snow. They were the first I had seen and I was not pleased with the angry bulbuls for seeing them off.

After I had taken a few more pictures of a bird that seemed well able to take care of itself and a match for any invader, I turned for home. Harold and Guy should have turned up by now.

To get my bearings, I listened for the sound of voices. When I had entered the bulbul copse, laughter and rapid-fire Créole talk could still be heard coming from the camp site. Now there was dead silence. Even the bulbuls had stopped chattering. I squirmed out of the thicket following, as I thought, the direction by which I had entered. To avoid disturbing the birds, and because even my machete was almost useless in the twisted teak-hard branches, I had refrained from hacking a way through and therefore had no clear track to follow. Back on the rocky plain I saw, with relief, the line of trees marking the camp site, but when I reached the first screw pine, the shallow rock pool had vanished.

Stop and think! How far had I walked? Not more than a quarter of a mile, I was certain. There was now a clear all-round view. I studied the shimmering landscape slowly. There were two more groups of trees exactly like those I had so carefully memorized. This was absurd. The sun reflected blistering heat from the rocky slabs and I wondered if it was affecting my vision. There was no doubt that it was harming the film in my camera. I lurched over to a patch of half-shade under a bush and sat down. Foolishly I had set out without water or a compass. Warnings given to me in London came back:

'There are no landmarks. You can get lost fifty yards from camp.

Even the tortoises die of exposure and thirst. Incineration . . .'

It would be dangerous to start walking aimlessly. It might be better to wait until the sun pointed to the west. If I then went north I would probably hit the track from the lagoon! I tried a feeble yodel such as we used in the jungle over vast distances. There was no reply, not even an echo. After a few minutes in the sweltering shade, watched pitilessly by several par-boiled crabs, I hit on a plan. Dumping my brightly-coloured bag in a conspicuous position in the centre of the stony plain and leaving the camera in the shade, I started to reconnoitre in a wide sweep, looking for a familiar bush or rock. There were few tortoises around, it was far too hot, but I came across a monster drinking in a stagnant pool. The water was flecked with brown scum but I was now so thirsty I longed to join him – a stretch of the imagination and it could be beer! Above the pool was a bush bearing what looked like tiny plums, the black ones ripe and inviting.

'*Beaucoup sucré, bon manger,*' said a voice behind me.

It was Laporte. He proceeded to eat several plums and picked a handful for me. They were delicious – sweet and juicy. I was ashamed at getting lost on so short a journey but said nothing about it and Laporte, who had heard my yodel, made no comment. I learned later that even the creoles constantly lose their way on Aldabra and keep in touch by calling at regular intervals. But it was a salutary lesson. I reclaimed my camera and bag and returned in time for *déjeuner*. The camp may have been more than fifty yards away, but it did not seem like it.

It looked most inviting now. An outcrop of champignon was again being used as a cooker, with steaming iron pots wedged in convenient holes. Canvas awnings had been slung under the spindly trees. Several round glass floats were hanging up filled with water. My fellow explorers, exhausted from their trek round the coast, were fast asleep in the shade. This Takamaka camp was one of the best we had, and as it rained heavily that night we were grateful for the creoles' skill. I had already begun to admire the speed and efficiency they showed, not only in getting the camp working, but in moving from one inaccessible place to another. Some of their adaptations were highly ingenious. Later at Cinq Cases I was surprised to see smoke rising from the middle of a large round *mapou* tree. The porters were using the inside as a kitchen and dormitory! The heavy canopy of leathery leaves provided shelter from the sun and rain and the interior branches had been knitted to reinforce the roof. It was a perfect green igloo.

Stewed green turtle was on the menu for lunch. The first time I had eaten it on board the *Lady Esmé* I liked the taste, but now it did not seem so good. The cotton wool texture of the meat and the dull green colour, particularly of the fat, that persists even after cooking, are unappetising and it was hard to understand why the Seychellois esteemed it so highly. Perhaps it is only because all the other meat of the islands is of such poor quality and it's a change from the eternal fish. But we were all so hungry we could have eaten anything. That evening we explored the unknown frontiers of gastronomy and it was Takamaka Grove itself that yielded the delicatessen.

While the American professor rested after several sleepless nights

turtle hunting, Guy, Archangel, François and I explored the grove.
There is nothing else like it on Aldabra. Several fresh water pools, up
to eighty yards across, lead to an expanse of woodland dominated
by the splendid shapes of a stand of takamaka and *Ficus* trees that
dwarf the surrounding scrub. It is cool and dark inside and you can
sense at once that it is throbbing with life. The stilt roots of a bewildering variety of tropical trees and shrubs give the grove a look so
primaeval that if a pterodactyl were suddenly to clatter through the
branches, it would not seem out of place.

With enormous relief we threw our gear down in the green shade
and took stock of this weird and isolated woodland that has been a
magnet for every naturalist who has visited the atoll in the past
hundred years.

Giant tortoises were pottering around everywhere, some marked
with splodges of bright green paint on the back of the shell, a reminder
of Roger Gaymer's work in this spot two years before when he did a
detailed survey of the grove's tortoise population. Though it was
now mid-afternoon the tortoises were actively feeding, unlike their
sleeping cousins outside, grubbing under a thick carpet of dead leaves.
One beast seemed to be imprisoned behind the silvery stilt roots of
a tree, but it was only an illusion.

Guy told me that the tortoises were inhibiting further growth of
the grove by devouring all the tree seedlings and certainly, when we
looked for young takamaka trees, we were able to find only very few.
A part of the grove seemed to have been struck recently by a cyclone,
for huge takamakas, with fresh-looking roots, were lying spread-
eagled in all directions, their heads supported by smaller trees
beneath. While this disorder provided good cover for animal life, and
we counted several nests of the Aldabra cardinal and sunbird in one
small area of destruction, it made one wonder how long the grove
could survive, with tortoises eating the new growth.

The sacred ibis colony overlooking one of the pools, a series of
untidy nests making an almost continuous platform twelve feet above
the ground, was deserted after their breeding season, but there was no
lack of other birds. Loud cooing was coming from the undergrowth
and high in the canopy of *Ficus* trees at least a dozen blue pigeons were
feeding. Cardinals darted like small red verey lights in the green
gloom. The white-eye was everywhere too, but difficult to see and
virtually impossible to film. A perky white-spectacled face would

peer at you for a second and then vanish in the leaves. The light was poor for filming but I had to try.

Back where I had left my cameras, I could hardly believe my eyes. They were moving slowly across the carpet of leaves. An enormous crab, far bigger than anything I had confronted before, straddled the pile and, having hooked one leg through a strap, was beating a slow retreat with a Rolleiflex in tow. The animal was nearly two feet across and armed with powerful claws, held low in front like the business-end of a mechanical grab. The whole was painted blue-green. Keeping a wary distance, I prodded at it with a stick. It raised itself, disengaging the hooked claw, half-turned and backed away a few feet to face me, waving its claws sideways. I heard laughter behind me. Guy Lionnet and François had come up. The latter picked up the huge crab with a firm grip at the back of its body and brought it over for me to admire. With a small stick he demonstrated its grip. The four-inch claw closed very slowly on the stick and it needed most of the creole's strength to wrest it away, severed in two. I could now well understand the fright of the Ministry of Defence man when nuzzled by one of these monsters at dead of night, but Guy's amusement at crabs generally never failed, even when faced with this king-size specimen.

The robber crab of Aldabra is extremely common at Takamaka Grove and during the next day or two we encountered many hundreds of them. Some were blue-green, others were red. The red ones seemed to be larger and either more adventurous or more numerous for, whereas the blues were generally hiding in rock holes under the trees or in the champignon clefts, only roaming at night, the reds could be seen foraging all day. It is thought that the colour may show the stage of moult which the crab has reached. They are scavengers and will eat anything. Fryer said they were so numerous round his camp that he had to kill several hundred – the carcases being promptly devoured by the survivors – to get any peace and to stop pilfering of his supplies. There is no evidence that they ever attack man, but all the same I would not like to lie crippled and unable to move in their hunting grounds. Now that my eye was trained to watch out for these improbable nightmares, I saw them everywhere. As I stepped over a dark hole in the rock, pointed blue claws thicker than a cigar would jerkily withdraw. A red 'thing' would rise from under a bed of leaves and walk away sideways, glaring. I never found them easy company.

Having disengaged my cameras, I was free to track down the source
of the cooing. It had become louder and was now close at hand. I
climbed cautiously over a fallen takamaka trunk and practically trod
on a couple of red turtle doves, a cock displaying to his chosen hen,
bowing with grey and white tail feathers extended, moving three
paces forward, bowing again and sounding his urgent courting call.

There were more than a dozen of the doves, feeding off fallen
seeds in champignon crevices and courting. At least three pairs were
engaged in the latter pastime and it was amusing to see how often
the cocks were distracted from their courting by the call of the
stomach. They would stop in mid-bow to glean a few seeds then,
appetite satisfied, they would hurry after the hen and start the display
again from the beginning. Although the hens scuttled away, I noticed
they slowed down when the suitor stopped to feed, sometimes
glancing over their shoulders. These gentle birds, which would not
have looked out of place in Trafalgar Square, glowed a rich reddish-
purple among the sombre rocks. They were the first I had seen on
Aldabra but later, near the East Channel (Passe Houareau), I counted
over 150 of them in the space of thirty minutes just before sunset.
They were flying over the pass to Middle Island in groups of up to
six, presumably to roost on the north coast.

Filming them was almost impossible in the dim light but as the
doves paid no attention to me, I was able to watch the courting-
feeding flock for nearly an hour. Although I did not realize it, I was
being watched in turn. When I got up to go, I saw a strange object
on the trunk of the tree I had been leaning against. It was so unexpected I did not recognize it at once – a blue robber crab, ten feet
up, motionless. So they climbed too. I tapped the tree and one blue
claw waved a lethargic farewell.

Laporte was calling to me. He was holding in his hand an orange
furry creature the size of a rabbit. At my approach it turned its
head and two round black eyes looked out of a cute white face, like
a squirrel's

'*Lui blessé; cassé les ailes,*' Laporte said, stroking the thick fur.

It was the beautiful Aldabran fruit bat, the largest of the three bats
of the atoll and the only mammals represented in the native land
fauna. One of the bat's wings trailed loosely, the other was wrapped
tightly round the furry, plump, body. It had obviously been wounded.
Laporte had discovered it under the *Ficus* trees. He led me to where

he had found it, on the bank of one of the pools, and suddenly clutched me by the arm and pointed. Immediately above us, twisting acrobatically as they searched for ripe fruit, were two more bats, their white faces and reddish fur making them look like cuddly toys. We went out of the copse to get a wider view of the *Ficus* trees. It was only five o'clock and still broad daylight. Practically every tree had fruit bats moving about in it and there were several more flying above the grove on broad, birdlike wings. At first glance they might well have been birds, but somehow their flight was more silent. They seemed to glide rather than fly.

I had seen fruit bats often before on the Asian mainland, but never any so handsome. It is the white face and bright fur that distinguishes the Aldabran species from any other and I felt that even those who find bats repulsive would have been attracted to these. As the light began to fade, more and more bats planed in. They were obviously thriving at Takamaka Grove. The wounded bat had died, but this one casualty did not now seem so tragic.

Surprising as it may seem, fruit bats are easy to tame and are sometimes encountered as household pets in the Seychelles. The dead bat still nestled in Laporte's arms. I told him I would like it. Before I left England I had been asked by Lord Cranbrook to bring back some bat specimens for him and I thought I might try my hand at preserving this one. But Laporte must have misunderstood.

That night we had an unusual dinner. The main course was a curry of fruit bat and for the faint-hearted there was an alternative, curried crab. Whoever said robber crabs were inedible was way out. Although a bit tougher than lobster they have the flavour of their tribe and bulk to compensate for any lack of delicacy. The bat was delicious.

Whenever I am confronted by gastronomic exotica, I take courage from the memory of my friend and colleague of many expeditions, Dr Ivan Polunin, who used to eat with evident relish that *cordon bleu* dish of Borneo – fermented rat. And survived.

IX  *Search for the Flamingo*

THE radio set never worked. Punctually every morning and evening since we had left the settlement, Guy had tried to raise the *Lady Esmé* but without success. We were cut off from all contact with base and now accepted the situation. We were on our own. For all we knew the *Lady Esmé* had left the atoll, driven away by a storm. The only effect of this complete isolation was, I think, to make us a little more cautious. There was no hope of swift medical aid if one of us had an accident. When crossing the worst champignon, we took no chances. If a pinnacle looked too fragile to bear the weight of a man, we tried to make a detour. And I never went exploring again without a compass.

After several attempts to adjust the little Japanese transreceiver we gave up calling the ship. It was useless. In some ways I was glad, although I didn't say so. At least we could not suddenly be recalled. There was still much to explore. Captain Sauvage had said that if the weather remained calm, he might bring the *Lady Esmé* round to the east end of the atoll to contact us there and replenish our supplies, but the wind was rising, and it seemed unlikely he would risk the hazardous journey. The eastern tip of Aldabra, exposed to the prevailing winds, was no place to try and anchor in a storm.

An indigo sea was now flecked with white to the far horizon and the roar of broken waves on the undercut cliffs reverberated like a drum. The hollow land near the coast shook under the impact. It was like being aboard a fantastic aircraft carrier and the feeling of insecurity, of not being on dry land, was strengthened when columns of spray roared through giant blowholes twenty feet or more from the cliff edge.

By contrast, the lagoon was calm and emerald green when we set out in the early morning for the end of the world. Our destination was the beach at Cinq Cases or Five Huts, one of the few places where landing from the sea is possible and where turtle fishermen had long ago built some wooden shelters. In this area, and particularly in the platin country stretching from here to the north coast, I expected to find most of the land-birds I had not so far been able to film. On several occasions when I had seen birds like the blue pigeon, the coucal and the drongo in poor light or at a distance I had decided not to waste time on them. There would be much better opportunities near Cinq Cases, I told myself. In this I violated one of the first principles of nature filming – 'take it now (it may be your last chance)' – and I nearly paid dearly for my folly. That morning could have seen the end of the expedition for me.

We had entered the wide mouth of Bras Takamaka, the most easterly extension of the lagoon. Behind, silhouetted against the bright emerald water, was the mass of Ile Michel, the biggest of the lagoon islands, and just visible beyond was the mouth of the east channel, some three miles away. The fresh green mangroves grew larger and larger, shapely as trees in an English park. Used as I was to the smaller mangroves in the swamps around Singapore, I was still surprised by these majestic specimens, rising up to forty feet out of the clean white mud. Experts like Dr Stoddart tell me, however, that the Aldabran mangroves are not exceptionally tall, only an average height for mature trees in the region.

Guy, who was actively studying the botany as well as the lepidoptera of Aldabra, told me that there were five different kinds of mangrove on the atoll, most of which could be seen in the extensive swamp we were now entering, an area of more than three square miles flanking a broad creek. The flora of Aldabra is relatively well known and the standard reference is W. B. Hemsley's paper published in 1919. This records 173 species of flowering plant on the atoll, of which sixty-eight were said to be indigenous, that is not introduced by man, and of these eighteen occurred nowhere else. In other words, the very high proportion of 10 percent of flora of the atoll was unique. Hemsley believed that other species would be discovered and there is little doubt that in the next few years if opportunities for study are allowed to continue, the list of atoll plants will become longer, probably including several new to science.

Already Guy had collected a number of flowering creepers he had been unable to identify, and to me at least, many of the flowers we had seen looked strange. It was indeed quite a pleasure to meet an old acquaintance in the 'moon flower', a popular garden ornament in Malaysia, growing profusely over the bushes near a beach. Its four-inch green bud, standing straight like a candle on a Christmas tree, was unmistakable. And I had one infallible test whether it was one or not. The flowers I had filmed in my garden in Kuala Lumpur years before opened at precisely 6.30 p.m., at a speed which made time-lapse techniques quite unnecessary. Within five minutes, an elegant white-scented flower like a big convolvulus had twisted itself out of the bud. As all the flowers opened at the same time, the effect was astonishing. The green creeper was suddenly lit up with white lights as if someone had thrown a switch. I watched the Aldabran moon flower as the sun started to set. The green skin of the bud began to twist and unwind, revealing snow-white stripes. A sudden burst and half the flower was out. Pause for a deep breath. One more twist and it was open. It made me feel quite at home.

As the channel narrowed, more and more sea-birds could be seen roosting in the branches of the mangrove trees. In one big tree there were fifty large white birds, scattered evenly among the leaves, rather like fruit or moon flowers. We were not using the engine, and as the rowers silently approached, the birds made no attempt to fly away. We floated up to them and found ourselves being scrutinized by rows of gannet-like faces ending in long beaks of palest blue. One bird flew to a more convenient branch trailing a pair of large pink feet. It was a give-away. Until that moment I had thought they were blue-faced boobies, a bird reported from Aldabra, but they were

15. Nest of a drongo. This is the most distinct of all the land bird species of the atoll. (*Malcolm Penny*)

16. A male Aldabran sunbird in the pemphis bushes. *(Roger Gaymer)*

undoubtedly the red-footed variety, one of the commonest sea-birds of the atoll and yet rare elsewhere. Trees on both banks were loaded with the boobies watching our cautious progress up the inlet. We estimated there were more than 400 of them in Bras Takamaka that morning.

The sun emerged from a bank of cloud and threw dappled light on the mud flats criss-crossed by the soaring roots of the mangroves. I thought of the Everglades, a kaleidoscope of green and white and black. So brilliant was the effect that it was hard to make out some of the forms moving below the trees. A white egret, stalking, a black egret, a black and white egret, a white egret with a black egret. I thought I was imagining things, the light must be playing tricks, but surely the camera wouldn't lie. Then I saw a dark blue-grey egret in full sunlight. Guy must have sensed my puzzlement. All the birds looked exactly alike except for their colour.

'That's the dark variety of the dimorphic egret,' he explained, aiming his camera at it. 'It's very like the Madagascar little egret, but it may be a sub-species. The whites are commoner than the dark. There's also a piebald variety. I think that was one just now, but I'm not sure.'

We passed several more egrets, but they seemed more timid than the boobies and often hid when they saw the boat with its load of pointing humans. Despite the presence of so many birds (we had also spotted white and noddy terns) it was strangely silent in the creek. Even the sounds of the reef were blanketted out. The channel grew shallower and we glided slowly on a shining path of watered milk.

I had seen several fish jumping ahead. The atmosphere was weird, almost foreboding. Suddenly there was a shout and a shriek of laughter from astern. I swivelled just in time to see the giant negro Emil, who was poling, hit on the chest by a fat blue fish of at least four pounds in weight. It had jumped clean over the side of the boat to a height of five feet, bounced off Emil's body and disappeared in a splash to starboard.

'Something is frightening them, said Archangel. 'I don't think it's only the boat. Watch out.'

Emil picked himself up, cursing that the blue fish had not been deflected inboard.

Perhaps I should have been warned. Five minutes later we grounded in the white mud, throwing up little puffs of submarine smoke.

'We walk from here, ' said Guy. 'I hope they know the route.'

The only sure guide, Laporte, was not with us. He was accompanying Harold Hirth who was diligently pursuing his inspection of the coastline, looking for turtle beaches, even the smallest inlet that might not be marked on the map.

We came to a halt in mid-stream as there was not enough water near the banks. Just before I jumped overboard, I noticed a curious eddy ten yards upstream. Another of those acrobatic blue fish probably, and I thought no more about it. There were other preoccupations. The creek bed was like liquid cement, my feet sank deep into the gummy clay as I picked up a load of cameras, a tripod and a large haversack. I couldn't move. The others had disembarked on the far side. I was about to make the effort to extract one foot from the white morass and start towards the bank when a shout rang out:

'Requin. 'tention!'

I pivoted quickly in my bed of clay to see the shark. The eddy upstream had suddenly become turbulent and, as I watched, a dorsal fin rose above the surface and headed straight for me. Emil hurriedly picked up an oar and banged the water, but the shark did not change course, it just increased speed. At five yards, I could see a long black shape under the heaving water racing towards me like a torpedo. I made one superhuman effort to move but was stuck fast, the weight of my gear having driven me further into the ooze. Before I had time to try again, a terriffic backwash nearly toppled me over, cameras, film and all.

There was a moment of stunned silence. We looked at each other.

*'Gros requin fait peur les poissons,'* said Emil rubbing his chest. It had also *'fait peur'* to me! I did not like to think about it. The shark had escaped downstream through the small gap between me and the side of the boat. What the consequences of a one degree change in course might have been was too grim to contemplate. I wanted to get out of this. With a mighty heave, I dislodged my feet from the binding clay and struggled stickily to the shade of the mangroves.

We had seen many sharks before this but never at such close quarters, except for the one I caught from the *Lady Esmé* and which we later ate curried. Aldabra is noted for its big sharks but until recently I had not heard of a human victim. Early in 1968 a member of the Royal Society Expedition was gashed on the leg by a shark while working in the lagoon, but the creature fortunately did not close its jaws and the wound was slight. I had no idea whether that man-eater, the great white shark, was found in the waters around the atoll and had no particular wish to find out. Certainly the dangerous hammer-head is. I think it best to respect sharks from afar, particularly if they are scared, as ours was in the mangrove creek.

It seems quite likely that the fishermen are sometimes taken by sharks. Anyone who signs on for Aldabra must face the possibility of getting killed there. Death can be met in so many ways in this fantastic place. And still Fate keeps grisly surprises up its sleeve. A month or two after we had left the atoll, one of the creole labourers died after being struck by lightning!

For nearly two hours we waded through the swamp, sometimes coming on dry champignon islands which were almost worse than the pot-holed mud under which sharp blades of rock cut viciously at the feet. The odd giant tortoise was meandering about looking lost. All we could be thankful for was the shade. Then the going became easier, we passed through a barrier of scrub surrounding a series of deep holes, and, without warning, reached the platin.

A featureless plain of broken grey slabs of rock stretched ahead. It was such a relief to be on flat land that we did not at once appreciate that, in some ways, it was a poor swap. The heat was intense and there was no shade anywhere. The few pandanus clumps and thin sprinkling of low scrub were such poor screen from the vertical sun that they barely cast a shadow. We straggled across the burning plain, widely spaced out, not talking. Even speech dried the mouth and water would be short until we reached the famous well near Cinq Cases. This one never went dry the porters said. I prayed they were right.

In the absence of Laporte, our guides were Emil and a thin, bearded man with Indian features whose name sounded like Lulu but probably wasn't. They were fifty yards ahead. Through a curtain of sweat I noticed they had stopped. The straggling file closed up to find the men looking at a heap of stones and pointing in two different directions. Guy explained that the creoles mark established routes across the islands by cairns of rock but unfortunately these are often knocked down by giant tortoises and disintegrate. It seemed that this particular route to Cinq Cases had not been used for a long time. The guides found one cairn and were looking around for the next which, according to custom, should be in sight; they told us to wait while they went ahead to find more route markers.

We looked for some shade to sit under and had to settle for a spindly bush that seemed to have cornered all the sharpest champignon needles in its embrace. I longed for a tortoise to sit on but, being wise beasts, they had left this wilderness alone in the heat of mid-day. Half-an-hour passed. The guides re-appeared in the heat haze and waved us on. After twenty minutes walking with no sign of cairns, the party stopped again. There was even less shelter here. A yellow butterfly crossed in front of us and Guy leapt after it, the tireless entomologist. He caught the tiny creature, a perfect specimen of *Eurema*, and I remember thinking that he deserved to capture something much rarer. This time Archangel and the two guides fanned out in three directions. It seemed hours before they rejoined us. The new attempt to find the route was no more successful. Apparently all the cairns had been demolished. We moved slowly foward behind Archangel and stopped again – a few drops of water were shared. There was now a horrible empty look to the biggest water bag.

'The well at Cinq Cases is very sweet, the best on Aldabra,' remarked Archangel for the third time, trying to cheer us up. It was a pleasant prospect but not much consolation in our predicament. The water would remain untouched for a long time. We were lost.

We decided to give the compass a try. Wherever we were, the sea could not be more than two miles away if we went east. I looked at my own compass and watched the needle follow the movement of the exposure meter slung round my neck. It reminded me of a frightening occasion in the jungles of Pahang where we had walked in a complete circle late one afternoon. It was a dangerous area for terrorists, tigers, rhinos, the lot, and we were seeking a certain small river to camp by. Our excellent guide, an elderly Chinese jelutong tapper, had lost his way for the first time. What was even more remarkable, he had admitted it, and suggested the compass took over. I was wearing a Weston exposure meter and it never occurred to me that it could deflect the compass. Only when we stopped, appalled to find, after an hour of slashing and wading, that we were back where we started, did I notice the needle swinging with the movement of the light meter.

I had never forgotten that hard lesson; it is certainly a useful thing for explorer-photographers to remember. I stuffed the meter in my pocket and checked Guy's compass reading with mine.

Turning to the east I had the curious feeling we were retracing our steps but the guides, Lulu and Emil, were unconcerned. They went on peering into the distance for cairns. Perhaps there were a lot of these cairn-marked tracks and they could read more from a heap of rough grey stones than I could – some esoteric direction mark. At first the going was all right, hot pavement with scattered scrub, but after ten minutes we reached a denser growth of almost leafless bushes with tough stems intertwined like snakes. The machetes came into use again. We made slow, painful progress on the sharp rock harbouring this barrier of vegetation – the champignon again – but at least we were going east towards the coast.

Emil stopped dead, machete still raised. He was looking down. We joined him and saw, barring the way ahead, several dark holes in the centre of jagged craters twenty feet across, the sides overwrown with pemphis scrub, its writhing roots climbing snakelike to the dead rocks. The pits resembled a series of ancient bomb craters. It was impassable.

The detour we had to make took nearly forty minutes and, for the first time, I appreciated the limitations of a compass on Aldabra. But at last luck was with us. Archangel had sighted a cairn. There was a brief conference around it and then, with every sign of recognition, he set off again, more or less in the direction we had been travelling before.

We were back on the platin surface and now passed several shallow rock pools, one of which I estimated extended to half an acre. These did not look like permanent pools, the surrounding vegetation being half-drowned, and I suspected they were simply rainy season accumulations which would soon dry up. It was good to see water and a few giant tortoises. The line of march spread out again and we moved more quickly – all anxious to reach the famous Cinq Cases well in the shortest time. It was, therefore, with dismay and alarm that I saw the guides stop once more. But there was a difference this time. I heard a muffled call and Archangel went up swiftly to join them. With his hand he signalled to Emil and Lulu to stay where they were and ran back to me.

'Listen,' he whispered.

I could detect nothing but a very distant rumble, probably the sound of waves breaking on the reef.

'What is it?' I asked impatiently, tongue cleaving to dry mouth.

'They can hear the flamingoes! Over there. Follow me.'

Thirst, sore feet, exhaustion were forgotten. I ran like a panther behind Archangel towards a tangle of low trees dominated by several bunches of screw pines. My mind raced. It was probably a pool – the pandanus usually indicated water. Flamingoes are timid. I signalled to the guides to let me go first, crouching to keep below the level of the scrub. Now I heard it. The unmistakable honking of an Aldabran bird seen only once in thirty years!

There was a wide expanse of water that looked very shallow. The honking grew louder. We moved, cautiously now, along a line of rock slabs skirting one edge of the pool. The light was perfect and the vegetation was dense enough to screen our approach yet did not obstruct visibility. Still I saw nothing. Archangel tugged at my sleeve and pointed with his chin.

That moment was, for me, the most dramatic of our whole tour of Aldabra.

Moving sedately along the top of a pemphis hedge, like an apparition in a successful spiritualist séance, were the disembodied white heads and big Hapsburg beaks of two flamingos. A few yards to go, and they would reach open water directly ahead. I was sure they had not seen us. Before they had come to the end of the bushes, six more heads, including one towering on a thin white neck above the others, joined the ghostly procession. I held my breath, finger on the camera release.

Thirty flamingos slowly emerged into full view on the bright stage of the pond. They were almost pure white and all sizes, from what appeared to be juveniles to one gigantic fellow bringing up the rear – possibly the platoon commander. Most of them were feeding in the shallow water but a few, with heads held high, were obviously on the alert. They were the biggest birds we had met on Aldabra, and the noisiest.

As I rolled off yard after yard of film, the first movie taken of these birds, I had time to marvel that they had remained undetected so long. Were they residents of the atoll or just migrants from Africa? Could they be a new sub-species of the greater flamingo? From the specimens collected three-quarters of a century before, it had not been possible to determine their status. There were differences of opinion, though the latest view of the Cambridge ornithologist, C. W. Benson, is that they are not an endemic form.

In 1895, the American naturalist Dr W. L. Abbott, who took five specimens, estimated a population of between 500 and 1,000 birds and considered they were breeding residents. Another bird was shot in 1906 and the skin sent to the British Museum for study. After that comes a long gap in the record and it was not until 1965, when Roger Gaymer was on his second visit to Aldabra, that they were definitely reported again by a qualified eye-witness. He thought there were about fifty flamingos living in the south-east of the atoll and that they probably bred there. He photographed the bird and suggested it might indeed belong to a new sub-species.

They looked anything but mysterious that afternoon. One stepped delicately past a giant tortoise lying half in shade under a mangrove bush. The whole flock was moving in our direction. If we could remain hidden they would pass within a few yards. Just as this happy thought came to me, there was an explosion of colour. The two leading flamingos unfurled the brilliant flag of their wings, carmine and black, and flapped them. I looked quickly behind me, following the gaze of the flamingo sentries. There, scattered over the rocks on the pool side, were the rest of our party, standing right in the open, making little effort to keep still or silent. It flashed through my mind that they were unused to timid birds and were lousy trackers!

But my disappointment was short-lived. For anyone who has not seen flamingos at take-off, the sight is breath-taking. In this case it was accentuated by the snow whiteness of the birds and the uniform grey-green of the background. Sixty huge red and black wings waved and, in a flurry of scrabbling stilt-like legs, the whole flamingo party took to the air following a leader, and rose steeply in an untidy cloud of red and black and white.

The colourful dots almost disappeared and I was about to put my camera away when Guy shouted. The flamingos had swung into formation and were heading back towards us at a height of several hundred feet – it was just like a fly-past by the R.A.F. Red Arrows at Farnborough. In perfect open arrowhead formation, with a huge bird at the apex and ten evenly-spaced on each arm (I wondered what had happened to the remainder of the thirty birds) they sailed over our heads and melted in the blue to the south. With long necks and legs extended, they looked enormous, masters of the sky. In a triumphant V-for-Victory, the lost flamingoes of the green atoll vanished.

We stood silently in the sun for several seconds when they had gone. I removed the precious film and tucked it into the darkest corner of my haversack.

'You are lucky,' said Guy. 'Now I've no doubt at all we shall see the flightless rail.'

I felt he was right on both counts. For the rest of the journey we spoke of nothing else but *flamants*. Even the porters, no longer tired, laughed and joked about Anglais Oiseaux's luck. Most of them had never seen the flamingoes before. But why? How could such a bird, such a dramatic aerial display, remain unseen? The flamingoes were still a mystery.

Now everything went right. In twenty-five minutes we reached the well, threw ourselved flat on the surrounding rock and drank. It was wonderfully cool, sweet – better than the finest château wine!

*The Rail, the Booby and the Man O' War*

I HAD been warned not to walk barefoot on Aldabra. There was therefore no excuse when I took a chunk out of my heel. Perhaps the sight, which never ceased to astonish me, of the creoles jumping shoeless from pinnacle to pinnacle, often with a heavy load on their heads, had blunted the warning.

I was sitting in the shade of a vast *Tournefortia* bush where we, and about forty giant tortoises, had made camp several yards from the sea at Cinq Cases. It was on the shoreward side of a sand dune that undulated gently towards a broad flat beach. The ground looked soft, but I should have been alerted by the odd grey stones that protruded here and there. In fact, it was just a carpet of wind-blown sand beginning to smother the champignon. A black and blue butterfly which I guessed was a *Precis* of the family Nymphalidae – the blue pansy I have mentioned before – flew past and settled near the 'burning bush' which the porters were using for a kitchen and dormitory. I chased it without bothering to put my boots on. After a few yards I felt a stabbing pain. The wound took nearly two weeks to heal and made travelling even more painful than before.

Dr Wharton's graphic account of the difficulties of walking on Aldabra, published in 1883 after the first survey of the atoll, came to mind:

'. . . the most aggravating and slowest piece of locomotion I have ever engaged in; nothing short of the patience, perseverence and general disregard of time of the tortoise tribe can make it an agreeable residence. Some of my Negro sailors were sent into the bush to hunt for tortoises and after three days' search brought back one, but they returned nearly as guiltless of artificial clothing as their captive . . .'

That evening I went back to the flamingo pool with only Laporte for company hoping to get closer to the birds. As we approached, we listened for the honking but not a sound disturbed the evening calm. Parting the bushes, a wide expanse of water came into view. It was not the right place. This pond was dotted at the far end with small stony islands.

'*Tortues manger*,' said Laporte, starting to move along the bank.

I looked through my binoculars. What I had thought to be islands were on the move, slowly. From them, horny reptilian heads plunged in the water and came out with weeds dripping from their jaws. There were about twenty tortoises feeding on the lush, trailing vegetation that carpetted the bottom of the pool. We stood on the bank above them and watched; more tortoises were arriving. They slid clumsily into the silky water, walked a few steps in their depth and without hesitation plunged in. Our experiment in the sea was not as impressive as this. Here were the giants cruising around freely, accomplished swimmers and bottom feeders. They looked as if they were enjoying the cool dip and the tender weed. One huge fellow surfaced a few feet from where we were standing with a yard of water grass trailing from his jaws. I could have sworn he was smiling. It looked like a challenge for us to jump in and join the feast!

This part of Aldabra was probably the place where tortoises were most hunted in the days before protection. On the way to the pool, where the reef rock barrier between the sand dunes and the platin began, we had passed a number of small enclosures made of lumps of coral rock. They were solidly constructed and looked old. In one or two of them someone must have tried to plant vegetables, for unusual plants, resembling spinach, could still be seen. But others were clearly pounds for captive tortoises. They might well have dated from the eighteenth-century heyday of the tortoise hunters.

On the rare occasions that I saw something man-made, I always examined it closely hoping to find some clue to what had happened to the party of Norwegians which had vanished on Aldabra nearly a hundred years before. I have recently heard that traces of human constructions have been seen on the hitherto unexplored south-west coast of South Island. It could be that the disappearance of this group of Nordic idealists, who planned to establish a fishing settlement on communist lines on the world's most inhospitable island will, before long, be explained. My own view is that they took one look at the champignon and beat it as fast as they could. Perhaps one day they will be discovered living on another forgotten island in pure Marxist bliss!

We were now more than twenty miles, as the frigate flies, from where we had left the *Lady Esmé*, so Guy tried the obstinate radio once more. Unbroken static was the only reply. He decided to send two men back to the settlement next morning by the motorpirogue to report our position to the skipper, to get the latest news and some more fuel for the outboard. The silence was a bit worrying.

It occurred to me that nowhere in the world could be more remote than this. In the moonlight, Cinq Cases looked like the perfect place to 'get away from it all' – the solitude and silence behind the growling sea gave the feeling of a landscape on another planet or of the earth in a past age. Dark against the silver, white-flecked ocean, the outlines of four huge trees crouched in silhouette, low and rounded like huge tortoises. Their level croplines stood out against the white sand, exposing a row of dark domes, sleeping giants too tired or lazy to go grazing, or replete after an evening constitutional. A light breeze rustled the heavy *Tournefortia* leaves sheltering our camp. The wind had dropped again and it looked as if we would have a fine day for our long walk around the coast to Anse Cèdres.

We no longer used mosquito nets – there was no need for them. To Guy's disappointment, moths were equally scarce, and on these open dunes even our sinister escort of robber crabs had thinned out. The only movement I could see as I stretched out on a camp-bed that had now become most precarious, with its canvas splitting ominously, was a small group of hermit crabs foraging on the sand and clicking quietly as they bumped into each other.

It may have been the excitement of the flamingoes but, for some reason, I couldn't sleep. Getting up quietly so as not to disturb the others, I walked to the top of a dune and peered out to sea. A ship with several lights showing was anchored half a mile from shore. So Sauvage has come, I thought. It meant the pirogue would not have to return to the settlement and we could get supplies quickly. I badly needed more batteries for my tape recorder.

'That's not the *Lady Esmé*,' said a voice beside me. I jumped with surprise. It was Harold, armed with his bag of turtle-tags setting out on a nocturnal inspection of the beach. 'It's too low in the water amidships.'

He was right. It was the same vessel I had seen from Anse Maïs. A bright light now shone from the side of the mystery ship and a rowing boat stood alongside.

'They're probably fishing, ' continued Harold, 'and I wouldn't be surprised if they were spearing turtles. I wonder if Captain Sauvage has seen them.'

Sauvage, as Head of the Seychelles Port Department, had magisterial rights in the island waters and could stop a ship to enquire its business. I hoped he had spotted these poachers, if indeed they were, and would catch them. Harold, I was sure, felt the same. In all his arduous climbing around the coast, he had thus far tagged only four laying female turtles.

Our camp was now dark but both Harold and I carried torches. The ship must have seen us yet it gave no sign of concern; the bustling activity around the rowing boat continued and I thought I saw a derrick moving on deck. Perhaps they knew we were powerless, that Aldabra's defences face both ways.

I went back to bed and was just taking off my boots when an enormous crab stalked into sight. It was walking, with a purposeful glint in its black eye, straight for the pole intended for my mosquito net. Discretion being the better part of valour, I decided to use the net after all.

At first light the mystery of the ship was solved. I was woken by the sound of Guy Lionnet talking to Archangel:

'Do they come here often?'

'There have been two or three in the last month or so.'

'I wonder why it is only the Japs who have mastered the technique. Long-line fishing. They've got quite a big syndicate set-up in Mahé now. It's mostly tuna they're after.'

I sat up quickly and peered out to sea. Bobbing on the waves, which looked yellow in the rising sun, was a small fishing boat with a dinghy tied astern. Its rusty grey stern half faced the land and on it Japanese lettering could clearly be seen.

'Do the Japanese have fishing rights in these territorial waters?' I asked Guy.

'They've just signed an agreement with the Seychelles government,' he replied, 'and are making quite a big business. We need the fish and they know how to catch it. There's a mother-ship at Victoria and several boats out fishing all the time at this season. The Japs were the first to do something practical, in a big way. They've got the technique of long-line fishing developed to a fine art. They use enormous lines, thousands of yards long, with hundreds of hooks. It's a very tricky job.'

Why was it, I wondered, that the British, who administer the islands, had not taken the initiative? Long before, I had read Dr Ommanney's book *The Shoals of Capricorn*, written after his two years' work on a commercial fisheries survey. This had been completed in 1949 and showed that there were enough fish, in certain parts of the banks, to make a commercial venture worth while. It recommended a modest start with two or three ships based on the Seychelles and a small drying and salting plant at Port Victoria. The idea had apparently been followed up by the Colonial Development Corporation but what had happened since then? Nothing, it would seem, until the enterprising Japanese came along eighteen years later.

Guy explained that, even in the capital of the Seychelles, fish supplies are scarce at seasons when in-shore fishermen are unable to go out because of rough seas. What are needed above all are cold storage facilities to ensure that fish, the main diet of the Seychellois, is available throughout the year. It was re-assuring to hear that concrete plans were now being laid to provide this in Mahé. The next step should be to exploit the fishing in the outer islands and in the open seas between. The Japanese were now starting to do this and from all accounts their plans extended to the whole Indian Ocean. Good luck to them, I said to myself, looking at the innocent mystery ship braving Aldabra's east coast.

Dr Sato, a Japanese expert whom I later got to know well in Mahé, gave me some idea of the scope of the enterprise. He felt that the Indian Ocean had been badly neglected in the past and that its fishing potential had been underestimated. Another group of his compatriots was now operating successfully from Mauritius. There seemed to be some jealousy of the Japanese initiative mainly, as might be expected, from those who had the chance and never took it but also, more surprisingly, because of the name of the Indian Ocean itself. In Ceylon and India, the Japanese have been asked, 'What are you doing taking our fish? It's the Indian, repeat Indian, Ocean, isn't it?' An extensive back yard. On my 1626 map of the region, the one that doesn't show Aldabra at all, the ocean is called the 'East Ocean.' One way and another the title 'Indian' has been used very loosely all over the world. Confusing for the politicians!

Thinking about fish and politics made me hungry for breakfast. Smoke was rising again from the burning bush, accompanied by the smell of coffee. No more bat curry, fortunately, and crab mayonnaise did not attract at this hour. Over a simple meal of spam and biscuits, we took stock of the situation and discussed plans. As we were out of touch with the *Lady Esmé*, there was no firm date for our return and there was still a lot to do and see. The useless radio had some of the advantages of Nelson's blind eye.

In order of priority, my list included the frigate bird and booby colonies, the herons and tropic birds, the nightjar which I thought I had heard two nights earlier and, of course, the flightless rail. I also wanted to get close to the flamingoes and to explore other pools in the platin to the north-west.

Immediately after breakfast I returned to the flamingo pool, hobbling on a sore foot. The tortoises were out for their morning stroll and we stopped to feed several by hand when we saw them straining for a leaf out of reach. On the back of one I noticed a six-inch green lizard bumming a lift, a curious association that Dr Wright had told me about when I saw him at the Natural History Museum in London. The animal was a green geoko and it was thought that this was an example of symbiosis, a mutually beneficial relationship between two different animals.

I could see at once what the gecko, whose colour changed from light green to brown the further the tortoise walked from the bushes, was getting out of it – a free lift and a warm seat – but it was harder to see how the tortoise profited. I understood that the gecko normally paid for the ride by eating the mosquitoes that pestered its steed, particularly those attacking the tortoise's soft neck but, as there were no mosquitoes at all at this season, the relationship looked one-sided. On the way to the pool I saw four of these strange natural associations. The geckos jumped on to a tortoise's back when he was sheltering under a tree but never remained for long when the reptile ventured outside. After a few yards in the open, the gecko took a mighty leap to the ground and scuttled back to the shade of the branches.

Although there were no mosquitoes, the butterflies, mainly small yellow Pieridae and *Precis*, were more numerous here than at any other place I had seen. I netted a few of them for the British Museum and for Guy Lionnet's collection. By contrast to the other coral atolls and islands of the region, with the notable exception of Astove which we planned to visit later, Aldabra is particularly rich in lepidoptera. But to someone like myself, used to the fantastic abundance of brightly-coloured butterflies of the Asian jungle – I had travelled over roads literally carpetted with insects for miles at a stretch – the Aldabran display was pathetically small and dull.

The Percy Sladen expeditions early in the century recorded sixty-six species of lepidoptera, with seven of them endemic, and this list was recently extended to one hundred and twenty-seven species of which no less than thirty-five were endemic. The French entomologist, Legrand, had himself collected on Aldabra a few years previously, and his monograph, including the results of the Italian Zoological Expedition of 1953, was the most recent work on the subject of the atoll's butterflies and moths. I guessed that Guy must be having a field day.

Distant honking could now be heard. I told Laporte to wait where he was and went forward alone, keeping as much under cover as possible. The water looked empty but, by their calls, I could tell that the flamingo flock was very near, hidden by the bushes flanking an arm of the pool. Very quietly I edged forward to a position under the vegetation on the bank from which I would have an uninterrupted view of the birds as they emerged. After ten minutes or so, I began to see white heads gliding along the hedge towards me. The first flamingo came out into the open thirty feet from where I sat. I started to film. The flamingo looked round at the source of the buzzing then, apparently satisfied, went on feeding. Many times before, when filming wild animals, I have observed that they are not frightened by continuous sound. It is better to go on filming when they are looking in your direction than to stop, even if it means wasting some footage.

This is *the* film – to make Jeffery Boswall say 'ooh-aah', I reflected joyously. At that instant the carmine and black flags were unfurled. Commotion behind the bushes. The spectacular take-off. The sky was flecked with colour. Nothing was left but the ripples on the glassy water.

I swung round.

'*Déjeuner, m'zieu,*' said Laporte, a gangling figure standing on the bank looking up at the magnificent V-formation in the distant sky. He had no idea that he had spoiled a wild life epic – the penalty of living on an island of tame birds. I resolved to come to Aldabra alone next time!

The flamingoes did not return that day and next morning we set off along the coast for Anse Cèdres, the biggest cove on the north-east coast. I thought it was goodbye to these timid birds, but I was wrong.

With my sore foot, the blistering journey around the nose of the atoll was a thirsty nightmare. Most of the time we walked along the cliff platform of bare champignon, over land unfit for mountain goats, or so I thought at first. We were approaching Pointe Hodoul, the eastern extremity of Aldabra named after an 18th century corsair, when Guy called me over to admire several handfuls of small round pellets of dung in the champignon. Goat droppings! So it was fit for the animals after all. This was the first and last time we saw of the celebrated feral goats of Aldabra unless you count the kid Archangel had brought from the settlement and which we had already eaten.

What had happened to these creatures? Ommanney wrote that he had seen a herd of about 200 less than 20 years before. A former governor of the Seychelles, Sir William Addis, whom I had known earlier in Singapore, had told me to look out for these animals – on a short visit to the atoll more recently, he had seen a number of them. But none of us had either seen or heard any. These fresh droppings were the only evidence we had that the creatures still inhabited the atoll. Had the goat finally met his match, in the terrain, the tortoises or the creoles?

17. Giant tortoises feeding on weed in a rain water pond on South Island near the site of the proposed airfield. These heavy reptiles swim comfortably. *(The Author)*

18. In the hot dry season every tree that affords any shade shelters a
group of huge tortoises. *(The Royal Society)*

Although I am fond of animals, it would have been quite a cheering thought. The goat has probably been responsible for as many deserts on earth as man has. Ruthless root-tearing habits of feeding have made him the most lively ally of the forces of erosion and he is mighty tough and philoprogenitive. In the blinding heat, my tears were not for this vanished invader. They were just sweat.

Goats were introduced to Aldabra by 'nature lover' Spurs, the lessee in 1890 who was also responsible for bringing cats to the atoll, ostensibly to control rats that were damaging his coconut trees. He rejected the advice that only one sex of cat should be introduced. If the native animals of Aldabra could get together for a party, I felt sure they would curse the memory of this over-rated lessee. But despite these vicious thoughts, it must be admitted that our expedition, after covering more than half of Aldabra on foot, had not seen or heard a single introduced predator – cat, dog or rat – since leaving the settlement. And we were on the look-out for them.

At Pointe Hodoul we turned away from the sea but, although exhausted, we still paused to admire the coast at this point. It was awe-inspiring, a shipwrecked sailor's bad dream of landfall. The undercut cliffs were nearly twenty feet high and the tearing waves had cut a sharp inlet in the coast. In this jagged vortex a dark blue sea banged and bounced, sending spouts of white water through blow-holes far inland. To the north, a hellish road of black minarets led around the promontory behind a curtain of spray. Some optimist had stuck a post on the far edge of the inlet, presumably as a marker. One hoped it was to warn people away rather than to lead them on. It was no place for a stroll.

After the exposed cliffs, the green undergrowth inland looked inviting, but as usual it was too low to afford any shade. Here I had my first fall on the champignon. Tripped by a vine straddling the track I plunged across a dark hole with cameras flying in all directions. I ended up bridging the abyss. It might have been much worse and Guy was able to haul me upright without too much damage, but if I had been alone, it would have been a nasty situation. We struggled on, choosing footholds even more carefully now, until the splendid news filtered back from the front of the column that the trees of Anse Cèdres had been sighted.

Half-an-hour later we found ourselved on a real picnic beach, a two hundred yard crescent of soft sand backing a deep horseshoe cove and shaded by a plantation of tall casuarina trees, the '*cèdres*' from which the anse took its name.

There were many signs that earlier expeditions had used this delightful spot, the usual litter of broken packing cases, strange tripods and gibbets of driftwood and rusty drums. To keep us company, a grey heron stood motionless on the concave cliff at the mouth of the inlet and a solitary sacred ibis gleaned peacefully among the fallen casuarina needles.

The bearded porter who looked like a 'Malabari' – the Créole name for an Indian – pointed to one of the drums and said *militaire*. I asked him how long it had been there and, with his fingers, he indicated five years. As far as I knew, no military had visited Aldabra then, and it was not until I returned to England, and the conservation battle was in full spate, that I learned that an R.A.F. team had indeed made a survey of the atoll in 1962. This was long before the creation of BIOT and the survey must have been done in some secrecy, certainly without the knowledge of conservationists, for it caused no alarm at the time.

Looking at this rusty iron surrounded by litter of turtle bones, it was disturbing to think that the plan to build a military airfield on Aldabra had been on the files for more than five years. So it was not a new idea as I had thought. How far had the planners got? I knew from experience that a government machine grinding for so long around the corridors of power would be hard to stop, well-nigh impossible to put into reverse. Not for the first time I had the feeling we might be among the last to see this fantastic island in its natural state. It made me forget the fatigue of our trek from Cinq Cases and want to go exploring at once.

Dr Wright had told me it would be easy to reach the platin from Anse Cèdres. He and his colleagues had cut a track through the pemphis jungle only three months before and marked it clearly with strips of scarlet cloth tied to the trees. He warned me to follow this direct route to the south because the champignon surface was particularly bad here and the scrub, in parts, almost impenetrable. I had not seen any sign of the track markers as we approached the beach, so I sent a porter to find the first piece of red cloth to enable us to make an early start in the morning; meanwhile I busied myself filming a couple of fairy terns.

This exquisite creature, the pride of Seychelles sea-birds, is of a whiteness that would do credit to the most avant-garde detergent advertisement, with long graceful wings and a pointed beak of navy blue. It is smaller than the noddy and has a large round head and big eyes. It is not only attractive but very friendly, approaching to within a few feet of your head where it stands on the air, wings flapping and extended like a brass eagle on a lectern. The fairy or white tern is not common on Aldabra, at least we saw few of them, but I doubt whether it is the prey of the barn owl here as it is on the granite islands of the central group. I say this only because the barn owl itself was conspicuous by its absence. According to Benson, this owl, a ferocious immigrant from Africa, probably came to Aldabra via the Comoros. It was said to be quite common on Aldabra at the end of last century but it has not often been reported since then. We saw none and no evidence of its presence.

Unfortunately the fairy terns were not busy at the nest or, to be precise, were not hatching eggs. This was something I wanted badly to see, for the fairy tern has extraordinary habits. It lays a solitary egg in positions so precarious that for a long time it was thought the egg must be glued in place with some sticky substance. It will choose the narrow branch of a tree or the step on a coconut palm, sometimes a rock on the ground or even the steps of a deserted house. The egg is so exposed to predators like skinks, to a footstep or to the wind, that one wonders how any can hatch out. And for the chicks, early days must be alarming. They need a good head for heights. Although I was unable to film a sitting tern on Aldabra, in the Seychelles I had many such chances and achieved a shot I never thought possible – of an egg from below with the hen installed on top. This egg was balanced in the fork of a young tree.

When I returned to our camp on the beach, I found a puzzled Archangel examining a piece of white cloth with the porter who had gone in search of the route to the platin. He showed it to me.

'I thought you said the cloth was red. This piece was tied to a tree about eight feet up. He saw others further on. It looked like a track but it's overgrown now. Must be the place. No one else has marked tracks here.'

I looked carefully at the white cloth. Dr Wright had chosen red to be conspicuous; white would hardly show at all in such a bleached landscape. One end of the rag was stitched over. Underneath was a tell-tale flush of pink. This was it – we would have to try to follow the white route. In three months the Aldabra sun had drained away all colour from the material. I already knew from the unbelievable readings I was getting on my meter that the light on the atoll was brilliant at midday, and we knew all about the heat, but this proof of solar power was still impressive. It was not a place to get lost in the open. The snow-white and empty tortoise shells lying on the beaches and arid plains were more understandable than ever.

'Follow the pandanus and the frigates if you want to find water,' they told me in London. With some difficulty we got through the worst champignon, using the marked trail, and found ourselves once more on the platin. It was about eight o'clock in the morning and very still. I reminded Guy of the injunction, but the trouble was there were no pandanus or frigates in sight! A glance at the map showed three pools to the west of us, and, sure enough, after a short walk, untidy stands of screw pine came into view. The undergrowth, mixed mangrove and pemphis, grew denser, and slowly we hacked a way through. We had no idea of what we would find on the other side – so far we had seen very few signs of wild life – but the sight that greeted us was so dramatic and beautiful it might have been a stage set for our benefit. It was like a reconstruction of an Aldabran landscape in a museum. Standing on the edge of the pool, my first thought was that we were trespassing, but this soon passed, for most of the animals treated our sudden appearance through the bushes with no more signs of concern than if we had been a couple of upstanding tortoises.

The expanse of water was almost circular, pale blue in the morning sun. It was big enough to be called a lake, about a hundred yards in diameter, and the banks of stone slabs were overgrown with mangrove and stands of pandanus. These provided shelter and perches for what looked, at first glance, to be a complete check-list of Aldabran fauna.

Most outstanding, on a dead branch opposite, stood a pair of dimorphic egrets, both white, peering down at the teeming water like works overseers. Sacred ibis were gleaning on the banks and one of them, a juvenile from its white feathery neck, strutted calmly on to the rock slab where we stood taking in the scene. At least a hundred giant tortoises were deployed around the banks while several, more adventurous, made dark domes in the centre of the lake, apparently afloat.

In a small inlet to the right, half-screened by a rocky promontory, two flamingoes stalked majestically in the shallows, pausing occasionally to feed on the bottom. An enormous grey heron stared at them and then, perhaps deciding there was too much competition, flew off on giant wings low over the mangroves. As we watched, a squadron of half-a-dozen red turtle doves crossed the lake in a diagonal, straight and swiftly as if in a hurry to get to some more attractive feeding ground. Not to be outdone, several smaller birds moved noisily in the bushes around us – a jabbering bulbul drawing attention to itself as usual, and two sunbirds catching flies. One of these was a male and when he perched momentarily in the direct sunlight, I was struck again by the green metallic armour covering his breast. A comoro blue pigeon flashed a red eye in our direction from the top of a nearby tree. It was one of those moments on a wild-life expedition when you cannot quite believe the scene is real, that you aren't dreaming. I had experienced them once or twice before – when I suddenly burst on a hundred Rajah Brooke's birdwing butterflies drinking in a hot spring in Perak; and by the banks of the Mekong on the Lao-Cambodian border when I watched a flock of eagles catching the fish jumping out of the water ahead of fresh-water dolphins on the hunt – but there was a difference this time. This was only the curtain raiser. The real show was about to begin.

Guy Lionett grabbed me by the arm. 'Look! The frigates.'

In the sky above the pool, fifty black shapes were now circling. They must have been 2,000 feet up. I made out the forked tail, the white patch on the breast, the enormous pointed scimitar wings, motionless in the blue. Occasionally one of the birds half-shut its wings and dropped like a stone for hundreds of feet – variable geometry at its most graceful. The soaring and wheeling went on for several minutes and then, as if at a signal, the gaunt black shapes swung away to disappear from sight.

Never mind, I thought, tomorrow we will see thousands of them on Malabar Island, site of the two biggest frigate colonies in the Western Indian Ocean. But we did not have to wait that long.

The frigates were just doing a reconnaissance – they were coming back. With a whoosh of outstretched wings they dived low over the bushes from two directions, skimming the water at such speed that they left a wake on the calm surface. They came in single file, evenly spaced. At the end of the glide there was a loud plop and a sucking sound before the huge bird rose steeply, forked tail outspread, banked and returned the way he had come. Sometimes the two streams of frigates crossed in mid-water and there was a double beat of plops and sucks. When the frigate's body was nearest to the water, its neck and head were quickly lowered and its open bill scooped up a mouthful. Drinking at fifty miles an hour. It was an astonishing display of aerial acrobatics, shattering the calm of a primaeval scene. When the glassy surface had been furrowed by at least a hundred thirsty gulps, the languid flamingoes, obviously deciding the club was getting too full and noisy, took off, dwarfing the frigates as they passed overhead, triangles of crimson and black supporting parallel match-stick legs and long white necks stretched out to their fullest extent. 'We're bigger and brighter than you noisy so-and-so's,' they seemed to say as they vanished to the south.

'This is it.' Guy muttered, 'This is the place.'

I knew exactly what he meant.

We were standing squarely on the site of the runway of a military airfield, if Mr Healey and the Anglo-American Defence planners had their way. The lake would vanish, filled with rubble by a bull-dozer. The tortoises and the birds would have to go elsewhere to drink. If there were any tortoises and birds left. If there was anywhere left to go.

We did not feel much like talking but I know our thoughts were the same. It would be madness, a scandal, to destroy this lost paradise of wild life. A steely determination to do something, anything, to save it, gripped me so strongly that, for a moment, I wanted to leave Aldabra and get home quickly to join the fight. Did Whitehall and the Pentagon know what they were about to destroy? I doubted it. Did the remote planners care? Midway, Gan, Christmas and Ascension Islands had worked out all right, despite the belated outcry of eccentric conservationists, why not Aldabra? Even if they did not mind the destruction of one of the last natural sanctuaries left on earth, others would and my film would show them what was at stake. These thoughts passed quickly through my mind as we returned to camp, but the desire to leave at once was short-lived. The film was unfinished. I hadn't yet seen the most intriguing creature of all – the flightless rail. He would be my next target.

Passe Houareau, the East Channel, was on its best behaviour when we went through on the rising tide. Even the reef provided only a few switchbacks and once we were through the mouth, the waves completely disappeared. Deep in the glassy water, it was exciting to see living coral again, and swimming among the round convoluted heads, shoals of red and blue parrot fish. The sea in this area abounded in fish and during the short journey from Anse Cèdres our boatmen had landed several bonitos and barracuda that promised a fresh diet for a change. The crabs had not been a favourite dish and we had not eaten them for days.

Standing out of the lagoon, just inside the mouth of the channel, were a series of mushroom islets which looked even more brittle and thin on top than those we had seen before. All were covered by a tangle of vegetation, coarse grasses and some spindly scrub. Outstanding on the nearest champignon was a grey heron mounting guard. As we came nearer it flew off in a wide arc and returned to the far side of the platform. It suggested a nest and I was not sure at the time whether it was a breeding resident of Aldabra or not.

Climbing on to the islet was much harder then it looked. I had to wait until the boat rose on the swell and then jump, hoping that the lace-like overhang would support my weight. It did, although a small fragment of the lip cracked off alarmingly as I landed. But the effort was rewarded.

On this rock table, the size of a large carpet, there were not one but two nests of the grey heron, both with young. Before we could stop him, François had picked up an atrociously ugly chick in each hand and held them out for me to photograph. I put them back in the nest and then took portraits of them while they squawked deafeningly and fixed me with ferocious amber-coloured eyes. Meanwhile the gigantic mothers circled the mushroom and looked about to attack. It seemed the right moment to leave but just as I was going to climb back aboard the pirogue a head darted out of the tussocks and made a stab at my leg. It was a red-tailed tropic bird reminding me to tread carefully. Her nest, hidden under a dome of grass, was less than two feet away from where I was standing, yet she had made no attempt to fly away. I stooped to admire her. A red down-curving beak and two lambent eyes stared straight at me unflinching; so immobile was she that even a large ant crawling across her head did not make a muscle move.

The red-tailed tropic bird is one of the most magnificent of all sea-birds of the tropic zone. Much bigger than the terns, its white feathers shine like silk, but its most outstanding feature is a long red tail that streams in flight like a banner. These long tail feathers have earned the bird, and its cousin the white-tailed tropic bird, the sailors' nickname of bos'n bird, in recognition of the bos'n's spike they carry. I suspect the red-tailed species has been hunted in the past for its feathers. There are conflicting reports about its occurrence on Aldabra, but Roger Gaymer estimated there may be a population of several hundreds along the northern part of the lagoon. I never found it anywhere else, not even on the Seychelles granitic islands where the white-tailed tropic bird is quite common.

Its courage in the face of an intruder was remarkable. But although the nest was well hidden it was given away by two stems of red grass that rose behind it.

The two angry herons had returned to their nests before we left the islet. I thought the creoles looked a bit disappointed.

'They would have eaten those young if we hadn't been here,' Guy explained.

Not being on the protected list and living outside the nature reserve of South Island, I suppose they were fair game. The grey heron is one of few native land-birds of Aldabra that cannot be distinguished from the same species in nearby areas.

We headed now for Malabar, or Middle Island, the northern rim of Aldabra, where we hoped to find the white-throated rail. Only a few hundred yards from the beach, on the lagoon side, the mangroves began and already above them I could see what looked like a swarm of midges rising to a height of several thousand feet. This was one of the two huge frigate colonies on the island. As the tide was low and it was possible to walk along the lagoon flats, Guy and I decided to go and watch the birds coming home to roost. It was long past the breeding season, unfortunately, but to all appearances there were still thousands of birds among the mangroves.

Estimates of the resident frigate population of Aldabra have varied widely, some having put the score of birds as high as half a million. They are certainly to be counted in tens, if not hundreds, of thousands and their habit of soaring to heights up to 4,000 feet, filling the whole sky with black dots and dashes, is a constant reminder of their overwhelming presence.

The frigate is a large bird with a wingspan approaching seven feet and with its glossy black plumage and powerful beak it looks something like an elegant vulture at rest. It too has nasty habits. A marauder preying upon the boobies, it soars all day on air currents above the atoll, watching. Sometimes it will come down to do a bit of fishing itself, but its main occupation is waiting for the return of the boobies with their catch. When the frigate spots a likely victim, it 'buzzes' the hapless creature until, in desperation and to lighten load, the booby disgorges and drops its fish. The swift and acrobatic frigate then catches the fish in mid-air. I had already seen this happen several times. The frigate's skill is so remarkable one forgets to deplore the dirty trick.

To get away from the pursuer the booby, itself no mean aeronaut, takes all kinds of evasive action, often diving low to skim the seas in a last dash for home. Nevertheless the frigate generally gets what it wants. I had been told that the boobies themselves were never hurt in the encounter but this is not true. At Cinq Cases we had seen a collision between the two birds. The booby was obviously wounded and fluttered away to land on the beach.

On the way to the colony, I noticed a great number of grey moray eels writhing among the coral in water barely deep enough to cover them. These creatures, mostly about two feet long, got out of our path but never withdrew very far. They are said to be one of the most aggressive of sea creatures with a ferocious bite and I knew that fishermen treated them with the greatest respect.

It so happened that I stopped to look at a frigate just as one of these eels had retreated. I was obliged to take a step or two in its direction. Fortunately I was looking down watching for footholds because, as I moved forward, the moray eel did an about face and, with its mouth open exposing rows of teeth, advanced slowly towards me in turn. When I halted, the eel did likewise. As I did not feel inclined to proceed with the confrontation I beat a dignified retreat. Out of interest, though, I tested the reactions of others and it was always the same – a readiness to fight an animal fifty times its size. This was another Aldabran creature well able to take care of itself.

But the moray eels were forgotten when I rounded the next headland. The mangroves here were taller and denser and the branches were alive with white birds, the red-footed boobies. So striking was the colour contrast between the whiteness of the boobies and the deep green of the mangrove trees, that I did not, at first, see the black frigates roosting with them. In the sky above, hundreds of frigates were circling and it was only when I saw them land in the branches that I realized there were as many marauders as victims perched there. It was not the frigate's breeding season or the birds, at least the cocks, would have been much more visible, for it is then that they blow up their red neck balloon in display. Photographs I had seen of the colony at this season made the mangroves look like exotic cherry trees. As it was, a few small red balloons were still to be seen here and there as if a bird had been unable to deflate completely.

On wading closer I saw that frigates were often sitting side by side with boobies on the same branch, apparently good friends and neighbours. Was this an example of the balance of nature or could it be that the booby had been well-named? Too stupid to resent the parasite. Perhaps the booby enjoyed the excitement of the chase and treated the giant frigate as an idiot child, unable to fish for itself. In French, the booby is called *l'oiseau fou*, or the crazy bird, which I have always thought is too unkind. The booby is a friendly bird and perhaps is simply misunderstood. After all, the dodo got its name from the Portuguese word for 'stupid' but, in the final reckoning, who deserved it most – the dodo or man the exterminator?

While I was filming this immense concentration of sea-birds, and particularly when I glanced at the sky full of wheeling frigates, I wondered how the atoll could ever be used by aircraft. Would not the presence of this soaring multitude, rising out of sight in the high thermals, be a great danger to aircraft? Bird-strikes were already a hazard in many countries and surely Aldabra would present a problem greater than any encountered before. Or was it the intention of the airfield planners to destroy the frigate population or a large part of it? On Midway Island in the Pacific Ocean, the United States Air Force had had to kill vast numbers of the Laysan albatross to make the skies safe but, although they had clubbed or gassed more than 60,000 birds in ten years, the menace was still there. The 60,000 birds had died in vain.

By now I had learned enough about the frigate to know that efforts to limit the airstrike danger on Aldabra by killing the birds were even less likely to succeed. Not only was there a large non-breeding population here, but juveniles would keep returning to breed for as long as seven years after the first slaughter. Was the Air Force prepared to consider a yearly massacre of the frigates until the mid-1970s? The prospect was too grim and fantastic. Yet how else could landing be made safe? A popular name for the frigate is man o'war bird.

Perhaps it, too, had been well-named. The frigate might prove to be the final defender of Aldabra.

Archangel's voice sounded from the direction of the camp. We turned and saw him calling.

'I've heard the r–a–a–i–l. Come quickly,' he shouted, as several frigates shot into the air disturbed by the noise.

'Where?'

'Behind the beach.'

It was still light enough to film. We hurried back past the ferocious eels, to find several of the creoles peering into the bushes at the back of the fisherman's hut. Dr Abbott had remarked years before that the rail was so tame and curious it would come close to investigate any unusual sound, like the tapping of a stick or somebody walking. I knew the nearly flightless bird had been exterminated by cats, its greatest enemy, on Picard Island and that it now survived only on this northern rim of the atoll, Malabar and tiny Polymnie Islands, and perhaps on the two biggest islands in the lagoon. Was it still unafraid of man or had it been frightened by persecution? The best way to find out was to try an Abbott-type experiment. The beach was, as usual, littered with turtle bones. I asked Archangel to make a tapping sound with a couple of them while I stood ready with the camera. On purpose we made no attempt at concealment. He started to beat a rhythmic tattoo, reminding me of the many times I had tried to attract the Malayan mouse-deer by the same methods, but only once with success.

I anticipated a long wait, but he had been tapping the bones for less than a minute when we saw movement in the bushes – a small white object was advancing jerkily. And suddenly the rail was there. A plump little body of chestnut and olive brown, carried on strong stilt legs and surmounted by a white throat patch, and pointed red beak. The rail looked at the ring of faces and then, focussing attention on Archangel's hands, zigzagged forward in full sunlight. Ten feet – five feet – two feet from the tapping bones. It was so near I could hardly get it into focus. For half a minute the bird watched Archangel and evidently deciding the activity was futile and there was nothing around to eat, steered a drunken course back into the shade of the undergrowth.

'I ought to catch a pair of them for the aviary in Mahé,' said Guy. 'I wonder how many there are around here.'

We were interested in the rails, and it seemed that the rails were equally interested in us. For the rest of the evening we were startled by an amazing variety of loud calls coming from the bushes around the beach. We saw two more birds, both in sandy places, but none on the champignon rock that started fifty yards down the coast and looked more forbidding and impassable than ever. Harold, who had joined in the rail search, suddenly called me over. A huge brown rat, the first I had seen on Aldabra, was scurrying through the rocks. It was alarming to see this creature so near to the flightless bird. It must be a menace, certainly to their eggs and young. We tried to kill it but it escaped.

Although several recent visitors had told me that the white-throated rail of Aldabra, the last of the flightless birds of the Indian Ocean Islands, could easily be seen it was, nevertheless, an astonishing experience. When the rail first came to the atoll it could, presumably, fly but with no predators to fear it gave up the use of its wings. Why bother when it is so much easier to walk? (For rails if not for humans!) As it came out to inspect us, its innocent confidence was almost agonizing. How could a defenceless creature like this possibly survive when the bulldozers came? Dodo of Mauritius, extinct 1681. Rail of Aldabra, extinct 1971. I could see it in the textbooks.

Plans for the development of Aldabra into an 'air staging post' (euphemism for a base) envisaged the building of a road the full length of the north coast from Main to East Channel. The narrow islands are nowhere more than one-and-a-half miles wide. When the construction machines started to work, the curious rail would certainly come out to investigate. Its restricted breeding grounds would be flattened. In a matter of months, although it is a tough and fearless fighter in defence of its nest, the rail would join the dodo. It seemed to me inevitable, unless the Anglo-American defence plans were scrapped.

Next morning I was awoken just before dawn by the sound of a tremendous explosion in the lagoon. I went outside. A creole was peering in the direction of the channel.

'What was that?'

'*Un rai*,' said the black face smiling.

I had always wanted to see the giant manta ray, the size of a billiard table, jumping. We watched the grey water for some time but it never rose again. These enormous creatures leap clear out of the water and come down with a resounding belly flop, the object probably being to dislodge lice and other irritants.

I returned to the dark tent and lay down on the camp bed. With a loud rending of the last shreds of canvas it collapsed – a warning perhaps that it was nearly time to leave Aldabra. Guy sat up laughing as I struggled in the sand and debris. I knew his bed was tearing too, but he was lighter then I. Hopefully I looked at it, then gasped in amazement.

'Guy,' I whispered, 'there's a rail under your bed.'

He had his mosquito net up as a protection against crabs. 'Let the net down to the ground and you'll catch it for the aviary. Quick!' He bent and looked down. The rail was gleaning in the sand. Guy hesitated.

'No. I don't think I will. They're probably rarer than we think. Just live around these few sandy beaches. It might be a hen with young.'

The rail drifted out of the tent.

Guy Lionnet, Chairman of the Fauna Conservation Board of the Seychelles, was the perfect conservationist. I knew how much he wanted a rail for the Mahé Botanical Gardens.

He lay back on the bed. There was another rending crash and it was my turn to laugh.

It wasn't fair really.

# XI    *The World's Most Valuable Reptile*

Nᴇᴡs on the turtle front never got any better. After a tour of the atoll in which he examined every beach, except for a few small inlets on Malabar and Polymnie Islands, Harold Hirth had found only seven female green turtles. And this was at the height of the nesting season.

In his book *The Green Turtle and Man*, James J. Parsons describes the Aldabran group of islands as having 'the greatest concentration of breeding turtles in the Indian Ocean in modern times, and perhaps in antiquity'. Reports at the end of the last century told of 500 females a night coming up to lay on one strip of sand of Assumption Island, Aldabra's nearest neighbour twenty miles away. Harold saw only two on all the beaches of Assumption. On both this island and Cosmoledo, which we visited briefly, he was able to locate small breeding populations and to do some more tagging, but the general impression he obtained after this field study of the Aldabran group of islands was depressing.

The American professor, an associate of the world's foremost authority on the reptile, Professor Archie Carr of Florida University, told the Seychelles Society at a lecture in Mahé on our return from the islands: 'I would say that the female green sea turtles in the Seychelles area are near the point of extinction,' a view he had earlier expressed to me in more graphic terms – that for the day of the reptile on Aldabra it was already a quarter to midnight. The audience heard the sombre news in shocked silence but should it really have come as a surprise? Most of them were turtle eaters, and the fact that Professor Hirth's investigation, made on behalf of the Food and Agriculture Organization of the United Nations with the support of the Seychelles government, was the first since the general fisheries survey of 1948, itself showed a lack of concern for an animal that was known as the world's most valuable reptile. Harold Hirth explained how it had earned this title. If properly prepared, over 50 percent of its meat is edible, he said. One would have thought this reason alone might have led to earlier action to protect it.

There is a great deal of misunderstanding about marine turtles. Of the two commonest species in tropic seas, the larger green turtle is edible but has a commercially useless shell, while the hawksbill turtle, itself becoming rare in Seychelles waters, provides tortoiseshell but is not so good to eat. A common fallacy is that turtle meat is good only for making soup, whereas this is the most wasteful use of the reptile. Only two or three pounds of 'calipee' (the cartilage linking the upper and lower shell) can be taken from a beast weighing as much as 600 pounds, and in the process of extraction, carried out on remote beaches, the rest of the edible meat has to be thrown away for want of cold storage if it cannot be dried and salted. There is also a misconception about the growing rarity of sea turtles, for being so conspicuous while mating, their numbers are easily exaggerated. Indeed, few people remain alive who can remember the days of the multitudes.

Clearly the local exploiters, both in the Indian Ocean and the Atlantic, must take most of the blame for the near extermination of an animal that could have been as valuable in a hungry world as beef cattle, which it resembles in converting marine grass into nourishing meat. But often, when I saw the grey litter of bones on the deserted beaches of Aldabra, I felt others were guilty too. Some in high places, like the Lord Mayor of London. His banquet makes one think automatically of turtle soup. Now that it is well known that the turtle is in danger of extinction, and that the making of calipee is wasteful, what a splendid example it would be if it were announced that the soup was no longer on the menu? Yet what happens? Conservationists were delighted that at the last banquet there was a break with tradition – eel soup was to be served for a change. The editor of the magazine *Animals*, Nigel Sitwell, immediately rang the Mansion House for confirmation of the good news. He was told that the Mayoral palate had dictated the change. The Lord Mayor was sympathetic to the plight of the green turtle and glad to hear his altered menu would 'also help conservation' but he was not prepared to make suggestions to his successor about turtle soup.

It looks as if this ostrich-like attitude may persist among importers and dealers too until the supply of soup meat dries up because there are no more turtles to slaughter.

Killing of the females as they wait offshore preparatory to laying has been prohibited by legislation in the Seychelles since 1925, when Hornell enquired into the state of the industry. He said 'the policy of the lessee (of Aldabra) cannot but lead to an early extinction of the trade'. Most of his recommendations were accepted, but the most vital one, the institution of a close season, was not. Full protection of the females in law was not given until 1962 when a close season from December 1st to March 31st was finally declared. It may have come too late and even now it is hard to enforce. Until I spoke to Harold Hirth I had little idea how vulnerable the females were and how quickly their slaughter could lead to extermination of the species.

They lay only once every three years, usually in six batches of up to 200 eggs a time. There is a two-week gap between each visit to the beach and during the whole three-month period the females lie offshore never moving far from one spot. They are therefore an easy target, and if they happen to be taken before the first visit to the beach, not one, but up to 1,200 turtles perish. During the act of laying, in a carefully excavated hole in soft sand above the high tide mark, they are defenceless too; in some parts of the world females are still 'turned' at this moment, sometimes even before the eggs have been buried.

My previous experience of turtles, on Egg Island near Penang and with Tom Harrisson on his turtle reserves in Sarawak, had not prepared me for this attack on the reptile itself. In South East Asia only the

19. Gigantic robber crabs invaded most of our camps. *(Roger Gaymer)*

20. The last surviving flightless bird of a region once famous for the dodo. On Malabar or North Island the Aldabran white-throated rail displays aggressively to defend its ground nest. *(Malcolm Penny)*

eggs are taken; the flesh is never eaten for Muslim law prohibits it as unclean. I was surprised to find that the raw eggs, a delicacy in the Far East, are not liked in the Seychelles. Here they are cooked, if eaten at all. It is hard to say which of the two practices most endangers the species. I suspect that of the Seychelles, although the egg collectors of Malaysia and Indonesia are very skilful.

Once on Egg Island I watched a turtle lay her clutch at dead of night. She took such trouble finding the right spot and the ovipositing itself was such an arduous business, I made up my mind to see that this nest, at least, escaped. Earlier I had noticed that, despite all the turtle's painstaking efforts to hide the nesting hole, there were two monstrous give-aways. The sand she used for filling in was wet and darker than the surrounding beach and she left two unmistakable tracks, like those of a small tank, on her journey to and from the hole. Early next morning I knew an Indian collector would arrive to take the eggs – an Indian '*kongsi*' had the turtling concession – so my colleague and I spent the rest of the night making an artificial turtle out of driftwood and dragging tracks all over the beach. We also dug a number of holes and filled them in with wet sand.

I felt quite sorry for the Indian egg collector. His face lit up on seeing such a maze of new tracks. He hurried to the back of the beach to cut a sharp stick with which to locate the eggs and started work. For half-an-hour he prodded around the nest marks but the point of his stick always came up dry. Finally, with a resigned look, he came over to the hut where we were camping and said, 'The Malays have been here'. I tried to look sympathetic and innocent. In our track-laying frenzy I now noticed that one of the turtle paths led up to a tree – the first arborial turtle. It was amazing that he had been taken in and that 200 babies had been saved.

Incidentally, it was at this time I discovered that turtle eggs bounce. They not only look and feel like ping-pong balls, they act like them.

The green turtle takes five to eight years to mature. As an adult it has few enemies, but on leaving the nest the young have a hard time. First they have to get out of the sand and only the combined efforts of the group enables them to scramble to the surface. It is therefore no use leaving a few eggs in the nest hoping they will hatch out, as was sometimes done on the Trengganu beaches where the world's biggest turtle, the giant leatherback, breeds. Then the babies have to get to the sea. For a creature the size of a silver dollar, at night or even by day among the sandhills, this is no mean achievement. It is believed that they locate the sea by light sensitivity, the light over water being always brighter. Now there is the journey across the sand, fraught with danger from crabs, birds like herons or frigates, rats, and a host of other predators. And when they reach the water they remain for the first year or so very vulnerable to attack by sharks and other large fish. Only a tiny fraction of the brood survives these hazards. It is quite surprising that any do. Then comes man.

We have heard how a lessee of Aldabra at the end of last century proposed to take 12,000 turtles a year. There was nothing very unusual about this for killing on such a scale had by that time started in many parts of the world.  From now onwards the reptile was commercially exploited, and the result was immediate and rapid decline in numbers. Already by 1909, Fryer could deplore the 'wasteful slaughter' on Aldabra and a glance at the annual returns tells its own story. By 1925, as Hornell noted, the number of turtles taken on the atoll had dropped to three or four thousand and by 1948, when Ommanney was there, the figure was fifteen hundred. Under the terms of the present lease signed in 1955, not more than five hundred turtles may be taken annually 'on or within three miles of Aldabra'. The legacy had been reduced in a few years to a pittance.

Meanwhile the Atlantic species had fared no better, perhaps even worse. A once vast breeding area in the Caribbean was shrunk to a single protected beach in Costa Rica. Highly efficient 'exploitation' decimated the turtles on the East African coast, and in the Malaysian region, unrestricted egg collection produced the same results.

But for the efforts in recent years of Tom Harrisson in Sarawak and Professor Carr in Costa Rica, where the breeding grounds are given real protection and hatcheries bring the new-born young safely through their most vulnerable years, the green turtle might well be off the menu altogether by now.

In the light of this appalling story of wastefulness and greed, it would be nice to say that man had learned a lesson but clearly he has not. One of the few places left in the world where, until recently, the green turtle was able to breed in peace was the coast of South Arabia. Harold Hirth had been there just before his Aldabra survey and had found a good population. The local people being Muslim did not eat the reptile and the beaches, remote and inaccessible, had not attracted commercial exploiters. But it was too good to last.

Just before he left he saw a truck crossing the desert. It was loaded with living turtles, stacked in layers like sides of bacon. He discovered that one of the biggest East African turtle exporters had just moved in. There was nothing left in their old hunting grounds. The forgotten Arabian beaches had given the business a new lease of life.

The scale of trade seems to be increasing as the turtle population declines. Recently, in a single year, 1,200 frozen carcases reached London and nearly 20,000 live turtles were sent to New York. In 1956, Grand Cayman Island alone exported more than 4,000 live turtles and 24,000 pounds of products. The growth in popularity of turtle soup is the root cause of continuing pressure on a vanishing species.

Efforts are now being made by the International Union for the Conservation of Nature to persuade all governments concerned to 'take note of the danger to all turtles and to initiate and give assistance to projects for ecological research and survey on which conservation measures may be based'. This resolution was passed in 1963 and referred specifically to the green and hawksbill turtles. It was followed by another, Resolution No. 30, concerned only with the green. It congratulated the Government of Costa Rica on its timely action at the Tortuguero nesting ground and expressed the hope that 'all steps will be taken in future to safeguard the precarious stocks of this species wherever they are found'.

Not only is this destruction of a natural food resource shortsighted, it is executed with quite unnecessary cruelty. Age-old techniques are still in use. One gets the impression that the hunters and shippers have no feeling at all for the suffering of the animal. I saw this with my own eyes.

Turtles can be caught in a number of ways.

On Aldabra, where the turning of females on the beach is now illegal, the most popular method is by spearing, mainly of mating pairs flapping around near the surface. The male animal, being on top, is the usual victim. The sight of turtles ahead causes an almost compulsive reaction in creole fishermen to grab for a spear.

I followed one of these chases over the reef by Malabar Island. The moment the flippers were spotted, whoops of joy rose from the boatmen. The pirogue we were towing rapidly unhitched the line and two men from the motor boat jumped in to join the rowers. Everyone pointed and shouted but there was no recognizable word of command. It looked like an automatic drill. A tall young negro stood in the bows holding his spear aloft, looking like a heroic figure in a battle-scene of antiquity. The rowers pulled away laughing, muscular backs straining at the oars, the lethargy of the past hours suddenly transformed into a frenzy. In the white breakers of the reef, the pirogue vanished momentarily, re-appeared with bows almost vertical, dived again, the black marble spearsman still standing ready to strike.

Although the hunters were now almost out of sight, the creoles in our boat knew exactly what was happening. 'The spearsman's got one turtle with his first strike. It's been hauled aboard. Now they are after another' [there are often several males waiting to pay court and disputing with each other] 'he's got that one too.' Happy, hungry looks lit up the faces of our men. There was a feast and a reward in store.

As the pirogue drew alongside, I saw the butter-yellow underparts of the two male turtles filling the boat. One had his head raised and gazed sadly from huge, gummy eyes at his captors, while his front flippers waved feebly. The other lay quite helpless, his head at the end of a wrinkled, rubbery neck resting on the bottom of the boat. He looked like an old man falling out of a yellow-draped bed. While everyone admired the catch, one tortoise sighed noisily, gulping in air. It was a long time before I heard the breath exhaled.

Turtles are rarely killed on the spot unless the hunters are hungry. The idea is to take them alive to market. Sometimes, from Aldabra, this involves a journey of hundreds of miles and temporary storage in a pound, like the one we had seen near West Channel. It is during this journey the turtle suffers most.

Like most reptiles, the turtle is hardy and can endure discomfort and privation that would kill most other animals. It doesn't seem to matter much to the buyers in what state the reptile arrives provided it is still breathing. This may account for the brutality with which they are treated, particularly in the Caribbean trade where all four flippers are pierced and a rope is passed through the hole to tie fore and hind flippers on each side firmly together. On its back, the huge creature is helpless, relying entirely on the kindness of humans to give it shade and an occasional cold douche. On the *Lady Esmé*, I was once shocked to see a wretched creature whose eyes had been pecked out by a chicken running loose on deck. There is something about the treatment of turtles that recalls the worst excesses of the slave trade. They are left starving, parched and helpless in over-crowded conditions and then banged, bounced and dragged on arrival.

Although I suspect the treatment of turtles in the Seychelles is less cruel than elsewhere – I never saw turtles with pierced flippers or crushed by stacking – it was still sickening to a newcomer, and I am obliged to say that I rarely saw any sympathy expressed for the suffering beast. Half-dead turtles, lying on the dockside at Port Victoria with concave plastrons showing they had not eaten for a long time, and with spear wounds still bleeding, evoked nothing more than humorous appraisal of their market value in a crowd of onlookers, idling in the sun.

But the news from this region is getting better. Even while I was in Mahé, a much improved turtle pound was provided – the reptile likes clean, clear water – and drastic conservation measures were being worked out.

Of all the recent threats to the survival of the marine turtle, the underwater speargunner is certainly the worst. These 'sportsmen,' often travelling far out to sea, discover a 'dormitory' of sleeping turtles and shoot as many as they can, regardless of size or sex. If the massacre happens to occur in the close season, the hunters store the wounded beasts on some remote island and bring them back to market in Mahé when the period of prohibition ends.

Looking at the starving creatures on the dockside, it occurred to me that this could explain the condition they were in and why Guy Lionnet, who came to see them, was so angry. In March 1964 the use of underwater equipment against turtles was made illegal.

While the local government takes steps to arrest the slide to extinction of the 'world's most valuable reptile', immense fields of turtle grass wave uncropped around the islands and on the vast submarine plateau. Can anything be done at this late hour to bring the once enormous herds back to this pastureland?

Harold Hirth, in his talk to the Seychelles Society, said:

'One solution might be a re-stocking programme whereby eggs are collected and incubated in wired-off enclosures, the young turtles reared in safety up to the age of one month and then released outside the shallow waters where so many of their natural enemies lurk.

Alternatively, a more ambitious scheme might be to raise the young on special 'turtle farms' until they reach the age of one year and are big enough to escape the attention of their predators.'

If the turtle is saved and the industry can, in future, be intelligently and humanely controlled, not only will the world regain a rich natural food supply, but scientists will benefit. Recent research has uncovered some remarkable facts about this maltreated creature. Harold had fascinated me with accounts of two in particular, both of which, he said, had aroused the interest of the United States Navy.

Turtles travel up to a thousand miles, possibly more, from the beaches where they are born, yet unerringly, the females return to exactly the same strip of sand to lay their eggs eight years later. How do they navigate? The process still eludes the experts, but it is obvious that the location must be imprinted by some sensory reception of physical conditions in that particular area.

And turtle tears are not, as once thought, simply the accompaniment of labour pains. Analysis of the tears has shown that they contain superconcentrated sodium chloride. All animals need fresh water and the turtle acts as its own desalination plant. A special gland in the eye separates the salt from the water and the salt is exuded in the tears.

So, after all, the captive turtles I saw were not weeping at the stupidity and cruelty of man. They were simply demonstrating a process so advanced as to be beyond man's comprehension.

All the same, it seemed to me they had enough to cry about.

# XII  *Assumption, Cosmoledo, Astove, Mahé*

THE *Lady Esmé's* dinghy was hauled inboard and the crew stood by to raise the anchor, clearly visible in six fathoms of water. It was time to go.

Captain Sauvage had waited patiently for us off West Island. The sea had been too rough for him to risk a journey to the east end of the atoll and the radio silence had not worried him unduly. He had found on the first day that the sets were not powerful enough for the conditions. He knew we would have sent the pirogue back if there had been an accident.

I looked over the stern at the green atoll. A tiny Union Jack was being lowered from the mast in front of the manager's bungalow. Black figures like chessmen lined the beach below the boatshed, looking out to sea. There was Mrs Archangel with the baby in her arms and her other child beside her, our porters waving and, to the right, a little apart, the spidery figure of Laporte. Fearsome Aldabra had been kind to us and we were sorry to go.

Above the shining water the settlement looked beautiful, the undercut cliffs beyond the beach smooth and graceful, the pemphis scrub a mere dusting of soft green. Three frigates floated motionless in the unclouded sky. On this last day the weather, which had favoured us all the way, was putting on its blandest show. The scene was like a 'come to Aldabra' poster. I almost felt we were leaving a favourite holiday resort and that we would be back next year with the family. As we drew slowly away through the deeper blue water it was hard to remember the trials – champignon, the parched feature-less plains, the impenetrable bush. But we had plenty of mementos and it was not a place one could easily forget.

The precious film and my hundreds of still photographs had been safely stowed in the cabin I shared with the ship's engineer. Guy's flourishing beard had been liquidated and shredded boots had been shed. A cool breeze replaced the stifling heat of the land and we were on our way to another island, Assumption. But somehow the magic of Aldabra clung to us. We could speak of nothing else. It was as if an invisible cord bound us to the mysterious atoll, as if we had to fix in our minds every detail of the 'living natural history museum' because we might be the last to see it thus. Every conversation ended with speculation about the airfield plans. One reason why we were anxious to get back to Mahé was to get the latest news.

We were unanimous that to develop the atoll in any way would be a tragedy. Aldabra deserved absolute and immediate protection and it should at once be declared a wild life sanctuary, if necessary under an international umbrella. Even cautious Guy, who clearly wanted to see the place for himself before making up his mind, was in full agreement that Aldabra, the whole of Aldabra, must be saved.

As we discussed this, always with a sense of foreboding, one memory kept coming back to me – the lowering of the flag on the rickety mast. If the atoll was to be despoiled, at least there would be no doubt who was to blame. The buck could not be passed.

Were there no alternative sites for an airfield on other islands of less scientific importance than Aldabra? Within two hours Assumption came into view. I had already studied it on the Captain's chart and knew that it was, unlike Aldabra, a solid reef island; it was nearly four miles long and up to a mile wide with, according to Sauvage, one of the few good anchorages in the whole Aldabra group. More significantly, it was a man-made desert as a result of guano digging.

Early this century, it was found to have enormous deposits of guano, the solid accumulation of birds' droppings over millions of years. Over 160,000 tons of this loamlike deposit was scraped off the tiny island in the twenty years up to 1945 and it was believed that an equal amount was still left.

Before the invention of chemical substitutes, guano was the best fertilizer available and its discovery on these islands brought wealth to the private individuals and companies who leased them. It is formed by the interaction of bird droppings on the coral foundations beneath, promoted by rain. Layers of this phosphatic deposit were found as much as fifty feet thick. To get at the source of the wealth, natural vegetation and top soil had to be removed, and so, inevitably, within a few years the guano-producing islands were wrecked. Weeds replaced the natural vegetation, wild life disappeared with its habitat, and introduced predators like rats finished the job. Fortunately, Aldabra had no guano deposits worth exploiting – Assumption, on on the other hand, was said to have been the best endowed. I picked up my binoculars to look at the victim.

Above a long white beach, a row of wooden shacks stood unshaded in the sun. It was like the Aldabra settlement only shabbier and almost treeless. The only relief from the tropic glare was at a small headland. Here, among a grove of dusty casuarinas and coconuts, was a larger house – the manager's – where the inevitable Union Jack was now flapping limply. Behind and beyond the beach, a shelf of green extended flatly into the distance. A bald hill rose on the horizon. From where we were anchored, the interior of the island looked like an unkempt cornfield, with every fifty yards or so a huge weed standing out like a scarecrow. The blue sea, the white sand, the flat green land – at first sight it was a stockbroker's dream. On closer inspection, a nightmare.

The island that Abbott had described so enthusiastically only seventy years before as having some of the most interesting land and sea-birds of the region, including the booby that bears his name, was now a silent wreck. The carpet of green was a tangle of pantropical weeds hiding the scarred earth. The central plateau was pitted with innumerable craters, filled with stagnant water and overgrown, which told of the relentless probing for phosphates. There were few birds and the most noticeable were the black and white pied crows of Africa. Even butterflies were scarce. There were no trees to offer shade and a rusty small-gauge railway, that looked disused, wandered across the wounded plain and enhanced the feeling of desolation.

Guano is still being mined on Assumption, now mostly under water, and conditions for the forty-odd creole labourers must be appalling. The settlement seemed to lack even such amenities as shower-baths – an essential for men engaged in so dirty a trade – and there was no provision at all for their recreation or refreshment. I was not surprised that they looked miserable, nor to be warned to keep the cabins locked when a party came aboard. They were obviously dying for a glass of beer or a cigarette and I handed out all I could spare.

My most vivid memory of this pitiful island which, I thought hopefully, must surely be suitable for a military airfield with an extension into the reef if necessary, was a big shoal of yellow and turquoise mackerel and two man-made mountains. These were mounds of guano awaiting a buyer and a ship. It was irony worthy of a Greek tragedy.

Here were the guts and riches of Assumption, extracted at such terrible cost, and no one wanted them any more. I learned that Harry Savy, the lessee, was having great difficulty in getting this huge aromatic heap removed.

It was good to get back to the ship and plan for our next landfall, the atoll of Astove or Astova.

Most atolls, like those in the Pacific, are sandy and at sea level, often overrun by waves in a storm, but the four atolls of the Aldabra group are different. They are platforms of dead coral standing up to fifteen feet above the sea. They come in the rarer and biologically important category of 'elevated atolls', uplifted in some distant past either by a submarine convulsion or by a fall in sea level. They are important because on the platform thus created plants and animals can establish themselves without interference from the sea.

According to Darwin's theory, an atoll is formed when an island fringed by a coral reef starts to sink; as the central land gradually disappears, the encircling reef goes on growing until finally it is the only dry land left ringing a lagoon where once the island stood. The stages of normal atoll development therefore are: first an island surrounded by a submerged reef, then a barrier reef around a vanishing island and finally just the enclosed reef itself with a central lagoon. But Darwin did not directly consider the uplifted limestone islands, the class of elevated atoll in which the Aldabra group falls.

At first sight, Assumption, which we had just left, seemed to represent the start of atoll formation, but in fact all four islands of the group are at the same stage of development. In the centre of Assumption there are traces of a lagoonal depression which is, however, now quite dry. To find the first stage in Darwin's theory in this area one would have to look at the Comoros – high volcanic islands with small fringing reefs. The island of Mayotte in this group comes in the second stage, a high island with a well-developed barrier reef, and the third stage, of sea level atolls, can be seen in the Maldives and Chagos archipelagoes.

Astove, where we were now headed, is a nearly perfect example of an elevated atoll, consisting of a coral rim surrounding a shallow lagoon, broken at only one point by the sea. It contrasts with Aldabra itself, where the rim is cut in four places with a fifth channel in the making, and the last of the group, Cosmoledo. The latter has been so eroded by the sea that it is now no more than a broken circlet of small islands and sand-spits. The presence of a lagoon twelve miles in circumference is merely suggested. Cosmoledo could be described as the memory of an elevated atoll.

The nearer we got to Astove, the most southerly of the group, the more anxious Captain Sauvage became. He had no wish to linger at a place renowned principally for the number of wrecks it has caused. He stressed that there was no possible anchorage (a chain mooring on the reef had long since broken up), that if the weather looked ominous we would have to get away quickly, that it was uninhabited and even water supplies were doubtful. Over dinner he regaled us with stories of giant garoupas on a reef that dropped to 200 fathoms in a matter of yards and of buried treasure, the only sensible reason for visiting such a hellish island. Although I felt sorry for the skipper, I was now keener than ever to get there!

It looked harmless enough next morning when we hove to – unable to anchor of course – and the *Lady Esmé*'s dinghy was lowered to take us ashore. Priority passengers were twelve young Aldabran tortoises with which Guy hoped to re-establish a population on the atoll. There is evidence that tortoises once inhabited Astove, but they became extinct in the distant past.

'Listen out for the siren, ' warned Sauvage as we pulled away, upturned tortoises rattling in the bottom of the boat. 'Drop everything and come to the beach at once when you hear it.'

The sea was rougher now and white waves broke on the vertical reef, but we had no difficulty in landing. A grey heron watched from the end of the beach and went on fishing undisturbed.

Half-a-dozen ruined buildings, including a reservoir with a broken roof and the skeleton of a boatshed, under which were two rotting boats, marked the site of the deserted settlement. Part of the ruin was just decay but some of it was clearly the work of a cyclone. At the back of the beach was a large, overgrown coconut plantation and vegetable gardens gone to seed. Several fruit trees grew luxuriantly round the broken huts.

The tortoises were carried ashore safely, righted and pointed towards the interior. They walked swiftly over the sand, relieved to get away from us, and at the first sight of green vegetation, stopped to feed. This was a good start. The one I was filming peered up and I am sure I saw a glint in its eye as it surveyed the lush vegetation. The new tortoise population of Astove was already quite at home. An hour later one of them was indeed walking about with a green gecko on its back. For the tortoise it must have been just like Aldabra, or better.

We humans, on the other hand, noticed some big differences. In the first place the mosquitoes. There had been almost none on Aldabra, even at night, but here they were intolerable. They descended on our exposed skin in droves, behaving as if they hadn't had a good drink of blood for months. It was impossible to stand still and even a blast insecticide kept them at bay for only a few seconds. Against the instructions on the tin, I sprayed the stuff all over me in desperation. It worked a bit better that way.

But when I saw the butterflies I almost forgot the mosquitoes. For some unknown reason, Astove has the most flourishing lepidoptera of any island of the region. You could see at a glance that they were far more numerous and varied than on Aldabra. Fryer had noted this in his report and had singled out for special mention the magnificent blue *Precis rhadama*. While Guy and I hared around with our nets catching as many insects as we could and praying the siren would not suddenly interrupt the chase, we kept a keen eye open for the flash of blue. At last he saw one but it escaped. Among the species we took, however, all within a quarter of a mile of the landing place, were nine *Acraea ranavalona Boisduval* and a number of Pieridae and Nymphalidae we had not seen on Aldabra. I was delighted to learn later that the insects I gave to the British Museum were the first they had got from this atoll.

After the desert of Assumption, it was exciting to see plenty of land-birds too. The bird I was most anxious to meet was a sunbird, believed to be a distinct sub-species, and, to my surprise, this presented no difficulty. They were flitting everywhere in the abandoned plantation, showing even less fear of man than their Aldabran cousins. Cockbirds, their metallic heads and shoulders glinting in the sun, perched in the coconut palms watching as I chased the butterflies, but only in the hen did I detect any difference in coloration. She seemed to be yellower than the Aldabran species. In the tussocky grass near the lagoon I found a nest of *Cisticola cherina*, a common Madagascar bird which for some reason has avoided Aldabra. It contained six eggs. Little attempt had been made to conceal it which suggested that predators were few.

On the boat I had been reading the account of a party of English people who were shipwrecked on the island at the end of last century. Their vessel, the *Lion*, was on its way to Bombay and hit the Astove reef in the dark. Everyone on board escaped with their lives and they lived in reasonable comfort on the atoll, at the time uninhabited, for five months until rescued by a passing man-of-war. An army officer in the shipwrecked party was a keen naturalist and he described finding a number of nests of the red-tailed tropic bird near the beach. I was anxious to see this bird again, particularly in flight when it must look magnificent, but although I searched diligently I found none.

A dark cloud was building up on the horizon. The siren sounded and we returned reluctantly to the *Lady Esmé*.

Astove, like Assumption, has been mined for guano but the deposits were more localized and it has therefore suffered much less damage. Remains of wrecks on several parts of the coast tell their own story. It is not a place that man has often gone to voluntarily, although it must have a strong appeal to treasure hunters as well as to those who enjoy real isolation! In Mahé I met a former manager of the atoll who told me of buried treasure found there by one of the creole labourers. Finders of such hoards are always secretive, and particularly so in the Seychelles, but I have good reason to believe that this story was true. But I knew nothing about this at the time. On our brief visit I got the impression that Astove deserves much further scientific study, certainly for its insects.

And now it has a chance to get it. The atoll has just been leased again, this time to an Englishman, the former Director of Fisheries of the Seychelles, Mark Veevers-Carter. While I was writing this book I received a letter from him datelined Astove. He had moved there with his American wife and family and was busily engaged in rebuilding the settlement while combatting unimaginable hordes of mosquitoes. There was good news of the butterflies and he noted that 'our sunbirds show tremendous variation in colouring; it seems hardly possible they are all of the same species.'

Astove is a place I will certainly visit again. I am not so sure about Cosmoledo.

The fine weather broke at last as we approached this crumbling atoll. Cosmoledo was probably sighted and named by Vasco da Gama on his pioneer voyage to the Indies in the spring of 1498. Through a grey pall of driving rain the chunks of its broken rim stood out darkly. Many of the fragments, barely visible above the waves, had been eroded almost to sea level but the larger islands brought back memories of Aldabra, with undercut grey cliffs covered in low scrub. They looked more than ever like aircraft carriers, half-dismantled in a breaker's yard.

We stopped for a few hours at the two biggest islands, Wizard and Menai, but as there was nothing much to see and the rain made filming almost impossible, I soon accepted an invitation from my cabin mate, Esmé Jumeau, to go fishing in the ship's dinghy. Everyone said the sport was excellent here and they were right. We zoomed up and down the reef, hundred-pound nylon handlines armed with three-inch hooks streaming astern; the boat soon began to fill with barracudas and bonitos. A golden dorado, the dolphin that adorns old maps, joined the pile. The largest barracuda was over four feet long. I was surprised at how little fight they showed after the first heavy tug, a signal to slow the engine and begin the swift haul in. There were now almost enough fish to feed the crew for a day. It was too easy. Suddenly I was pulled forward by a tremendous jolt on the line. '*Touché!*' but there was no time to take the strain. A pain like fire on my forefinger and the line parted. The engine stopped. Esmé and the helmsman were on their feet staring excitedly astern.

'Did you see that?' gasped the tall engineer. 'A yellow-fin tuna – as big as me. It jumped six feet out of the water.'

'Sorry about the line,' I said, sucking the red-hot blister on my finger.

'Oh, don't worry about that. But what a pity – that fish could have fed us for a week.'

I did not care at the moment. The finger tip felt as if it were about to fall off. The moral of the story – use a rod for fishing off Cosmoledo unless you have armour-plated hands.

Now the wind was rising and the clouds to the south growing darker. Captain Sauvage decided it was time to leave. We towed the local fishermen in their pirogue back to the settlement, escorted by a skyful of brown boobies. These birds, clumsy on land yet spectacularly graceful in flight, came even closer than gulls. There must have been at least two hundred of them. A man was standing in the bows of the pirogue astern, holding a stick with a noose at the end of it. Boobies were wheeling so close to his head that if he had put a hand out he could easily have caught one, but he had a surer technique. A flick of the stick and there was a brown flurry of wings. The prize was grasped by eager hands and thrown into the boat. He did this twice – enough for a good meal.

The brown boobies dive-bombed us all the time we lay off Cosmoledo, so I was surprised to read in C. W. Benson's chapter on the Birds of Aldabra, published in the Smithsonian's Atoll Research Bulletin of November 1967, that 'one was seen off Aldabra in 1964 . . . No further evidence has been traced of the occurrence of this species anywhere in the archipelago . . .'.

I did not think the heavy brown birds could have been anything else, though it's possible they were red-foots in the brown phase or even immatures. Several times they landed on the rigging, balancing like amateur tight-rope walkers; we could not have had a closer view and we got some good film of them. As the pirogue was unhitched and black hands waved farewell in the dancing spray, the boobies wheeled and swept upwards to vanish in the direction of the mist-wrapped land.

They were the last wild creatures we saw in the Aldabran Islands.

    *      *      *      *      *      *      *

Four days later we reached Mahé, the biggest island in the thousand mile chain stretching north-east from the coast of Africa. There was tremendous excitement on deck as our crew neared the home they had not seen for two months. We were now well clear of the cyclone belt. It was a fine blue morning. Through the thinning mist, the towering outline of a mountain appeared ahead and soon the peaks called the Trois Frères, dominated by the 3,000 foot mass of Morne Seychellois, were discernible.

After the flat low coral islands of the southern zone, the effect was overpowering, and again I thought how incredible it was that these granite islands had remained uninhabited by man for so long. They must have been seen by countless trading vessels, men-of-war and pirates on their way to the East. Why had no one settled here until the French came barely two hundred years ago? The islands had timber, water, a pleasant climate, and, according to the first visitors, teamed with wild life both tame and tasty. Turtles and tortoises abounded and the surrounding seas were full of fish and sea-cows, the mermaids of legend. Splendid forests were the home of so many strange and beautiful birds that even the most unscientific travellers never failed to comment on them.

The morning sun now lit up the steep green slopes tumbling to the sea. Coconut palms lined the rocky shore and above them, breaking the canopy of green, giant granite boulders hung precariously. What a place for a landslide, I thought. The remains of natural forest nestled in the high valleys, and crowning all were the brooding granite faces of the mountain tops, curiously marked with vertical stripes sculpted by the rain of ages. I had been told that the basic granite and basalt of these unique islands was between 600 and 800 million years old. Dots of light showed among the trees and on the headlands.

Perhaps it was fortunate for these mountains peeping above the Indian Ocean a thousand miles from land that they had been spared earlier attention by man because, even in the short time he had lived there, havoc had been wrought among their wild life. The tortoises and sea-cows, both defenceless, had been wiped out, at least two of the land-birds had become extinct and others teetered on the brink. Even the green turtle had all but abandoned this vast ancestral breeding ground.

But it was time to interrupt the musings. We were now entering the harbour of Victoria, capital of the Seychelles. I thought then and believe still that it is the most beautiful in the world. Sheltered by a scatter of green islands, a small township nestles under the bulk of the Three Brothers, behind a sea of brilliant blue, streaked with mauve. The breathtaking beauty of the scene is enhanced by a blaze of flowering trees on the hillsides and a row of schooners, anchored

21. The birds which even the optimists thought we would not see: greater flamingoes in a pool at the east extremity of South Island. *(The Royal Society)*

22. Anse Cèdres, the isolated cove near Passe Houareau. A small beach backed by large casuarina trees which are a landmark in the trackless hinterland. This was a deceptively calm day on the north coast of the atoll. (*The Author*)

along the harbour, gives the place an 18th century look. One of these schooners, Guy told me, was the celebrated *Argo* that plies between Mahé and Aldabra.

A dapper, dynamic-looking man of about fifty with straight black hair was waiting on the dockside to welcome us. Guy introduced me to Harry Savy, the lessee of Aldabra and Assumption. I thanked him for the introductory letters and all the help his men had given us on both islands.

'Do you not agree that the whole of Aldabra should be made into a permanent sanctuary for wild life?' he asked me.

I did.

Before the memory of the distant atoll faded, I poured out my convictions to three friends in England. My cousin, Sir Tufton Beamish, who had recently been elected President of the Royal Society for the Protection of Birds, Jeffrey Boswell of the BBC, who had promoted my expedition and for whom I was making the films, and the ornithologist, Dr Bourne, who I knew was tireless and outspoken in the cause of conservation. I told them what I had seen on the threatened atoll and made suggestions of other possible sites for the military airfield. Although we had no news of what was happening in England, or how the defenders were faring in their fight, I had a feeling that time was short and the days of the forgotten atoll were numbered unless something could be done to arouse public opinion before the bureaucratic juggernaut had ground too far.

On Mahé itself, everyone I spoke to seemed unanimous that it would be a scandal to wreck the last unspoiled island of the region. The local newspaper gave us full support. On March 16th I went on record in the *Seychelles Bulletin* as saying:

'I hope the film will arouse world-wide interest to ensure [Aldabra] remains a paradise for wild life.'

Guy Lionnet, who as a senior Government servant could have been excused for reticence, felt obliged to write in this paper on March 29th:

'Aldabra is something unique, something to be prized and preserved at all cost!'

Going on to list the wonders of the atoll, he ended the article:

'Virtually unspoilt by man, Aldabra is a virgin land where plants and animals exist in a natural but fragile equilibrium. This could easily be upset by man and his machines. To preserve and protect [it], so that our children's children may enjoy it, Aldabra should be left to itself. It should be turned into a sanctuary, untouched and untouchable. It deserves no less.'

Although he never told me so, I suspect, as a former civil servant myself, that he got a rocket for these heartfelt views. A few days before, he and I had been on the local radio together in French, pressing strongly the case to spare the atoll. Judging by the reactions, we were speaking to the converted.

After Harold Hirth's warnings about the green turtle, the newspaper *Le Seychellois* declared on April 3rd in a front page banner headline:

## 'PROTECT THEM'

and in the French style of mixing news with editorial comment, went on:

'We feel that something drastic, and perhaps unpopular must be done. The mass killing of our turtles must be stopped and Government should do all it can to protect this main source of food for our community. Turtle meat is now the only regularly available meat on the local market, but if the present mass slaughter continues we will have no turtles left. Our own reporter has seen turtles of even minute size killed. [Poachers] should be severely punished and the turtles confiscated.'

On the subject of Aldabra, only the government officials were guarded and referred vaguely to a decision in Whitehall. It was out of their hands now the new colony of BIOT had taken over responsibility. I gained the impression that in some way the United Kingdom's promise to build a much-needed civil airport on Mahé was linked with acquiescence to their plans for the development of Aldabra. In conversation with them I tried tactfully to avoid mentioning the atoll; it would not have been fair.

By now my films were on their way to the laboratories in England. I waited impatiently for news; had they negotiated the roundabout journey by sea, land and air? Had they survived the heat of Aldabra?

There was much to occupy my mind in the meantime. Birds even more rare than those of Aldabra were to be filmed. The paradise flycatcher, reported extinct ten years earlier, the magpie robin on Frigate Island, of which less than a score still existed, and the black parrot. While trying to film the latter in the Vallée de Mai, the Garden of Eden of tradition, I broke my ankle and had to spend a week in hospital. Then the telegram arrived.

'All films generally OK stop exposures correct stop awaiting further instructions . . .'

There was only one thing to do – return home and use the film in defence of an island that could not speak for itself.

XIII  *The Fight for Aldabra*

E VEN in distant Mahé, we knew the battle was under way. The
muffled boom of gunfire reached us in English newspapers, six
weeks out-of-date:

'Healey versus the Pink-footed Booby'
'Battle for Survival – Flightless Rail against the VC 10'

and from *The Times* of London:

'Airfield Scheme as Threat to Island'.

Following the January conference on Aldabra, which had studied
the report of Drs Stoddart and Wright, the Royal Society had issued
a press notice. This voiced 'considerable concern' over the defence
proposals, announced plans for an expedition to the atoll and revealed
that the Royal Society was having discussions with the Ministry of
Defence about the 'strong case for preserving the island for scientific

investigation by abandoning the airfield proposal'. At the conference it had been generally agreed that the Royal Society should lead the campaign. The first shot had been fired.

Although few newspapers can ever have heard of Aldabra before, Press reaction to the Royal Society's appeal for its protection was immediately sympathetic. An article in the *Evening Standard* of March 3rd was typical:

'As a romantic, with emotions that warm at the idea of giant tortoises lazing in the sun and a flight of pink-footed boobies skimming the lagoon, I am right behind the Royal Society'

wrote the correspondent,

'and I would be delighted to forward any protests from readers to the Minister responsible.'

There was a lively response from the other side of the Atlantic too. Professor Evelyn Hutchinson, Professor of Zoology at Yale University, declared that 'the destruction of Aldabran wild life would lead to a permanent gap in our understanding of the living world' and the *New York Times* on February 24th reminded its readers that this was not the first time scientists had rallied to the defence of Aldabra. Darwin himself had done so nearly a hundred years before. And, with a cynicism that was nearly prophetic, the *New Yorker* magazine urged conservationists 'to cheer up and take a broad view of the matter'.

'The coming decimation of the atoll,' the leading article said, 'is itself a splendid specimen of evolution in action, illustrating, as it does the universal tendency of man's evolving machinery to destroy all forms of life that are less noisy, brutal and demented than itself.'

We searched the Seychelles papers eagerly and remained glued to the crackling radio to find the British Government's attitude to to these appeals and protests. The first indication came in a report of a House of Commons statement about the defence estimates made on March 15th by the Under-Secretary of State for the R.A.F., Mr Merlyn Rees. Declaring that virtually a new air force was being built, he went on:

'We are considering the possibility of establishing a staging airfield on the island of Aldabra. This has caused concern in scientific circles as the island has a unique ecosystem. The Ministry has assured the Royal Society that scientific considerations would be taken into account in coming to a decision . . .'

This statement, that no decision had yet been reached and that the scientific importance of Aldabra was understood by the British government, would have been more reassuring had it not been followed immediately by a disturbing revelation from the Liberal Member of Parliament, Mr Lubbock:

'Maps have been published in British and American journals showing how the F-111-K would operate from bases in the Indian Ocean . . .'

He then asked:

'Why does the Minister persist in refusing to give this information to the House directly?'

There was no reply.

By now a more detailed memorandum on Aldabra had been prepared by Dr Stoddart for the Royal Society and proposals for a research station on the atoll had been drafted. The memorandum was approved by both the Natural Environment Research Council and the British Museum of Natural History and was circulated to the Ministry of Defence and other departments on May 17th. A few days later, in an unprecedented move, a delegation of the Royal Society, led by its President, Professor P. M. S. Blackett, called on the Minister of Defence, Mr Healey. It was clear from the press notice issued after this meeting that the Royal Society's views had hardened further. It was 'convinced that any extensive development will inevitably destroy the greater part of those biological features – the result of a long period of evolution in isolation – which make [Aldabra] unique among the atolls of the world.'

Mr Healey was unable to give any assurance that Aldabra would not be developed. He stated that a decision would be taken within twelve months, that alternative sites had been ruled out for 'compelling reasons' and that 'scientific bodies concerned would be consulted if it were decided to go ahead with the defence plans for an airfield and harbour'.

There was nothing to cheer about in this reply but, at least, it showed that the Minister was now taking the matter seriously. He had not always done so. Until then he had treated Aldabra as a joke to be used in the best prima donna style for scoring points off the Opposition. One particularly good wisecrack he would probably like to have buried, when confronted by the President of the Royal Society. Replying to a question in the House a month before, he had said:

'As I understand it, the island of Aldabra is inhabited – like Her Majesty's Opposition Front Bench – by giant turtles, frigate birds and boobies. Nevertheless, it may well provide useful facilities for aircraft.'

What, no tortoises? Or had someone not done his homework?

Further exchanges in the House of Commons threw no more light on the government's intentions and, in midsummer, the author of the 'homework', Dr Stoddart, a world authority on atolls, returned to the Indian Ocean leading a party of eleven scientists in the survey ship H.M.S. *Vidal*. This was the first phase of the expedition mounted by the Royal Society with the main object of gathering as much information as possible about Aldabra before any construction work began. There was little time left. The scientific survey was to be conducted in three phases, covering the dry and wet seasons from August 1967 to March 1968. Also on board *Vidal* was an official survey party concerned with the practical problems of airfield and dock construction.

The arguments for sparing Aldabra were now better known, at least in scientific and government circles, but what was the military case for building the airfield? This had been vaguely outlined by spokesmen of the Defence Ministry with an obvious reluctance to fill in the details. It seemed that the staging post on Aldabra was needed to complete a planned 'sovereign route' to the Far East for Anglo-American military use. Aldabra was to be another Gan, the next link in a chain of airfields after Ascension Island in the Atlantic, off the west coast of Africa, and ending in Cocos-Keeling Islands off Australia. It was not intended to be a base. In their opinion, Aldabra alone among the islands of the region had the size and situation to satisfy all the planners' needs.

It was not surprising that the public should have been taken aback by the violence of this sudden confrontation of scientists and military. Very little had been heard before about the strategic importance of

Aldabra and BIOT itself had been created in such secrecy that its ominous significance had been overlooked. The military survey of the atoll in 1962 had been conducted without the advice or presence of any scientist, a fact which may also explain the pile of tortoise bones left behind. Even as late as the autumn of 1966, the defence boffins were pleading for silence on the grounds that no decision had yet been taken. Fortunately the Royal Society could not agree to this; it decided that to delay remonstrance would leave it too late. The Defence Ministry obviously hoped to have advanced so far with its plans by the time the 'eccentric' naturalists heard about them that it would have been impossible to turn back, however loud the outcry. Resolute action at an early stage might well have discouraged the protagonists.

The exact role envisaged for Aldabra was first spelt out to the public much later in a letter to *The Times* from Air Marshal Sir Dermot Boyle, former Chief of Staff, published on August 14th. He pointed out that the new defence policy was to rely on United Kingdom-based forces and 'rapid deployment to areas overseas where our help may be needed', and continued:

'To be certain of meeting obligations quickly and economically we must be able to reach a variety of possible destinations in circumstances which cannot be foreseen. For this we need the flexibility which can be provided only by staging posts under our direct control, which will be immediately available whatever the political circumstances of the time. Aldabra is well-located for a such a purpose. Equally it would form a useful focal point from which the R.A.F. could discharge its future responsibilities for protecting shipping with land-based aircraft.'

More questions were put to the Minister in Parliament, notably by Sir Tufton Beamish, a former opposition defence spokesman, but the answers were invariably the same – that no decision had yet been taken, that the scientific importance of Aldabra was appreciated and that, if it were decided to go ahead with the development, scientists would be consulted at all stages. Aldabra began to sink dangerously from the news. A verbal stalemate had been reached.

I was certain that my film and photographs of the atoll could help to bring the debate into the public eye and ear and, shortly after my return, I was invited by Dr Bourne to show them to a group of naturalists he had convened. On July 14th we met at Malcolm Penny's house in London to see the films and discuss further action.

Although the meeting was informal, an impressive group of 'Aldabra fighters' attended, among them several conservation experts and three members of the Bristol University Expedition, Roger Gaymer and Malcolm and Mary Penny, the latter probably the first Englishwoman ever to visit Aldabra. Major conservation societies were represented by Sir Tufton Beamish (Royal Society for the Protection of Birds), Miss Phyllis Barclay-Smith (International Council for Bird Preservation), Mr and Mrs R. S. R. Fitter (Fauna Preservation Society) and Peter Scott (Survival Service Commission of the International Union for the Conservation of Nature and the World Wildlife Fund), for whose natural history series on BBC Television my film had been made.

We agreed that more must be done, urgently, to draw attention to the issues involved, in view of the government's non-committal replies both to the President of the Royal Society and in the House of Commons. It was also felt that while the scientific case for sparing Aldabra had been made, this did not seem to carry much weight with the military, and attention should now be concentrated on the practical difficulties of the scheme. The public must be brought into the debate. It was decided to launch a campaign in the press.

The opening shot was fired on August 5th by a letter to *The Times* signed by the heads of the main protection societies, Sir Tufton Beamish, Peter Scott, Professor W. H. Thorpe and the Marquess of Willingdon. It said that it was not the object to question the need for a staging airfield, although 'it would be helpful if the Government would give its reasons' and proceeded to pinpoint the problems and hazards of the scheme:

'The island has no harbour and is composed of coral rock, undermined and dissected by the sea. The plan is to dam the lagoon, which is tidal and the size of the Thames estuary, to make a port and then to build a causeway twenty miles long . . . Even before the construction is complete, the scientific value of the island will have been irreversibly damaged. Then the authorities will have to overcome the problem of bird-aircraft collisions – likely at Aldabra to be the worst in the world . . . it appears incredible folly to embark on such a project without a proper on-the-site survey and costing of the various other islands in the area to which there is no scientific objection and where the frigate-bird problem does not arise. The whole project, besides involving enormous and unstated expense, appears extremely hazardous.'

This provoked a lively correspondence which lasted three weeks. Of the twelve letters published only two, both from Sir Dermot Boyle, supported the use of Aldabra for an airfield.

Lord Ridley, who made the survey of the sea-bird egg industry in the Seychelles, asked what were the 'compelling reasons' that had ruled out the use of other islands of the BIOT, some of which, he thought, could well prove equally suitable. He added:

'The bird-strike problem cannot be overstressed; American experience at Midway should be sufficient warning . . . The Public Accounts Committee should investigate the idea before and not after the construction of the base . . . The cost may well be fantastic.'

Several Bristol Expedition members joined in. Roger Gaymer mentioned the unsound rock and the difficulties of clearing the vegetation and warned about the dangers and effects of the dam:

'At its narrowest the channel is over 600 yards wide . . . The sea roars through at every tide bringing turtles, manta rays, and dangerous sharks . . . Once complete, the dam would kill acres of coral at present irrigated by tidal currents and this may poison the entire lagoon.'

Mary Penny recommended Assumption, the ruined island nearby, as a good alternative. 'There is no evidence,' she wrote, 'that Assumption has ever been surveyed.' This was followed by a letter from Professor Wynne-Edwards, Roger Bailey – one of those who had been at our meeting – and Dr Bourne, speaking for the Seabird Group, which underlined alarmingly the bird-strike problem:

'It is difficult to think of a much greater bird hazard than (Aldabra) presents. Frigate birds have a wing span of seven feet. They are long-lived birds and their young are known to wander far and wide at sea during adolescence . . . If an airfield were built on Aldabra it is virtually certain that sooner or later the authorities would be forced into trying to destroy the frigates, as the Americans were with the albatrosses nesting on Midway Island . . . They would be hard to kill and every year for possibly six to ten years a new crop of recruits would arrive from the sea to nest. Thinking of large transport aircraft . . . we believe that Aldabra might be found in practice unacceptably dangerous. We urge that alternative neighbouring islands should be carefully considered.'

Not a word came from the Defence side until after a letter from Alistair Buchan of the Institute for Strategic Studies. This questioned for the first time the defence strategy that had led to the choice of Aldabra:

'I have great difficulty in understanding what function a base tucked away in that corner of the Indian Ocean would serve, unless it is for British or American intervention in Southern and East Africa – a role that has dubious credibility. Gan, Diego Garcia and the Cocos Islands provide natural staging bases for South East Asia, unless one is to contemplate the bizarre alternative of trooping from Britain to Asia via Ascension and Aldabra which are 4,500 miles apart, the extreme loaded range of the most powerful aircraft under development.'

This elicited from Air Marshal Boyle the letter which first exposed clearly Defence policy and intentions. He was surprised that 'so eminent an authority as Mr Buchan' should have difficulty in understanding the purpose of a staging post on Aldabra, and thought he had overlooked 'our increased capability due to the range of the VC 10 and flight re-fuelling facilities'. He pointed out 'there are routes between Ascension and Aldabra much shorter than 4,500 miles'. On the question of the bird-strike hazard, he said:

'The R.A.F. has considerable experience in dealing with this . . . and I assume it would not wish to proceed unless it was confident, after detailed study . . . that the frigate-bird problem can be overcome satisfactorily.'

He was challenged on the last statement by R. S. R. Fitter who claimed that the Americans were unable to cope with the albatrosses of Midway till they had 'consulated scientific ornithologists . . . when shall we hear that the R.A.F. have done just this . . .'

A powerful plea to save Aldabra now came from the President of the Charles Darwin Foundations for the Galapagos Isles, the only

other remaining home of the giant tortoise. Sir Julian Huxley's letter,
which appeared on August 22nd, told of the effects that 'a concentrated human irruption' had had on the native animals and plants
of the Galapagos:

'In little more than a century some of the evidence on which
Darwin based his theory of evolution has already disappeared, and
much that remains is in danger.'

After congratulating the Ecuadorian government for the 'far-sighted
measures which she is taking to check this process' by designating
the vital areas as national parks, he went on:

'The animals and plants of Aldabra have much in common with
those of the Galapagos . . . They can fairly claim to have international
value and, as such, the owner into whose hands they happen to have
fallen, surely has a responsibility to exercise some degree of limitation
of his activities in their favour.

If construction of an airfield goes ahead, it must be doubtful,
judging by our own tortoise reserve, whether it would be practicable
to set aside a viable reserved area for the tortoises . . . It is greatly to
be hoped that Britain can solve her defence problems without in-
vading Aldabra and that, in consequence, she will save for posterity
this valuable asset in the Indian Ocean.'

At this point the Defence Correspondent of *The Times*, Charles
Douglas-Home, questioned again the strategic value of an airfield
on the atoll; and once more the Air Marshal leapt into print.

'Aldabra would give us more strategic mobility,' he declared. 'It
would help to provide a means of access under our own control to the
Far East . . . The need for strategic mobility grows more not less.'
He then turned to the conservation arguments:

'I suggest that it is an exaggeration to speak of this project as
"scientifically tragic" when only an extremely small proportion of
the total area of the island would be affected . . . With an airfield, the
island would become much more accessible to scientists . . . The
R.A.F. have for many years taken expert ornithological advice on
the bird-strike problems in general and the Aldabra problem in
particular. I would stress that, in addition to the strategic gains,
the R.A.F. could, with the aid of scientists, preserve from destruction
the natural assets of the island and would, I fancy, be proud to do so.'

Sir Dermot Boyle, who appeared to be the government's spokesman, had the last word. Alone he defended the project against the onslaught of the conservationists. I could not help admiring him, but all the same I reached for my pen. Too late. The correspondence had been closed. A number of the Air Marshal's statements needed answer, particularly the suggestion that only a small part of the atoll would be affected. In fact, the construction work would involve at least a third of the dry land of Aldabra – not counting the BBC's transmitter station project – and, more seriously, it was that part with the greatest concentration of wild life. This provoked me to write an article for the Listener about the 'curate's egg' that was being offered as a sop to the Royal Society:

'Don't worry, chaps, even it we do go ahead with an airfield, roads, a dock for 20,000 ton tankers, bridges, and a dam, Aldabra will still be good in parts.'

But the ball was rolling well now. *The Times* was temporarily closed, but correspondence was promptly opened in other British newspapers and in the United States.

*Time* magazine reported the devastating reminder to Mr Healey, published in the *New Scientist*:

'The Union Jack flying over Aldabra is evidence of our cusodianship of a biological treasure house. It is not a licence to kill.'

The American journal, *Science* of August 18th said:

'The preservationists are now trying to drive home the point that there is no established mechanism by which the scientific community is consulted when such government decisions are made. So, as important as an Aldabra preserved is to science, even more is at stake than whether the atoll of the 1970's is to be the home of the flightless rail or the F.111!'

In the *New Statesman* of August 25th, under the headline 'Aldabra Does Not Exist', Nigel Calder wrote:

'Aldabra is one of nature's last ditches . . . There are practical and philosophical imperatives for grasping the global facts of life before we perish of hunger or turn the planet into a virtual desert.' . . . . . .

A major article by Pearson Phillips in the *Daily Mail* was headed: 'Before this New Imbecility in High Places goes too far . . .'

'Aldabra is a place reminiscent of those stories in schoolboy annuals about miraculous territories beyond inaccessible mountain ranges peopled by dinosaurs . . . but we can't allow that sort of place to exist undisturbed nowadays . . . This is the kind of high-placed imbecility which makes me, personally almost incoherent with rage. So bear with me while I try to splutter it out . . .

You can safely say that most – if not all – of this natural treasure house would be as dead as the dodo on the coming of man with his docks and his dams, his airstrips and his refuelling installations . . . The giant tortoises for one thing live where the airstrip is planned to go.'

The *Spectator* probably hit the nail smack on the head in remarking:

'Poor Mr Healey must have been rather surprised when the Royal Society decided to put its weight against his little scheme and (oh horrors) make its opposition public so that we would all know just what was going on. He may have envisaged a few wooly-headed die-hard preservationists with little organization. He can hardly have expected a head-on collision with the world's greatest scientific society.'

Some small consolation may, however, have come to him later from an article in the *Economist* which said that the airfield plan should go ahead. Stating with magnificent patronage that the case for sparing Aldabra 'is a perfectly respectable one, but it was not as unanswerable as the scientists seem to think it is', the *Economist* proceeded to show that Aldabra alone was suitable to provide the missing link in a 'third military air route into the Indian Ocean'. This article, the only opposition to the conservation case, other than the letters of Sir Dermot Boyle, to appear in print on either side of the Atlantic, exhorted Mr Healey to say 'yes, and say it soon'. The writer seemed to be well-informed on the question of comparative costs; it still intrigues me how he or she knew that Aldabra would be 'the cheapest island to develop'; it might almost have been the Treasury speaking.

In the meantime even bigger guns were taking up position in Aldabra's defence. On August 10th, the American National Academy of Sciences, counterpart in the United States of the Royal Society, issued a historic statement. It declared that it joined the Royal Society in its concern about the proposals to use Aldabra for a military airfield.

Any extensive man-made development . . . would do irreparable damage to this world science resource. The Academy and the Royal Society have urged their governments to exert every effort to elim- 'Aldabra is a biological treasure house that has a unique ecosystem . . . inate this threat of incalculable damage to one of the world's unique resources for scientific investigation . . .'

        ★      ★      ★      ★      ★      ★      ★

On my return to England in July, I had been interviewed on the radio and had stated strongly my views that an alternative site for the airfield should be sought among the 'ruined' islands of the Lost Corner, like Assumption. The programme was broadcast twice at peak times and, judging by the letters I received from strangers, none of them sounding eccentric, there was already widespread public concern about the fate of the forgotten atoll.

Now it was time to get to work on the film. The footage was satisfactory, considering the conditions under which it was shot, although as usual I felt it did not do justice to the subject. The calm weather we had enjoyed made Aldabra look, in parts, like a holiday resort, but *Testudo gigantea,* the inevitable star, came out well in several sequences and the flightless rail acted on film like the ac-complished performer he had shown himself to be.

From the outset, the producers, Jeffery Boswall and Keith Hopkins, went to great pains to get the scientific facts as accurate as possible in a film about a place so little known. Roger Gaymer was made zoological adviser and when it came to writing the script, every statement was checked and cross-checked, finally by Dr Stoddart himself on his return from the latest expedition to Aldabra. I think I learned more about Aldabra at this time than when I was actually there and some of the facts that emerged, such as the importance of the drongo among the land-birds, made me wish I had altered my priorities. The film was unusual in the television series called 'Look' in that it was intensely topical. It was to be the powerful plea for conservation to be expected from the Natural History Unit of the BBC. While it would try to explain the Defence needs as far as these were known, its main object was to give an accurate and up-to-date picture of what the world of science stood to lose. At the time very few people knew. In the cutting room we had a sense of red-blooded purpose – Save Aldabra. The atmosphere was bracing. I loved it.

As the film took shape, it was given the title 'Island in Danger' and Peter Scott recorded an introduction in which he referred to Aldabra as 'a natural wonder, in mortal danger'. Sequences from the film taken earlier by the Bristol Expedition were woven in to illustrate the value of the atoll for scientific research and by mid-October everything was ready. Jeffery Boswall, feeling as we all did that a decision was imminent, managed to get the date for its screening put forward – no easy task. The latter part of the film showed what damage would be caused to Aldabra and what danger would arise if the airfield were built and, to be thoroughly fair, the producer sent a copy of the commentary to the Ministry of Defence and himself went to London from Bristol to verify the accuracy of our statements.

It was only to be expected that the Ministry should feel the commentary was too strong; to talk of Aldabra being 'ruined' was surely an exaggeration, the spokesman said. He also stated that the settlement labourers must have damaged the island already and that 'conservation would be more practical with the kind of community that would be on the island if an airfield were established there'. Where we thought he had a valid point, the commentary was amended but it remained, unashamedly, as strong a plea for conservation of the whole atoll as we could make it.

Simultaneously I worked on a radio programme for 'The Living World' series of natural history programmes. I remember writing this bubbling with missionary zeal to such an extent that I felt the BBC would probably wish to tone it down. It came, therefore, as a pleasant surprise when the producer, Dr John Sparks, accepted it and considered that in certain respects it needed strengthening to get the issues in true perspective. I had hesitated to use the word 'scandal' in regard to the secretive way the military planners had worked to develop the atoll, ignoring scientific advice. He put it in. As the full facts emerged he was shown to be quite correct.

Years before I had been on the BBC staff myself, but I had almost forgotten the feeling of freedom that work in an independent radio

23. Seven-foot wingspan frigate birds drinking on the wing. (*The Royal Society*)

24. Dawn in the Seychelles. *(The Author)*

service gives. For a long time I had been associated with government-controlled broadcasting in newly-independent countries of Asia where even the mildest criticism of government actions would be unthinkable. Here there was no attempt to muzzle the conservation case, despite the fact that the BBC itself stood to lose if it should prevail. I almost forgot that the BBC planned to build a transmitter station on Picard Island!

To give the other side a chance to answer and criticise the film, a debate was arranged on the BBC's second television channel for later in the evening of transmission and the Minister himself was invited to take part. He nominated the Under-Secretary for the R.A.F., Mr Merlyn Rees, to represent him. The big night was to be November 6th.

In late September the scientists on the first phase of the Royal Society's Aldabra Expedition returned to England. The information they brought confirmed that 'the atoll is of high scientific interest and fully substantiates the memorandum presented to the Ministry of Defence . . .' In the press statement, a point was made that nullified one of the protests of the Defence Ministry about our film commentary, namely:

'There appears to have been very little disturbance of the natural ecology of the atoll.' In other words, the settlement creoles had not caused anything like the damage that the Defence spokesman had attributed to them.

And for the airfield planners there was little comfort in the latest estimate of the bird-strike hazard. The government's own adviser, Mr E. N. Wright, who was on the expedition, said: 'Man should not over-rate his ability to fly in direct competition with birds. What happened on Midway Island can happen elsewhere too.'

The Society again put its views to the Ministry, but what was most needed now was a good airing in parliament. Simple questions were being deftly brushed aside. Sir Tufton Beamish, who was in close contact with the Biological Secretary of the Royal Society, Sir Ashley Miles, applied to raise the Aldabra question on an adjournment motion, but was not successful in the ballot. All Defence Minister Healey would promise was a debate after a decision had been taken – a kind of post-mortem and discussion of the funeral arrangements. He held the whip hand and did not waver even when more cold scientific blasts crossed the Atlantic.

On October 13th, the journal *Science* carried a letter from the Secretary of the Smithsonian Institution, S. Dillon Ripley, saying they were 'deeply concerned over the possibility of military development on the most scientifically interesting atoll in the world'. And a few days later, the *Washington Evening Star* declared that 'nowhere is man's inability to leave well alone more vividly illustrated than on Aldabra'. Even more significant was the publication of an exchange of letters between the National Wildlife Federation of the United States and the then Secretary for Defence, Robert S. McNamara. The federation 'speaking for more than two million persons' expressed concern over the atoll's fate and asked that the Pentagon should use its influence to persuade the British government to select an alternative site for the airfield. In his reply, Mr McNamara assured the Federation that the 'importance of Aldabra as a scientific laboratory is fully recognised throughout our Government. We have notified officially the concern of the U.S. scientific community to the British'.

A statement by Dr Bourne, published in *Science* at the same time, evoked from Dr Ripley the assurance that 'it is my strong impression that our defence authorities have been willing to consider alternative sites.' The common practice of blaming the Americans would no longer work. The British and Mr Healey were on their own.

A surprising new champion now entered the lists. Seizing an unexpected and lucky opportunity, the Member of Parliament for West Lothian, Mr Dalyell, a Labour Party Defence rebel with some interest in science, made a fifty minute speech on Aldabra to a near-empty House of Commons on October 25th. He had been well briefed by the Royal Society and thrust forward all the arguments against the airfield plan. He made great play with the practical difficulties – moving 94 million cubic feet of honeycombed coral, submarine quarrying and many others – and the probable cost of the project: 'Would it really cost £20 million – or nearer £100 million?' His imagination boggled. In reply Mr Merlyn Rees repeated all the stock answers – no decision had yet been reached, everything that had been said would be carefully considered, there would later be an opportunity to debate fully. He also revealed a modification in the development plan whereby the dam across the Main Channel and the road along Middle Island would be replaced by a dam in East Channel, thus reducing the area of military construction.

Though it was obvious that Dalyell's chief concern was not conservation, that he had not charged on to the field flying the banner of voiceless tortoises, his speech was well-informed and constructive and it was a pity that it got almost no coverage in the press.

But far from discouraged, he followed it up with a barrage of questions to the different Ministries on all the most embarrassing and complex problems involved. Eighteen questions were answered on November 6th and twelve more during the next few days. By November 7th, he had tabled more than fifty questions and the Speaker then ruled that no more on the subject of Aldabra would be accepted from him. Dalyell raised this constitutional ruling on a point of order but it was upheld, and thereafter other members continued the onslaught on his behalf. By November 21st, twenty-five more questions had been answered and eight more were pending for the next day. At this point the inherent weakness of the questioning system in parliament on a subject as broad as this became apparent. Many of the vital questions were not reached. Nevertheless, the first object of the exercise had been attained. Aldabra had been thoroughly aired in the House of Commons. On the initiative of Lord Ridley, a debate in the Upper House was planned for the end of the month.

Public interest was further aroused by the showing of my film on BBC Television on November 6th and by the televised debate that followed it. Although nothing new came out of this discussion, in which Dr Stoddart and Dr J. Morton Boyd of the Nature Conservancy took part with the Socialist *enfant terrible* and the Under-Secretary of State, upwards of seven million viewers had now seen Aldabra for the first time and had heard the conservation issues forcefully presented. The battle was well and truly public. As Peter Fiddick wrote in the magazine *Nova*:

'What in the summer had been a somewhat acerbic correspondence in *The Times*, with more tempered backing from the *New Scientist*, had by November escalated into a full-scale propaganda exercise by the BBC with telefilm, Late Night Line-Ups, (the evening debate) and some of the most splendidly biased radio programmes in the grey history of the medium. In Parliament it raised constitutional questions. Outrage was the order of the day. If by then you did not know about [Aldabra] you must have been trying.'

Though I do not agree that my programme was biased, it certainly generated some remarkable reactions from listeners, the overwhelming majority of whom supported the case to spare the atoll. 'I was almost ready to lead a protest march!' declared a retired headmistress. But there was no need for it. Between the first and the repeat broadcasts of this radio documentary the pound had been devalued and Aldabra saved.

There could hardly have been a bigger anti-climax. As an economy measure, the government had decided not to proceed with the defence plan for a staging post on the atoll.

XIV    *After the Cheers*

$B$UT Aldabra was still in danger. When the cheers that greeted the House of Commons announcement had died away, its full significance sank home. The atoll had been reprieved not saved. The little girl who wrote to the BBC's programme 'Junior Points of View' saying: 'Thank you, thank you, thank you for saving Aldabra' was being premature, but she had a point. The vital breathing space had been won.

In the jubilation, Mr Healey's warning that the project might be revived again, ('it would be for a future government to decide'), was widely ignored. A few days later he was asked point-blank in parliament whether the need for a staging post on Aldabra had been so urgent as to over-ride scientific arguments. The Minister replied that the government had in fact decided, subject to expected American approval and in spite of scientific arguments, to go ahead. What many of us suspected was therefore true. The case to spare 'the living natural history museum', advocated by all the leading conservation societies of Britain and America had cut little ice with what Professor Galbraith calls the 'technostructure'. The fight would have to go on.

But what had really happened behind the scenes? Had the unprecedented campaign to spare the atoll had no effect at all on the defence juggernaut? It seemed hardly possible. I tried to find out from Dalyell who was in a good position to know, but all he would say was 'the Prime Minister was impressed by the public outcry'.

Writing in the magazine *Nova*, Peter Fiddick summed it up neatly:

'No principle of science versus strategy had been resolved, no authority had had to give in to informed outside argument.'

and he concluded:

'The way the publicity had been shaping, until devaluation released him (Mr Healey), one thing was certain; whether it be the bird or the Minister, the last one on Aldabra's a booby.'

We will not know for sure which booby won until the Cabinet papers for this period are eventually published, and as the 'technostructure' is unlikely to unseal its lips before then, I feel free to give my own assessment of what happened.

The beleagured British government seized on devaluation like a hungry frigate to get itself off the hook. If there had been no devaluation, it would have thrashed around seeking for some other excuse. The announcement was one of the few popular ones at this grim time and no loss of face was involved. The Government did not have to admit a mistake.

I hope I am right because, if not, the prospects for the future of Aldabra remain bleak. There are several pointers for optimism.

The fact that Aldabra was dropped so quickly on devaluation. If it were vital for strategic reasons, how could the policy be changed so fast? The House of Commons announcement was greeted by 'laughter and prolonged ministerial cheers'. It sounded like relief or release or both. And, on the best authority, I have it that when the Prime Minister told American Defence Secretary McNamara on the telephone of the decision not to go ahead with the project, the latter replied, 'Thank God. I've had these scientist fellows on my back for months'. I think it's safe to say that the advocacy of the Royal

Society and the American Academy of Sciences triumphed, however obliquely, in the end.

Even if the campaign had not been as decisive as that led by Darwin nearly a century before, it had borne rich fruit. The spotlight of world attention was focussed firmly on the remote atoll. Aldabra was alone no longer – it now had a host of friends and admirers. Such had been the publicity that a new word had entered the English language. *The Guardian* described Dalyell as 'aldabrating' when he tabled the last of his brood of fifty questions for answer in the House of Commons.

One of the most tireless and active campaigners, Dr Bourne, felt that 'the weapon that scared them (the Defence Ministry) most was publicity. If they had had their way the issues would never have been discussed in public at all. As it was, the clamour nearly came too late'.

He also evaluated the choice of weapons in the fight and drew the moral that 'conservation arguments are not felt to be relevant by the military authorities, they do not enter into their cosmology. The arguments they listen to are the practical ones of bird-strikes, rotten rock or lack of harbour facilities.'

Military strategists might well say, at this point, that the needs of science are obstructing measures vital for defence; that the plea to spare uninhabited islands is unrealistic; that a showdown is bound to come in which someone will have to arbitrate the priorities. But this is looking at only part of the the map. Undisturbed islands are greatly outnumbered by man-made deserts. On occasions it may be necessary to spend a little more on development, but then the issue becomes clear – is it worth it? Do we perhaps owe the extra payment to future generations?

In the case of Aldabra, would it be true to say that the red-footed booby and the flightless rail were blocking the defence interests of the Free World? I think not.

It is worth looking again at the two sides of the political argument. The air staging post on Aldabra was needed to complete a new 'sovereign' route to the Far East. Though this was never admitted, it was probably also required as a springboard for intervention in East Africa. The opponents of the scheme felt it was badly costed, over-expensive if practicable and probably not practicable within the stated terms. Beyond that, it was liable to commit us to politically unsound adventures in Africa and the Middle East. They claimed that Aldabra would often have to be supplied by flights across Africa and this made nonsense of the claim of 'sovereign' status of the route.

Both sides had a strong case but there were alternatives open to the Anglo-American defence planners. They still exist.

The obvious one is aircraft carriers but assuming these are, for some reason, ruled out, what of the other islands of the region? I am convinced that use could be made of Assumption, Cosmoledo or the Farquhar Group, all of which are in the category of 'deserts'. Astove would be too small, but the huge shallow lagoon of Cosmoledo is quite big enough to accommodate the airfield planned for Aldabra, and there is a reassuring precedent in the airfield built on the reefs of the drowned atoll of Johnson Island, south of Hawaii. Is it possible the planners simply forgot to include Cosmoledo in BIOT and wouldn't risk the furore of adding it later?

Assumption, with its good natural anchorage, would require some extension into the reef and another monsoon harbour, but it could surely be adapted as a staging post. Farquhar has the size and the alignment required, and although it is over two hundred miles distant from the ideal spot, it still comes within range at lesser load. And there is always the possibility of military use of the pro- jected civil airport on Mahé Island, where an enormous capital saving – at the lowest estimate £20 million – might subsidise a certain flexibility in strategic planning. A modern airfield already exists on Grand Comoro Island and it does not seem unreasonable to suppose that our allies, the French, might be willing to allow its use in an emergency. Further study may show that several options are open for that missing link in the 'third route' to the East.

My television film ended with the question, 'For a defence facility that will last at most fifty years, is it right to destroy for ever a natural treasure house built up over 50,000 years?'

In a rhetorical way this drew attention to another aspect of the threat that dismayed conservationists. Aldabra was to be despoiled not for the permanent benefit of mankind but for a very temporary military advantage. It was to take the short cut to desert status. Even the Defence Ministry thought that the estimate of fifty years was exaggerated; it was more likely to be fifteen. And to make the sacrifice even less justifiable, the strategic value of the airfield was doubted by many experts.

The sort of philosophy which placed short-term strategic advantage above long-term conservation issues was vigorously decried by the Provost of King's College, Cambridge, Dr Edmund Leach, who gave the 1967 Reith Lectures. He called the airfield plan for Aldabra an 'international crime':

'What horrifies is not that air marshals should contemplate such things but that the whole administrative machine of our country, including ministers in the Cabinet, should operate with a system of values which makes such action seem morally respectable. It is the bland unquestioned assumption that national interests always over-ride human interests and that what is man-made and artificial always has priority over what is wild and natural. For me such attitudes are criminal – criminal in just the same sense as Hiroshima was criminal and Hitler's attempt to exterminate the Jews was criminal. The scale is different but the offence is of the same kind. It is the monstrous misuse of man's newly discovered supernatural power. Actions of this sort can only occur when the decision-maker is totally disorientated about the relations which link ourselves to other people and mankind to nature.'

But why did the scientific community fight so hard for Aldabra and not for some earlier victim, like Ascension or Bikini or Wake Islands? Behind the answer to this question is one of the tragic stories of our time. The cry to halt was overdue. Man is nibbling away so greedily at the few remaining wild places on earth that before long there may be none left. Unless the process is checked, the entire planet, except for a few deserts and mountains, will be left to our descendents as one glorious Los Angeles sprawl, an interminable Peacehaven, a fully-automated airfield and tracking station complex. Or perhaps, worse still, as an abandoned airfield. But there was another good reason to 'stick' on this atoll.

Of the four types of oceanic islands, the rarest is the elevated lime-stone reef, a mass of coral raised from the sea in the distant past, and Aldabra is one of the only two of these that remain undisturbed by man. The other is Henderson Island, smaller, more remote from land and therefore with a less varied wildlife community, but never-theless a place that must be defended if it is threatened with develop-ment. It is another British island, one of the Pitcairn Group in the central South Pacific. Never colonized by man because it has no water – the central lagoon has dried up – Henderson has an even bigger sea-bird population than Aldabra and its own very distinctive flightless rail.

Ocean islands generally are of especial scientific interest not only because they are breeding grounds for vast populations of sea-birds and marine mammals and reptiles, like seals and turtles, but because their flora and fauna, evolved in isolation, is often unique. Unfortunately, the policy of using the few that remained undamaged by guano diggers and ruthless settlers, for airbases, which was conceived less than twenty years ago, did not immediately alert scientists and conservationists. Many islands succumbed to the military strategist with hardly a word of protest, although the menace should have been forseen. With the traditional 'sovereign routes' no longer available, as independent Asian and African countries straddled the old bases and airfields, the eyes of Western strategists turned naturally to those dots in the blue with romantic names often underlined in red. The most attractive, of course, were the uninhabited ones. Tortoises would never clamour for independence whatever the provocation. It was up to others to fight for them.

What damage is actually caused by military development even with a disciplined force alerted to the needs of conservation? If the island is small, the total destruction of scientific individuality is only a matter of time. It is not just the land requirements of the developers that cause it, perhaps even more damaging are the introduced plants and the predators – cats, dogs and rats – as well as the farm animals which destroy native vegetation.

To give two examples. On Midway, as we have heard, the mighty Laysan Albatross suffered appalling casualties. Ascension lost practically all its native vegetation and its gigantic 'wide-awake fair' (tern nesting ground) was saved from destruction only by the foresight of an English engineer acting on his own initiative to divert an American runway. And there is always the danger of escalation of the military plans once entry has been gained.

A fantastic example of what could happen on Aldabra was published, quite seriously, in the *Royal Engineers Journal* of December 1967. Under the title, 'The Nuclear Island of Aldabra', Major G. J. Chave demonstrated how newly-developed nuclear explosives could be used on the atoll to build a harbour on South Island, inside Passe Houareau, to accept vessels up to 30,000 tons, and a power supply and water desalination plant for 'the airfield complex and a maximum population of 8,000 including fighting elements in transit'. A 240-kiloton fusion device would be detonated and although only thirty inches in diameter and fifteen feet long, fired at a depth of seven hundred and fifty feet under the coral rock, it would excavate 'in a fraction of a second a harbour 1,500 feet in diameter and 400 feet deep at the centre'. Four smaller devices would be used later, buried at two hundred feet, to enlarge Passe Houareau itself to make 'a clean-cut channel, 400 feet wide and 100 feet deep at the centre, with a 30-foot wall protecting either bank, a convenient side-product of the explosion'.

I need not ask, convenient for whom? The author gave himself away involuntarily in his final paragraph.

'If this should ever come about,' he wrote, '[I] hope that I will be well away from the wrath of the zoologists and botanists, who regard the island as an ecological paradise for their studies. But even the *New Scientist*'s biological consultant had to admit that it is a pretty dreadful place, where only tortoises can live happily'.

So that's it. If Aldabra is 'dreadful' for humans, it's fit to be blown up. The fact that countless millions of other creatures like it, is of no consequence. I wanted to transpose a word or two in the final sentence to make it read – 'the only place where tortoises can live happily'.

In this nuclear pipe dream, I saw a nice neat solution to the bird-strike problem too. How about another couple of 'devices' under the frigate breeding colonies on Middle Island? That should solve it all right!

But it is not only the military who cause damage to wild life and natural habitats. Albeit on a lesser scale, zoologists have done their share. In the old days one would have been worried by the influx of scientists into Aldabra. Many were trigger-happy but, mercifully, the early type of researcher has now been replaced by scientists who use the camera and tape-recorder to help in the identification of species. Taxonomy today embraces animal behaviour and habits, a requirement which also tends to reduce the need for slaughter. Long may it advance in this direction, for there have been, even in recent years, grisly stories of the killing of rare species to advance the cause of science, over the animals' dead bodies so to speak. Some taking of specimens is essential, of course, for new species cannot be determined without anatomical study, but modern techniques, such as the use of the mist net, make the shooting much less necessary. Apart from the loss and the cruelty, the example it sets to porters and guides is lamentable. The main victims are birds and I was delighted that our own expedition was able to live fully up to the injunctions we gave to the creoles who accompanied us.

It is a regrettable fact that the memory of scientific killing lives long in local tradition. Later, in the Seychelles, I met several creoles who told me that their father or uncle had helped Monsieur le Docteur (the name fortunately forgotten) on his 'hunting expedition'. The same word '*la chasse*' was used as for the sportsmen. I wondered whether one of these was speaking of the eminent scientist who, in his own words, found on a small granite island 'as many magpie robins as I could take in a whole day's shooting'. The Seychelles magpie robin is now, in all probability, the rarest bird in the world, numbering not more than twenty survivors. These days are almost gone and with them, one hopes, the kind of request I once read in a responsible check-list: 'Total population 15–20 pairs. Specimens needed'!

What lessons can be drawn from the campaign to save Aldabra?

In Dr Stoddart's words, Aldabra is important as an example of what can happen if adequate channels of advice between government and the scientific community do not exist or are not used early enough. There are two salient points. Firstly, that the British Indian Ocean Territory was created, with Aldabra quite obviously its prime object, before any scientific advice had been sought or given. Secondly, that an agreement was signed between the British and United States governments providing for the use of these islands for defence purposes, even after the Royal Society had appealed for the total preservation of one of them. In other words, while the debate on the future of Aldabra was actually in progress, the government quietly sealed its fate.

The lesson that stood out above all others was the need for regular and effective communication between independent scientists and the government. Unless consultation takes place from the earliest planning days in future it is inevitable, in the words of Dr Stoddart, that 'situations similar to that at Aldabra will recur, and islands lacking the unusual fauna of Aldabra, and failing to attract publicity, will continue to be lost to science'.

Another lesson that emerged was the international concern now felt for the preservation of the few wild places remaining on the planet. Sir Julian Huxley's words often came back to mind. Britain was the country into whose hands Aldabra 'happened to have fallen'; the atoll was Britain's trusteeship, but there was world-wide interest in its fate. United States scientists played a big part in its defence and their hopes were constructive too. In *Science*, of December 1967, John Walsh wrote:

'Following the government announcement, the feeling here is that plans for research on the island should be made immediately . . . The form of action is still unclear, but it is hoped that research, like the effort to preserve Aldabra, will be a transatlantic affair.'

Harold Hirth had expressed the same sentiments when we were on the atoll.

To me, one of the most surprising discoveries during the campaign was that the authorities do not hesitate to distort the facts even in a non-political and humane issue like this. Two examples illustrate the point.

Government spokesmen said repeatedly in parliament that alternative sites for the airfield had been ruled out for 'compelling reasons'. When asked directly whether Assumption Island had been studied, the answer was 'yes'. In fact no ground survey of any sort had been done, a fact well known of course to many labourers we had met on the island. Only under extreme pressure was it finally admitted that its unsuitability had been decided from aerial reconnaissance alone.

And on the subject of damage to the ecosystem of Aldabra caused by the settlement workers in the past, although the Ministry of Defence well knew, from the Royal Society's memorandum and other sources, that this had been minimal and had not affected the scientific value of the atoll, great play was made of it to the end. It was continually suggested that, as Aldabra had already been damaged by man, an airfield would do no harm. A good argument but without foundation in fact.

There was, however, another and brighter side to relations with the government. From the time the Royal Society took Aldabra under its wing, the military and civil authorities were co-operative and helpful to scientists in many practical ways, and this co-operation continues. Within the limits imposed on them by the Anglo-American treaty, the authorities are aiding the Society to carry out its plans for research. Reversing the former situation, the great hope now must be that these plans will have advanced so far by the time money is again available for building a military staging post, that the idea of developing Aldabra would look even more like 'incredible folly' than it did the first time.

Meanwhile Aldabra remains in danger and will be as long as Command Paper 3231 of April 1967 hangs over it. This treaty document records the exchange of notes between Britain and America concerning the use of BIOT islands for defence purposes. Specifically it allows either country to build defence facilities on Aldabra for the indefinite future, stated as fifty years in the first instance.

Aldabra remains British, but sites on the atoll are at the disposal of the United States government free of charge. One clause provides that there must be mutual agreement before any construction or installation is started. Until Aldabra is withdrawn from the BIOT or the Command Paper is repealed, fears must remain for the safety of the atoll.

And nowhere in this treaty is there any mention of the need for any form of conservation whatsoever. The 80,000 'gigantic tortoises' might as well not exist.

★　　　★　　　★　　　★　　　★　　　★　　　★

As soon as the reprieve was announced, the Royal Society proposed an indefinite extension of the expedition which was already working on the atoll. It was decided to keep a few scientists there until a permanent research station had been set up. By June 1968, plans for this permanent station, to include laboratories, were well advanced and programmes of research had been drawn up.

I was told by David Griffin of the Aldabra Research Committee Secretariat of the Royal Society that all the organisations which supported the case for the total preservation of the atoll had offered their help and it was clear from the list of scientists taking part in the various phases of the expedition that transatlantic co-operation continued actively. No less than four names from the Smithsonian Institution were on it, including their Special Adviser for Tropical Botany, Dr F. Raymond Fosberg, one of those who had attended the crucial conference in London in January 1967. It was Dr Fosberg who wrote in the *Atlantic Naturalist* magazine at the height of the controversy:

'Would we destroy the Parthenon in order to use the Acropolis as a radar site to save the cost of building an artificial platform? I hope not.'

The Acropolis of Aldabra was already putting new exhibits on show to the most concentrated scientific investigation the island had ever known, the 'crash' programme of research made necessary by the imminent threat of development. With the announcement of the reprieve, the Royal Society changed the emphasis to long-term research. In order to avoid the risk of disturbing the ecosystem by their presence and activites, the number of scientists working on the atoll at any one time was to be kept to a minimum. There would be work for many years. With practically every telegram that reached headquarters in London, exciting discoveries were announced.

The presence of two distinct limestones which make it necessary to revise the simple picture of Aldabra as an uplifted reef. The egg of a flamingo – might they possibly breed there after all? New species of plants. The first report of Audubon's shearwater nesting on Aldabra. The discovery of an islet containing a hundred breeding egrets, with a new record for the cattle egret and the Squacco heron. Many sightings of the hawksbill turtle in the east lagoon. Mussel bed at Trou Nenez, 5,000 per square metre. Colony of a thousand lesser frigates at Bras Takamaka.

To me the most exciting news was that my old tent-mate, the flightless rail, is much less rare than had been feared. There are probably more than a thousand of them. All the mysteries are being solved, I thought rather sadly. Soon Aldabra will be an open book like everywhere else. It was Malcolm Penny who proved how wrong I was.

I met him in January soon after his return from the atoll where he had been studying the land-birds again.

'You know,' he said casually, 'we've found a bird new to science, on Middle Island near Johnny Channel, a few weeks ago.'

I was speechless. The discovery of a new species of bird simply doesn't happen any more. He went on.

'Tony Diamond and I were looking for nightjars. On the way back down the track I saw a small grey bird leave its nest. It was a brush warbler. First time it's been seen – a new species. It's going to be called *Nesillas aldabranus*.'

In 1968 it was the sort of news you could expect from Aldabra alone. What other secrets has the green atoll still in store?

by W. R. P. Bourne

MOST natural groups of plants and animals, apart from the chelonians (tortoises and turtles), have not yet been sufficiently studied to reveal the most promising lines of investigation on Aldabra, but it may be useful to summarize some of the more interesting features of that important group of vertebrates, the birds (recently reviewed by C. W. Benson and Roger Gaymer in *Atoll Research Bulletin No. 118*) as a demonstration why the wildlife of Aldabra is of special interest and of the type of research which might be pursued there in the future. In addition to the two people mentioned above, I am also indebted to Lt Cdr Roger Morris and other members of the Royal Naval Bird-watching Society and Dr David Stoddart, Messrs Tony Diamond, Malcolm Penny and Ernest Wright of the Royal Society Expedition, for a variety of information.

In general, the birds (like the other wildlife) are best considered under three headings, land, shore and sea, which each present different problems for study. It is the land-birds which tend to be peculiar to the atoll to a varying degree, two of them being endemic species closely allied to others on nearby land masses, eight of them endemic races or sub-species also shared with these land masses, while three are widely distributed species which show little detectable local variation on Aldabra. This contrasts with only one local race among the seven breeding shore and water-birds, and none among the nine sea-birds.

On the other hand, while the shore, water and sea-birds show little local variation, they have a comparatively big impact on the natural history of the atoll because of their great numbers, often large size, and consequently the large amount of food that they eat and guano and carrion that they produce, so that they form just as important objects for study as the native island forms. The important features of the natural history of the three main groups of species may be summarized as follows:

## The Land-birds

The atoll is visited by occasional vagrant northern migrants to Africa, and rather larger numbers of at least one Madagascar migrant to Africa, the broad-billed roller *Eurystomus glaucurus*. However these have normally failed to colonize it (presumably because the local conditions are unsuitable), and the land-birds are mainly derived from the nearest land-masses, Madagascar and the Comoro Islands. Although on an evolutionary time scale the atoll has been raised from the sea for only the comparatively short period of a few thousand years, these local populations already show minor but still interesting variations of size, colour, proportions or habits from their presumed ancestors, which provide useful material for the study of evolution within the context of the Malagasy area as a whole, especially because Aldabra is the least disturbed place in the area. Here it will be possible to determine the conditions under which evolution originally took place.

If we consider the Malagasy region as a whole, as the context in which evolution on Aldabra is taking place, it consists of a single large central island, Madagascar, cut off from the main land masses in remote antiquity, and a series of more recent outlying archipelagoes. Madagascar itself possesses a rich and complex flora and fauna, composed partly of ancient forms such as the lemurs, dating back to the period of its first isolation, and partly of others that have arrived more recently over the sea. The outlying islands have been colonized mainly by the more successful and mobile elements of the Madagascar flora and fauna, either independently at the time when they also colonized Madagascar or by secondary spread from there, which have subsequently become modified to produce a variety of more or less distinct local forms adapted to differing local conditions.

By comparing the situation on Madagascar with that on the outlying islands it is therefore possible to examine the manner of evolution of related plants and animals in a series of different localities which vary in their environmental conditions and in the complexity and variety of species which occur together in the same community. All too often it is also possible to study the varying impact on these natural communities of man and the additional plants and animals which he has imported. The Aldabra archipelago and some lesser islands north of Madagascar provide the simplest situation for studying the condition of relatively little-modified Madagascar forms. These studies can be developed subsequently in outlying groups such as the Comoros to the west, the Seychelles to the north-east, and the Mascarenes (Réunion, Mauritius and Rodriguez) to the east, where there are populations of closely allied plant and animal species showing a higher degree of insular adaptation and also the effects of more prolonged human disturbance. The new nature reserve of Cousin Island in the Seychelles, in particular, has been almost as little affected by man as Aldabra, and has a rather similar animal community, so that it also seems likely to play a vital part in the development of a programme of investigations.

Research in the area started in the middle of the last century with the collection and description (largely by the Newton brothers of Cambridge) of specimens of the surviving birds of most of the islands together with the excavation of the subfossil bones of the lost ones such as the gigantic elephant birds *Aepyornis* of Madagascar (Sinbad's Roc), and the large flightless dodos and rails of the Mascarene Islands. It is to be hoped that this phase is now nearly over, since many of the birds still left are now becoming rare, due more to the destruction of habitat and the introduction of predators than to coliecting, although some recent activities in this direction give cause for anxiety. Once the character of the native birds and their local variation has been defined through the study of collected specimens in museums, the next stage, about to begin, involves further study of the behaviour of live birds in the field to discover reasons for the appearance of differences between the more closely related forms living under different environmental conditions. This requires investigation of behaviour, diet, breeding success, and the birds' relation to diverse combinations of competitors and predators to determine how they have adapted to varying situations on different islands.

Aldabra seems likely to serve as a base line indicating the original undisturbed natural situation that once prevailed throughout much of the Malagasy area. Studies can later be extended to the more complex and highly evolved bird communities on other archipelagoes modified by man, since many of the same or closely related bird species are found there as well. A main purpose of this check-list would be to indicate ways in which work on Aldabra could lead to comparative studies elsewhere.

*The Shore and Water-Birds*

These are widely dispersed and highly mobile species which visit Aldabra to feed on the broad flats in the tidal lagoon, some of them spending much time around the pools inland. The seven larger species, including five herons of different sizes and habits, an ibis and a flamingo seem to be more or less resident (though it seems likely a good many may come and go between the atoll and other islands or the mainland), while the smaller waders are all migrants from the north. There is nothing particularly remarkable about the local populations of these birds except for the occurrence of two rather poorly-defined local races, but they do provide a very interesting opportunity for studies of their feeding behaviour, which are currently being undertaken by Malcolm Penny.

Thus the diet of the herons, which catch large, mobile prey, is easy to investigate because the young birds commonly vomit their last meal when disturbed (although it is wise not to disturb them too often). It seems doubtful if the diet of the birds taking smaller prey can be identified so easily but there should be little difficulty in inferring it by watching where they feed and then netting the water or sieving the mud to see what they catch, and by weighing young birds regularly to see how much food they are receiving. It might eventually be possible by counting all the birds, estimating the amount of food that they take, and comparing the results with those obtained by specialists on other animal groups to assess the part which the birds are playing in the natural economy of Aldabra. Such studies would never be possible where large numbers of birds are able to come and go more freely.

*The Sea-Birds*

These are all extremely widespread pan-tropical species. In many cases their geographical variation has not yet been fully established but it seems unlikely that any occur on Aldabra that are either generally rare or peculiar to the atoll. They are chiefly of interest because while some species reported offshore, such as the blue-faced booby *Sula dactylatra* and sooty tern *Sterna fuscata,* have not been found breeding on the atoll and probably have their regional headquarters elsewhere (perhaps on Cosmoledo Atoll), certain tree-nesting species, and especially the two frigate-birds and the red-footed booby *Sula sula*, have their regional headquarters for the whole western Indian Ocean on Aldabra. In consequence, if these colonies were destroyed, it would not only impoverish Aldabra by removing a source of fertility in the form of guano, but would reduce the sea-bird population of the Indian Ocean as a whole.

Since part of the argument over an air base on the atoll revolved around the bird-strike danger to aircraft that these sea-birds would present, and it has been claimed by the military authorities that it is not serious, it is worth repeating what appears to be the unanimous opinion of informed observers, that it is likely to be if anything considerably more severe than was predicted. Apparently the boobies alone present at least as large a hazard as any previously encountered, such as that presented by the albatrosses on Midway Island, but this risk pales into insignificance beside that presented by the frigates, which are much more numerous and soar much higher than any of the other birds which have previously caused trouble at airfields.

It appears that in general, while the frigates do not breed in large numbers near the proposed airfield site, preferring the mangroves along the north-east side of the lagoon where they probably find an upward deflection of the wind that facilitates soaring, they also visit the east and south-east in numbers as well. Here they attract most attention where dense flocks gather to drink on the wing over the pools, but it appears that they may also start to soar along the windward south-east shore and then make more height as they drift to lee over thermals inland before they disperse very high to look for food out at sea.

It follows that the removal of the pools during construction of the airstrip would not eliminate soaring frigates which probably sometimes have to make several circuits at increasing heights before they are ready to leave the area. Indeed, it seems doubtful whether this menace to aircraft could ever be controlled short of the systematic slaughter of the entire population maintained over many years to catch young birds and visitors from other colonies.

The arguments over the bird-strike hazard if it has not convinced Air Force planners does at least seem to have revealed the need for a closer study of frigate feeding techniques. They were formerly supposed to live by robbing boobies but it is now clear that there are not

enough boobies to support them all, so that they must find a good
deal of their food in unexplained ways for themselves, presumably far
out at sea. Although they are rarely seen from large ships, possibly
because they avoid them, frigates come down on occasion to inspect
smaller boats and submarines. Presumably they do most of their
hunting from a great height and only come down to lower levels
when they see prey in the form of a shoal of fish or a laden booby
returning to its nest.

It would be interesting to know whether the two pairs of species
of frigate-birds and tropic-birds of different sizes breeding on
Aldabra take food of different sizes or perhaps have different feeding
techniques. While it may be difficult to watch them feeding at sea,
it should be possible to examine their respective diets, since they and
other sea-birds commonly vomit any undigested stomach contents
if they are disturbed at the nest. Dr and Mrs N. P. Ashmole have
recently shown on Christmas Island in the central Pacific that the
study of such offerings can reveal much useful information about
both the diet of birds and the fish of neighbouring seas, and it will be
interesting to see the results of similar investigations by Tony
Diamond on Aldabra.

Other observations on Christmas Island, and those of Dr and Mrs
D. W. Snow on the Galapagos, and James Chapin and subsequent
workers on Ascension in the Atlantic, have also revealed that many
tropical sea-birds have highly irregular breeding cycles. Some of the
smaller species such as the terns rear one chick, complete a subsequent moult, and return to breed again in little more than nine
months, whereas larger species such as the frigate-birds which feed
their young for a long time after fledging may take twice as long.
Similar non-annual cycles could explain the irregular seasonal occurrence of many sea-bird breeding records on Aldabra, and this
possibility, together with the comparative breeding success at the
growing number of different sites now under investigation in tropical
seas, also needs investigation.

There are clearly still opportunities for many years of useful
research on Aldabra alone. This can be infinitely extended as the
neighbouring islands are brought into the picture.

## BREEDING BIRDS

(Endemic forms peculiar to Aldabra are marked with an asterisk)

AUDUBON'S SHEARWATER *Puffinus lherminieri* ssp. This small brown and white shearwater which is very widespread in tropical seas was only found breeding on islets in the Aldabra lagoon by Tony Diamond as recently as 1967. A specimen differs little from those from the Seychelles and Maldives, whose subspecific status is currently under study by Christian Jouanin. In the Galapagos, David Snow found these birds were breeding at nine-month intervals.

RED-TAILED TROPIC-BIRD *Phaethon rubricauda rubricauda.* This is a large tropic-bird widespread in the Indian and Pacific oceans, but replaced by the closely-related Red-billed Tropic bird *P. aethereus* in the Atlantic.

WHITE-TAILED TROPIC-BIRD *Phaethon lepturus lepturus.* This is a smaller tropic-bird whose range overlaps that of the last two throughout the tropical seas. All three tend to have prolonged breeding seasons with some concentration in the summer except where competition for nest sites may lead to staggered breeding (Galapagos) or pressure on the smaller species to breed when the other is away (Ascension).

RED-FOOTED BOOBY *Sula sula rubripes.* This is a small, tree-nesting booby which is widespread in all tropical seas, and in the western Indian Ocean seems to have its main breeding station on Aldabra while the other boobies nest elsewhere. It is polymorphic, and may occur in white or brown phases when adult, although the young are normally brown; on Aldabra the adults usually seem to be white.

THE BLUE-FACED and BROWN BOOBIES *Sula dactylatra* and *S. leucogaster* have been reported offshore by members of the Royal Naval Bird-watching Society, and the former and Abbott's Booby *Sula abbotti* once nested on Assumption, while the Blue-faced at least still does on Cosmoledo Atoll, but there appears to be no evidence yet that any of them have ever bred on Aldabra.

GREAT FRIGATE-BIRD *Fregata minor aldabrensis.* A large frigate-bird widespread in tropical seas except for the North Atlantic (where it is replaced by the Magnificent Frigate-bird *F. magnificens*), but apparently rather scarce away from Aldabra in the western Indian Ocean, though there may be small colonies on neighbouring islands, Tromelin, the Carajas Cargados group, possibly the Chagos group, and elsewhere, while non-breeding birds visit the Amirantes, Seychelles, Comoros, and the coast of Madagascar as well.

LESSER FRIGATE-BIRD *Fregata ariel iredalei*. A small frigate-bird which occurs at many (but not all) the same places as the last species, and considerably outnumbers it on Aldabra. The mid-Pacific breeding populations have recently been shown by a Smithsonian Institution ringing programme to wander vast distances during the period of immaturity, and this probably also applies to the Indian Ocean birds, and perhaps to frigates generally.

GREY HERON *Ardea cinerea cinerea*. Aldabra and Comoro birds are intermediate between the nominate race of Europe and Africa and *A. C. firasa* of Madagascar, and may be reinforced regularly by continental migrants.

LITTLE EGRET *Egretta garzetta dimorpha*. Local birds belong to the race found in Madagascar which is very similar to the typical white form found in Europe, except that somewhat over a third of the birds occur in a dark phase which is very rare in northern populations (with occasional intermediates). It would be interesting to know more about the genetics of these birds.

SQUACCO HERON *Ardeola idae* sp. This Madagascar species has recently been found nesting with the other herons by Malcolm Penny. It may also occur on migration to Africa.

CATTLE EGRET *Bubulcus ibis ibis* Local birds resemble the nominate form occurring in Africa rather than those from the Seychelles, said to show more rufous markings, like birds from the east.

LITTLE GREEN HERON *Butorides striatus crawfordi*. This is a local race of a widespread species notable for its capacity to colonize islands where it shows marked geographical variation in colour. In common with the forms occurring in the Comoros, Mascarenes, and Chagos-Maldive-Laccadive island chain, the Aldabra form is of particular interest because it resembles pale races from the east rather than dark ones from the Seychelles, Madagascar and Africa to the west. It is not clear whether this is due to differences in the original place of origin of the birds or, as seems more probable, the effect of the local environment in causing a convergence in coloration.

SACRED IBIS *Threskiornis aethiopica abbotti**. The populations found in Africa, on Madagascar, and on Aldabra show a progressive reduction in the black on the wings, and in the Aldabra form, on the head of the juvenile as well. Otherwise the Aldabra race does not seem very remarkable, but the population is small and plays an important part in the ecology of the atoll, so surely needs careful conservation. One example of the typical form from Africa has also been reported recently.

FLAMINGO *Phoenicopterus ruber roseus*. It has seemed rather doubtful whether the local population, which seems to fluctuate erratically in size, breeds locally or comes from the vast colonies in East Africa, but the recent discovery of an abandoned egg by Malcolm Penny indicates that it does at least nest occasionally.

MADAGASCAR KESTREL *Falco newtoni aldabrana*★. Three species of kestrel occur in the Malagasy region, a small, rather brightly coloured one, *F. araea* in the Seychelles, which seems likely to be of independent origin, a rather streaked form *F. newtoni* with a rufous dark phase on Madagascar and a small race on Aldabra, and an even more heavily marked species *F. punctatus*, presumably derived from the previous one, on Mauritius. The first feeds in the open, the second both in the open and beneath trees, and the third entirely beneath the canopy of what is left of the native forests, where it is safe from cyclones, and comparative studies of their behaviour might prove interesting.

WHITE-THROATED RAIL *Dryolimnas cuvieri aldabrana*★. The nominate form of this bird on Madagascar apparently flies well enough, but the Aldabra race differs somewhat in colour and more in having wings only four-fifths the size, and appears to be flightless. There was formerly a rather pale intermediate population *abbotti* on Assumption and others which never received proper study on Cosmoledo, Astove and Mauritius.

CASPIAN TERN *Hydroprogne caspia*. A few pairs have recently been found breeding by Tony Diamond. While it breeds locally on shallow rivers and lagoons in various parts of the world, it is a surprising find on Aldabra.

LITTLE TERN *Sterna albifrons*. This widespread species which shows a good deal of geographical variation is said to breed locally, but there could be confusion with at least one other tern breeding in the area, the Roseate *S. dougalli* and winter visitors of these and other species as well.

BLACK-NAPED TERN *Sterna sumatrana mathewsi*. A widespread inhabitant of coral lagoons in the Indian Ocean and Pacific, perhaps with a non-annual breeding season.

SOOTY TERN *Sterna fuscata ssp.* Collected, and reported offshore, but it may have come from the colonies on Cosmoledo Atoll, where the allied Bridled Tern *Sterna anaethetus* is also said to occur, so that might reach Aldabra as well.

CRESTED or SWIFT TERN *Thalasseus bergii thalassina*. The big crested tern of coral reefs and lagoons in the Indian Ocean and Pacific.

COMMON or BROWN NODDY *Anous stolidus pileatus.* Another common pan-tropical tern. (The closely related Lesser or Black Noddy *Anous tenuirostris*, which nests in trees, also occurs widely elsewhere in the Indian Ocean, but has not been reported yet on Aldabra.)

WHITE or FAIRY TERN *Gygis alba monte.* Another species widespread in tropical seas other than the North Atlantic, recently shown by N. P. Ashmole to have a prolonged breeding season on Christmas Island in the Pacific, a completed cycle lasting about 10½ months.

COMORO BLUE PIGEON *Alectroenas sganzini minor*\*. A member of a Malagasy genus of fruit-pigeons of eastern origin, once represented by five species, including *A. rodericana*, only known from sub-fossil bones from Rodriguez, *A. nitidissima*, only known from a few ancient specimens from Mauritius, *A. madagascariensis* from Madagascar, *A. sganzini* from the Comoros with a small race on Aldabra, and *A. pulcherrima* from the Seychelles.

MADAGASCAR TURTLE DOVE *Streptopelia picturata coppingeri.* A Madagascar species with a considerable number of races which differ mainly in the colour of their plumage in the islands to the north, the most interesting of them in the Seychelles now largely lost through hybridisation with the mainland form. Birds from the Aldabra group are rather pale, and those from Aldabra itself are slightly smaller.

MADAGASCAR COUCAL *Centropus toulou insularis*\*. A long-tailed local race of a Madagascar species, which has unusually pale underparts outside the breeding season, formerly represented by an intermediate population on Assumption (*assumptionis*) as well.

BARN OWL *Tyto alba affinis.* The African and Madagascar race of this widespread species was collected a number of times at the turn of the century but has not been seen since. It seems to have been rather tame and might possibly have been killed off by the cats which were introduced about the time that it disappeared; otherwise its disappearance is entirely mysterious.

MADAGASCAR NIGHTJAR *Caprimulgus madagascariensis aldabrensis*\*. A rather large grey race of a Madagascar species.

MADAGASCAR BULBUL *Hypsipetes madagascariensis rostratus*\*. The species occurs in south-east Asia and on Madagascar, with ill-defined races on Aldabra (rather brown) and the Comoros (*parvirostris*, rather grey) overlapping in its distribution on Moheli with a second species, *H. crassirostris*, also found in the Seychelles, while a third, *H. borbonicus* is found on Mauritius and Réunion.

ALDABRA BRUSH-WARBLER *Bebrornis* (or *Nesillas*) *aldabranus**. The Malagasy brush-warblers are a rather distinct group represented by a variable streaked, long-tailed species *B. typica*, on Madagascar and the Comoros, a closely allied grey, even longer-tailed form *B. aldabranus* recently discovered by Malcolm Penny on Middle Island, Aldabra, and a series of increasingly green, short-tailed species on Moheli in the Comoros (*B. mariae*), Rodriguez in the Mascarenes (*B. rodericana*) and Cousin Island in the Seychelles (*B. sechellensis*). The extremes of variation are so different that they were long placed in separate genera, *Bebrornis* and *Nesillas*, but they are linked by *B. mariae*, another recent discovery only found by C. W. Benson in 1958, and show a type of variation between a specialized form on Madagascar and generalized ones on outlying islands remarkably similar to that also occurring in the genus *Foudia* (discussed below), so that it seems possible that they might be better combined in one genus under the older name *Bebrornis*.

ALDABRA DRONGO *Dicrurus aldabranus**. This is another local representative of a group undergoing active evolution in the Malagasy area, in this case to such an extent that the affinities of the various endemic species on Aldabra and the Comoros are completely obscured, though possibly the Aldabra bird is a primitive form of the Madagascar species *D. forficatus* while the two Comoro ones *D. fuscipennis* and *D. waldenii* come from the African species *D. adsimilis*. Comparative studies of the behaviour of the group might help to unravel their relationships where in this case museum studies fail.

PIED CROW *Corvus albus*. A common species, widely distributed in Africa and Madagascar, which has colonized both the Comoro and Aldabra groups without showing any local variation there.

SOUIMANGA SUNBIRD *Nectarinia souimanga aldabrensis**. A Madagascar species which shows much local variation and a variable amount of melanism in the islands to the north, culminating in the development of dark allied species in the Comoros (*N. comoroensis*) and Seychelles (*N. dussumieri*).

MADAGASCAR WHITE-EYE *Zosterops maderaspatana aldabrensis**. Another Madagascar representative of a very widespread group, with a series of races on islands to the north and more or less close allies in the Comoros (three, two of them of African origin and one shared with the Seychelles), the Seychelles (two) and the Mascarenes (one, showing much local variation).

FOREST FODY *Foudia eminentissima aldabrana**. The fodies are a rather distinct Malagasy genus of weaver-birds, represented by two species on Madagascar, *F. madagascariensis*, originally perhaps confined to open country on this island alone although it has followed man to most of the others in the area (and St Helena) as he developed them; and *F. eminentissima*, found in woodlands, with local races on all the Comoros and Aldabra, and two close allies on Rodriguez (*F. flavicans*) and the eastern Seychelles (*F. sechellarum*) which show generalized adaptations to the insular environment very similar in general character to those already described for the brush-warblers of the genus *Bebrornis*.

## MIGRANTS AND VAGRANTS

The commonest visitors are a variety of northern waders which occur in immaturity, on passage and in winter on the mudflats of the lagoon, including especially:

Crab Plover *Dromas ardeola*, Grey Plover *Squatarola squatarola*, Greater Sand-plover *Charadrius leschenaultii*, Turnstone *Arenaria interpres*, Sanderling *Crocethia alba* and Whimbrel *Numenius phaeopus*, while Common and Wood Sandpipers and Greenshank *Actitis hyboleucos*, *Tringa glareola* and *T. nebularia* and also a Lesser Black-backed Gull *Larus fuscus* have occurred.

The commonest visiting land-birds are migrants visiting Africa from the north, although strays from Madagascar and Africa also occur. They include Black Kites *Milvus migrans* (probably of the African race *M. m. parasiticus*), various dark falcons which must be either Eleonora's or Sooty Falcons *Falco eleonorae* or *F. concolor*, the Striped Crake *Porzana marginalis*, Cuckoo *Cuculus canorus*, Swift *Apus apus*, northern race of the Blue-cheeked Bee-eater *Merops persicus superciliosus*, Northern and Broad-billed Rollers *Coracias garrulus* and *Eurystomus glaucurus*, Swallow *Hirundo rustica*, Sand and Mascarene Martins *Riparia riparia* and *Phedina borbonica*, Golden Oriole *Oriolus oriolus*, Lesser Grey Shrike *Lanius minor*, Wheatear *Oenanthe oenanthe*, Spotted Flycatcher *Muscicapa striata*, Yellow Wagtail *Motacilla flava*, and an unidentified pipit *Anthus* sp.

Since a substantial number of bird species migrate from eastern Asia to Africa, doubtless the occurrence of more on Aldabra is merely a matter of time.

## APPENDIX 2  REFERENCES

I SEARCHED in vain for references to the Aldabran Group in the accounts of sixteenth and seventeenth-century travellers. Following the path of Vasco da Gama, these early voyagers in the Indian Ocean preferred the comparative safety of the Mozambique Channel to the unknown seas east of Madagascar and thereafter hugged East Africa until they reached the great island of Socotra off the south Arabian coast. This route was followed, for example, by Sir James Lancaster (1591–1603), Peter Floris (1611–1615), Nicholas Downton (1614–1615) and Sir Thomas Herbert (1626–1629), thus the only islands of the 'Lost Corner' chain they encountered were the Comoros. Herbert's comment in his log, when he was once blown off course, 'other dangerous Isles invironed us' explains the reluctance of these navigators to explore further, and their treatment at the hands of the Comoros 'Moores' must have been another discouragement.

Sir James Lancaster 'entertained in the best manner' the king of these islands on board his ship and shortly after had the harrowing experience of seeing thirty-three of his men, who were 'a-washing' and collecting water, butchered by the 'trecherous Moores', 'we being not able for want of a boat to yeeld them any succour'.

Sir Thomas Herbert is the most informative about these islands neighbouring the Aldabran Group and comes to the conclusion that they derived their name from the Welsh 'cumr-yne, the Welchman's Isle'. He describes the green turtle and the manatee or sea cow that abounded there:

'The Sea Tortoise is a fish not much differing from those at land; by overturning they are easily taken. Some we took for pastime more than food and upon trial found that they taste waterish and dispose to fluxes. They superabound in eggs, some having near 2,000, which are not easily made hard though extremely boiled.'

'The other fish, the Manatee, is good meat and has a fleshie taste. Her face is like a shrivelled Buffolo and the stone generated in her head is most valuable, being Soveraign (as some report) against choler adust, stone cholick and dysentry. A docible fish and apt to be made tame, famoused for their love of man whose face they delight to look upon.'

Despite the interest in the region these explorers showed, it is only in recent scientific literature that the atoll of Aldabra itself receives close attention. These publications include:

ABBOTT, W. L. 1893. 'Notes on the Natural History of Aldabra, Assumption and Glorioso Islands.' *Proc. U.S. Nat. Mus.* 16.

BENSON, C. W. 1967. 'The birds of Aldabra and their status.' *Atoll Research Bulletin of the Smithsonian Inst.* No. 118.

BOURNE, W. R. P. 1966. 'Observations on islands in the Indian Ocean.' *Sea Swallow (Ann. Rep. Royal Naval Bird Watching Society)*, **18**, 40–43.

CHERBONNIER, G. 1964. *Aldabra l'Isle aux Tortues Geantes.* Paris. Gedalge.

COUSTEAU, J-Y. 1963. *The Living Sea.* London. Hamish Hamilton.

CROOK, J. H. 1961. 'The Fodies of the Seychelles Islands.' *Ibis* **103a**, 517–48.

EDWARDS, F. W. 1912. Diptera, Tipulidae. *Trans. Linn. Soc. London*, ser 2, Zool. **15** (Percy Sladen Expedition Reports, 4.)

FOSBERG, F. R. 1967. 'Unique Aldabra.' *Atlantic Naturalist*, **22**, 160–165.

FRYER, J. C. F. 1910 'The SW Indian Ocean.' *Geog. Journal.* **37**, 249–268.

FRYER, J. C. F. 1911. 'The structure and formation of Aldabra and neighbouring islands – with notes on their flora and fauna.' *Trans. Linn. Soc. London.* ser. 2, Zool. **14** (Percy Sladen Expedition Reports, 3).

GARDINER, J. S. 1906. 'The Indian Ocean, being results largely based on the work of the Percy Sladen Expn. in H.M.S. *Sealark*, 1905.' *Geog. Journal* **28**, 313–332, 454–465.

GAYMER, R. D. T. 1966. 'Aldabra – The case for Conserving this Coral Atoll.' *Oryx*, **8**, 348–352.

GAYMER, R. D. T. 1967. 'The Indian Ocean Giant Tortoised on Aldabra.' *J. Zool. Lond.* **154**, 341–363.

HARTMANN, R. 1886. *Madagaskar und die Inseln Seychellen, Aldabra, Komoren, Maskarenen.* Leipzig: G. Freytag.

HEMSLEY, W. B. and others. 1919. 'Flora of Aldabra; with notes on the flora of neighbouring islands.' *Bull. Misc. Infm. Roy. Botanic Gardens Kew*, 1919, 108–153.

HONEGGER, R. E. 1966. 'Ornithologische Beobachtungen von den Seychellen.' *Natur und Museum*, **96**, 481–490.

HONEGGER, R. E. 1968. 'Beobachtungen an Riesenschildkroeten auf den Seychellen.' *Salamandra, Zeitschrift. f. Herpetologie und Terrarienkunde.*

HORNELL, JAMES. 1927. *The Turtle Fisheries of the Seychelles Islands.* London. H.M.S.O.

LEGRAND, H. 1965. 'Lepidoptères des Iles Seychelles et d'Aldabra.' *Mem. Mus. Nat. d'Hist. Natur.*, Ser. A. Zool. **37**, 1–210.

MERTENS, R. 1934. 'Die Insel-reptilien, ihre Ausbreitung, Variation und Artbildung.' *Zoologica* (Stuttgart), **84** (2), 1–209.

NICOLL, M. J. 1906. 'On the birds collected and observed during the voyage of the *Valhalla*, 1905–1906.' *Ibis* Ser. 8, **6**, 666–712.

OMMANNEY, F. D. 1952. *The Shoals of Capricorn*. London. Longmans Green.

PENNY, M. J. 1965. 'Bristol Seychelles Expedition, Part V. The Birds of Aldabra.' *Animals*, **7** (15). 409–411.

PETERSON, R. T. 1968. 'A plea for a magic island.' *Audubon*, **70**.

RIDGWAY, R. 1893–94. 'Descriptions of some new birds collected on the islands of Aldabra and Assumption by Dr W. L. Abbott.' *Proc. U.S. Nat. Mus.* **16** and **17**.

SMITH, J. L. B. and M. M. 1963. *Fishes of the Seychelles*. London, **1–215**.

STODDART, D. R. 1966b. *Report on the conservation of Aldabra*. Royal Soc. Mimeographed, 1–15.

STODDART, D. R. 1967. 'Threat to Aldabra.' *Geog. Mag.* **40**, 800.

STODDART, D. R. 1967. 'Various papers.' *Atoll Research Bulletin. Smithsonian Inst.* **118**.

THORPE, W. H. 1967. 'Aldabra and the vandals: the Scientists' case.' *New Scientist*, **36**, 471–472.

TRAVIS, W. 1959. *Beyond the Reefs*. London. George Allen and Unwin.

VESEY-FITZGERALD, D. 1940. 'The Birds of the Seychelles. The endemic birds.' *Ibis*, ser. 14, **4**, 480–489.

VOELTZKOW, A. 1897–99. 'Wissenschaftliche Ergebnisse der Reisen in Madagaskar und Ostafrika in den jahren 1889–95.' Band I. *Abhand. Senckenb. naturf. Gschft.* **21**, 1–664.

VOELTZKOW, A. 1902b. 'Die von Aldabra bis jetzt bekannte Flora und Fauna.' *Abhand. Senckenb. naturf. Gschft.* **26**, 539–565.

WALSH, J. 1967a. 'Aldabra: Biology may lose a unique island ecosystem.' *Science*, **157**, 788–90.

WATSON, G. E. and others, 1963. *Preliminary field guide to the birds of the Indian Ocean*. Washington: Smithsonian Inst. i–x, 1–214.

WHARTON, W. L. 1879. 'Letter on Aldabra from H.M.S. *Fawn*, off Zanzibar, 1878, included in Guenther's paper.' *Ann. Mag. Nat. Hist.* Ser. 5, **3**, 165–66.

WHEELER, J. F. G. and OMMANNEY, F. D. 1953. 'Report on the Seychelles-Mauritius Fisheries Survey 1948–1949.' *Colonial Fisheries Research Publications*, **1** (**3**), 1–145.